The View From the Corner Shop

The Diary of a Wartime Shop Assistant

The View From the Corner Shop

The Diary of a Wartime Shop Assistant

Kathleen Hey

Edited by

Patricia and Robert Malcolmson

**SIMON &
SCHUSTER**

London · New York · Sydney · Toronto · New Delhi

A CBS COMPANY

First published in Great Britain by Simon & Schuster UK Ltd, 2016
A CBS COMPANY

1 3 5 7 9 10 8 6 4 2

Simon & Schuster UK Ltd
1st Floor
222 Gray's Inn Road
London WC1X 8HB

www.simonandschuster.co.uk

Simon & Schuster Australia, Sydney
Simon & Schuster India, New Delhi

A CIP catalogue record for this book
is available from the British Library

Paperback ISBN: 978-1-47115-401-0
Ebook ISBN: 978-1-47115-402-7
920·1/HEY
Typeset in the UK by M Rules
Printed and bound by CPI Group (UK) Ltd, Croydon, CR0 4YY

One day I started chatting with a sailor home on leave from the Far East. What did we talk about? Food, of course.[*]

Curious how 'het up' everyone gets over food ... Food really hits the tender spot.

Kathleen Hey, 3 September 1941

[*] 'Food Inglorious Food', M. Dent memoirs, Second World War Experience Centre, LEEWW:2011.0045.5.

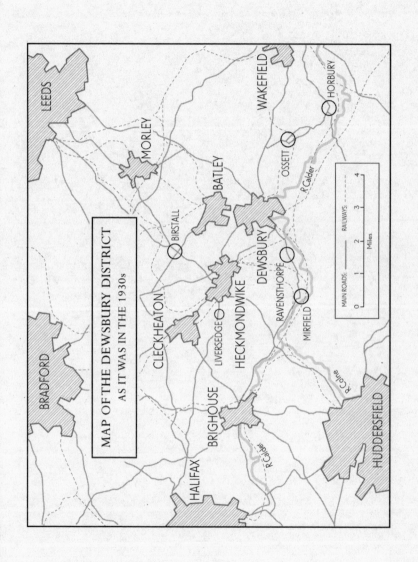

MAP OF THE DEWSBURY DISTRICT
AS IT WAS IN THE 1930s

MAIN ROADS: ———   RAILWAYS: – – –

0   1   2   3   4
Miles

LEEDS

MORLEY

BATLEY

BIRSTALL

CLECKHEATON

LIVERSEDGE

HECKMONDWIKE

BRIGHOUSE

HALIFAX

BRADFORD

WAKEFIELD

HORBURY

OSSETT

R. Calder

DEWSBURY

RAVENSTHORPE

MIRFIELD

R. Colne

R. Calder

HUDDERSFIELD

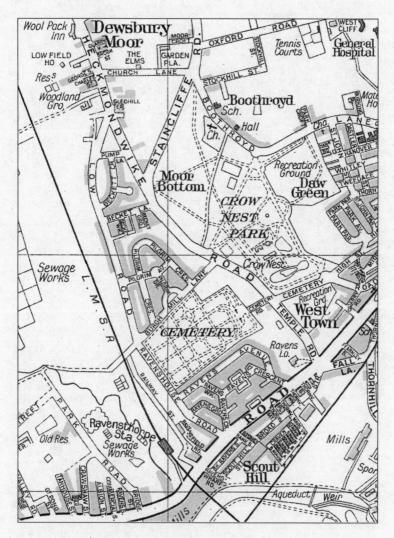

Dewsbury Moor, 1938. Kathleen Hey's brother-in-law's shop was situated on Heckmondwike Road, opposite the junction with Staincliffe Road.

Contents

Introduction

One feature of any good diary is that the reader is never sure what will come next. Life is often unpredictable; a person may be taken by surprise; incidents and revelations suddenly crop up, unexpectedly. One day's writing may be focused on public events, the next day on a personal worry or a memorable conversation, the day after that on shopping, prices, and material hardships. The diarist may, out of the blue and for whatever reason, disclose a feeling or attitude that she discloses nowhere else. Kathleen Hey's diary is very much of this sort: novel testimony appears again and again, new issues capture her attention, or perhaps old issues are re-evaluated. At the same time, though, there are matters of commonplace routine – spending most of one's hours under one roof, living with and hearing from the same people day after day, and navigating the predictable rhythms of the normal working week. For Kathleen, these rhythms were closely associated with assisting in a grocery shop in a working-class neighbourhood on the outskirts of Dewsbury, West Yorkshire. Work made up for her much of life (and most people's lives in West Yorkshire), and she wrote about it a lot, from various points of view, including those of her customers. Play was less prominent, but she sometimes wrote about that too. Wartime events in distant places were occasionally much discussed, at other times barely mentioned at all.

Kathleen Hey wrote her diary for Mass Observation, the social research organisation that had been launched in 1937 with a mission to help produce 'a science of ourselves'. Kathleen did not reveal her reasons for taking on this volunteer work. We can only surmise that she felt a degree of commitment to MO's function as an agency of social investigation, and its desire to learn as much as possible about the everyday lives of Britons during this extraordinary period of the nation's history. We do know that she found social history appealing, for in August 1943 she was reading the Penguin edition of Elie Halévy's *A History of the English People* and said that 'I like this immensely because the author is matter of fact, does not air his opinions, his language is simple and "graspable", and social history is much more fascinating than the old Kings and Queens and Battles and Dates kind. Have found nothing to dislike about it yet.'*

Diaries were valued by the leaders of Mass Observation – and we assume by most of those who volunteered to write for it – as an important tool for recording individual and social experiences. Diaries were a means of capturing the moment – perhaps an incident outside a shop, or reactions to war news, or behaviour on a bus, or an overheard conversation, or feelings (say) of exasperation, prejudice, or disgust. Diaries documented people's thoughts and feelings in all their confusion and uncertainty, *without the wisdom of hindsight.* Diaries gave 'ordinary' individuals a voice, or at least put these voices on record, and these Observers' voices – some 480 of them during

---

* These words were written in response to MO's Directive, or questionnaire, that month; for more on these Directives, see below, p. 10.

1939–1945 – were thought to contribute to a sort of social anthropology of contemporary Britain. It is virtually certain, too, that most Mass Observers felt that their writing would lead, in some small way, to a better understanding of the beliefs and behaviour of the modern society that they inhabited.*

One final point by way of setting the stage. In our opinion it is best to avoid characterising a diary in a particular way – as (say) personal or detached, as opinionated or clinically observational. This is partly because, whatever its dominant leanings, a strong diary is so often multifaceted: serious sometimes, at other times jokey; calmly analytical in one entry, ill-tempered in another; serene one day, anxious a day or two later; at one moment bored or depleted, at another keen and energised. Moods alter, perceptions vary, new circumstances prompt changed sentiments. In other words, diaries commonly reflect the rather messy manner in which most people live their lives. Some diaries are indeed rather repetitive and mechanistic, but Kathleen Hey's diary decidedly is not, and this is one of many reasons that it is worth reading and enjoying.

Kathleen Hey was born on 17 March 1906, the youngest of four children. In 1911, when she was five years old, her siblings were aged nineteen, seventeen, and thirteen. Their parents, Arthur Hey and Clara Parker, had married in 1889. He was then twenty-four and a painter in Dewsbury; Clara was twenty-three, living then in Heckmondwike but with recent roots in Northamptonshire, where her father was a boot and shoe maker. In 1911 the Hey family of six people was living at 17 Cambridge Street in Heckmondwike in the West Riding

---

* See the Appendix for further details on Mass Observation and its diarists. (In this book we follow modern usage and have eliminated the hyphen from the original name, Mass-Observation.)

of Yorkshire. The town's population was around 9,000 – there were more women than men: the former were very prominent as woollen workers – and its major industries were the manufacture of woollen blankets and carpets. There is no evidence that the Hey family had any direct connections with the woollen trade. Kathleen's father, Arthur, aged forty-six at that time, was listed in the census as a house painter – 'master house painter' on Kathleen's birth certificate. When his elder daughter, Margaret, and surviving son, Ben Rudolph, were married in 1926 and 1927 respectively, he was said to be a 'Musical Director'.* Many years later, in 1959, Clara Hey's death certificate recorded her late husband's occupation in the 1930s as 'Manager (painting department) retired'.

Regrettably, beyond these bare facts, we know almost nothing about Kathleen's life before the 1940s. This is mainly because, unlike most other writers for MO, she rarely reminisces, or speaks of past events, or places people who appear in the diary in any sort of historical context. Other diarists occasionally connect an incident in the present with some past experiences, or are reminded that day of something that happened years ago, and write about it. Kathleen does not do this. She never mentions her school days or what she did after leaving school, probably in 1920, at the age of fourteen. Given her command of English, as witnessed by this diary, she must have read a lot and been sensitive to good writing, but we have no information concerning the elements of her self-education. She says nothing about the jobs she held in her later teens and twenties. She reveals no details about significant events, whether happy or sad, in her family's history. We know that she

---

* We are much indebted to Ann Stephenson for her careful and revealing research into the history of Kathleen's family.

had relatives in Northamptonshire, but we can say little more about her family connections, for she almost never provides any background. An 'Auntie' appears from time to time in the diary, but is otherwise without identity (and it is possible that there were two aunts living nearby). The interwar past is largely absent from her writing, though we believe that up to 1941 she always (or almost always) lived in that part of West Yorkshire that encompassed Heckmondwike, Liversedge, Mirfield, Wakefield and Dewsbury – that is, the region west and south of Leeds. Her diary is remarkably present-centred; it is concerned almost entirely with her life and the lives of others in wartime. Occasionally, in dealing with wartime diarists, a surviving relative is available to answer questions for which there are no documentary sources, but for Kathleen Hey this is not the case.

During most of the Second World War, Kathleen lived on the outskirts of Dewsbury, an industrial town a few miles south-west of Leeds. On 30 July 1941, then aged thirty-five and unmarried, she wrote the following 'Details' as a preface to her Mass Observation diary, which she had actually started to write twelve days earlier.

I help my brother-in-law, B., in his grocer's and general shop. Our household consists of my brother-in-law, my sister, who does the housework, my mother, who does the cooking and helps generally, and myself. The shop, which stands in a good position at the edge of a large housing estate (chiefly slum clearance), was in a poor state and very dirty when we took it over six months ago, but we have doubled the trade and expect to have a great increase in registered customers this re-registration period [for rations]. Our customers are all 'working class' and most of them wear shawls on their heads and do not use soap too often but they are not as poor as they seem and do not mind what they spend on food if they can get it. There are many Irish, a few Scotch and a handful of Italians.* A good many women go out to work leaving their children in care of neighbours – that is, to be fed by the neighbours. Otherwise, they run the streets when they are not at school. Our shop faces the road, with the housing estate behind and below in a hollow, and overlooks the church, a field and the trees of the park. Buses pass the door between Dewsbury and Bradford.

This grocery shop, the setting for much of Kathleen's diary, was at 37 Heckmondwike Road, Dewsbury Moor, where the family also lived.† Dewsbury Moor is on the north-western edge of Dewsbury. Its predominantly working-class character is indicated by what one sees on detailed Ordnance Survey maps from the 1930s: a woollen mill on each side of Heckmondwike Road slightly up from the grocery shop, and a little further north-west a substantial chemical works. Large sewage works were sited between two sets of rail tracks going into Heckmondwike. There was still a lot of open land in Dewsbury Moor and between it and Heckmondwike. The housing estate Kathleen refers to was built in the later 1930s and has Becket (now Beckett) Crescent as one of its main arteries. St John's Church is to the north-east, across the field she mentions, and a few hundred yards to the east is Crow Nest Park, the principal open public space in the Dewsbury region. The shop on Heckmondwike Road, opposite the junction with Staincliffe Road, is about a mile and a half by road from the centre of Dewsbury, a town of some 50,000

* See also her diary for 31 July 1942.

† It was still a shop when the editors visited it in 2013 – not literally on a corner, but across from a corner. It has a fine perspective from its back windows towards Mirfield.

people that then specialised in manufacturing heavy woollen goods.

A grocery shop – the focal point of Kathleen's wartime exist-ence – was intimately involved in selling rationed goods, as her diary richly documents. Rationing was a major commitment, involving all sorts of complications, and was not embarked on lightly. As the still major authority on the subject has remarked, 'only foods possessing certain qualifications might be admit-ted to a rationing scheme. They must, to avoid overloading the mechanism, be necessities; they must preferably be non-perishable, to avoid the problems of sale off-the-ration; they must be in regular demand, and be capable of even supply, week by week; and the variation in demand for them as between individuals must not be so wide as to make a uniform ration inappropriate.'* (Thus, for example, cigarettes, which were heavily used by some people and not at all by others, were not formally rationed. Actual availability, however, was not ensured.) By the time Kathleen began her diary, almost two years after the start of the war, several basic commodities were rationed, consumers had to be registered for these goods with a particular retailer, price controls were applied to other items, supplies of some items were unpredictable, and lots of paper-work had to be done to keep the system going.

As Kathleen's diary makes clear, shopkeepers did not lead an easy life, though she was well aware that others, especially those living elsewhere, had to struggle a lot more. Her writ-ing is testimony to both the virtual universality of certain wartime constraints and the very selective impact of others,

---

* R. J. Hammond, *Food* (3 vols.; London: HMSO, 1951–1962), I, 195. Volume I is subtitled *The Growth of Policy*; volumes II (1956) and III (1962) are subtitled *Studies in Administration and Control*. This authoritative reference work is part of the *History of the Second World War, United Kingdom Civil Series*, edited by W. K. Hancock.

including those related to property damage and sudden death from enemy bombing. If most people in Dewsbury routinely faced the necessity for hard labour, they saw almost nothing of German aerial attacks, though others who did sometimes found themselves evacuated to Dewsbury and billeted in the region. Each British town experienced war differently. Kathleen's diary testifies both to matters that were distinctive to where she lived *and* to practices and concerns that would have been standard fare throughout Britain – notably rationing and the provisioning of food. Beyond these merits, her writing is also wide-ranging, thoughtful, often acerbic, and sometimes amusing. She was no sentimentalist.

No photograph of the shop as it was in Kathleen's day has been found. This Dewsbury tobacconist's, however, photographed in 1920, typifies the strongly working-class character of the town.
Photograph © Kirklees Image Archive

Notes on Editing

In Kathleen's diary, as in many other MO diaries, private individuals are not named, even the members of her immediate family. This practice was designed to help preserve the anonymity that diarists were then promised – and which has been relaxed only in recent years. As a consequence, Kathleen's diary is full of people identified as 'Mr C.', 'Mrs D.', 'M. G.', and the like, most of whom are untraceable. Here are those people who feature prominently in the diary that we can name:

Margaret (Preston), sister, aged 48 in 1941

Bert (Preston), brother-in-law, aged 53 in 1941

Ben Rudolph Hey, brother, aged 43/44 in 1941, lives in Heckmondwike

Zillah Hey, sister-in-law, aged 43/44 in 1941, lives in Heckmondwike

Mr Hobbs, landlord and next-door neighbour, at 35 Heckmondwike Road

Mrs Hobbs, his wife, and owner of a furrier shop in Dewsbury

Henry Hill, neighbour, at 33 Heckmondwike Road, a bus inspector

Bella Hill, his wife, and a friend of Kathleen

Alice, a cousin of Kathleen from Northamptonshire

Amy and Edna Naylor, unmarried sisters of Zillah; they live in Hull

We have reproduced everything that Kathleen wrote in her diary up to September 1944. Nothing has been omitted. Then, in the final chapter, covering October 1944 through August 1945, we present selections that highlight what we think are her most interesting observations from these last months of the war. We have also drawn on some of Kathleen's responses to Mass Observation's (usually) monthly questionnaires, known as Directives. Some of these passages are integrated into the text of her diary, others are placed in footnotes or paragraphs of editorial commentary. In all these cases this non-diary MO evidence is clearly identified by the letters 'DR' (Directive Response) with the relevant date. We use square brackets occasionally to supply a missing word or a few pertinent facts, commonly of identification, and a modest number of footnotes for longer explanations and elaborations. Other than a few minor corrections, Kathleen's sometimes idiosyncratic grammar has not been altered. As editors we play bit parts only. The diarist's voice is always centre stage.

PART ONE

1941–1942

1

Work, War, and Relaxation

July–September 1941

Friday, 18 July

A hectic day. Bert could not return from Blackpool until the late afternoon as the early bus was taken off without warning. Of course everyone came for their rations at once. Margaret did her best but had to keep asking prices and then I had to see that she gave people their rations as they liked them – that is, some prefer all marge instead of fat, and some (particularly the odious Mrs J.) had already had most of theirs during the week in driblets. We keep a record of this on a piece of card and woe betide us if we lose it! What arguments whether they have had all their sugar or whether it was a quarter or half [pound] of marge yesterday, and so on. Oh, Lord Woolton [Minister of Food]! Could you be in our shoes for a single day! How much wiser you would be. These people were coming with their new [ration] books and expecting them to be attended to there and then so they could take them to the butcher. This [is] impossible so I asked them to give the butcher first turn and let me have them for the weekend. I rang up for potatoes but their van had broken down. H. went down with the car after dinner but it was too late, potatoes had gone, although he nabbed a basket of tomatoes which Margaret weighed into half pounds and we reserved them for registered and 'best' customers. (A 'best' customer is not necessarily registered but spends a good deal of money and, more important, is no trouble to serve.) Mrs J. kicked up a fuss because the extra sugar ration was not yet available. She said she would go to the Food Office. I said I wished she *would* and then perhaps our wholesalers would get a move on.

The Food Controller and the newspapers proclaim these things to the world, and then when the machinery goes wrong the poor shopkeeper is the buffer as usual. We are three weeks overdue with that extra sugar-for-jam ration, and I am tired of trying to convince people we have not used it all ourselves, that we are not keeping it for spite, and that we have already 'seen about it' several times. It is just the same with eggs. The press proclaimed last week three eggs per head. We had 184 for 107 registered [customers] and do not know if that is a fortnight's or a week's supply. This fortnightly delivery business is trying when you have been used to two or three calls per week from the wholesaler. Who can gauge a fortnight's needs ahead in a shop of this kind?

Bert arrived at 5.30. We were both pretty well in by that time but carried on until closing time, 8 o'clock. After supper we 'did the books' and everything was satisfactory, barring a discrepancy of 4s in the cash, but Bert said that was near enough.

Saturday, 19 July

Today has been a little quieter but not much, but considerably easier with Bert at home. He took the car down for potatoes and had to go to the siding for them. Only one bag. We rationed them two pounds per customer. The peas went well at 4½d per lb. The kiddies kept us busy as we had a few sweets. We continue to keep them for the children as much as possible (not allowing anyone more than 2 oz) and it is our pride we make halfpennies when no other shop on the Moor will make pennies. Sometimes there is only two for a halfpenny if the sweets are large and dear. (Six pence per quarter [pound] seems to be the rule. I think it abominable the way cheap confectionary has risen in price. We have sold *stones* at 2d per gram.)* When we get sweets in word goes round like wild fire that 'Preston's have some spice', and then we have a riot. Most of the children pass the shop on their way to both the Catholic and the C. of E. schools. Then for half an hour I feel like a harassed mother bird with an unusually large brood clamouring to be fed. We do not 'bag' sweets now unless they are very sticky or the children are very small. Bags are too dear. I believe we are the only folk on the Moor to wrap up bread. I often meet women with an armful of bread and tea-cakes. Of course no one thinks of taking a basket. A few may use a paper carrier and the holding capacity and strength of these useful articles as demonstrated by our customers make me take my hat off to our paper makers. But usually they are content to carry things in their hands and can bestow all kinds of bulky and awkward parcels about their anatomy like a conjuror.

* Sweets were not rationed until June 1942.

Later. After closing at 7.30 went over to Mirfield to see how Ma was enjoying her holiday. Mr D. had plenty to say about Lord Woolton. He said he was the ruination of this country and was making everyone into thieves and liars and made a mess of everything he undertook. They are definitely giving up the retail egg business and have told all their customers so. They will merely keep the eggs to be collected. Mr D. said he had never given his customers a bad egg in twenty years and he was not going to have any old eggs out of a pool for them now. At first he said he would chuck up altogether but he has £200 laid out in hen houses and could get nothing for them at this present day. So he is carrying on with the few he has left, 200, instead of 2,000. Mrs D. rages because they told her she shouldn't have her own eggs but must be rationed like everyone else. 'I'll show the davals,' she says and gave us an egg each (three) to bring home. Also redcurrants, raspberries and three boxes of matches because I wrote during the week we were without. (We have since had some in but I did not throw her kindness in her face by telling her that. Margaret is 'keeping them squat' from Bert.) Mr D. talks about keeping a milking goat and rearing a few calves. They will manage alright. They both get the pension now and the apples and raspberries pay the rates.

Sunday, 20 July

Went for a run to Wakefield to see the old shop [at 9 Townley Road] and then to the country just outside for an hour or two. We marked a spot for blackberries in the autumn, at Walton. No one would dream we were only two miles from Wakefield. A farmer's wife came past while we were sitting reading the Sunday papers in the car. She was very indignant because some youngsters had been trampling in the corn and had left a gate open, and said they should not be allowed to roam about unwatched, it was not playing the game – [said] in such a vexed tone that we guessed she thought we were the 'owners' of the unruly ones. But I think our hearty agreement with her convinced her otherwise. It is too bad. People would not dream of roaming round a woollen mill or walking through the Council Offices leaving every door open, and yet they have no compunction in interfering with and damaging the farmer's land, which after all is his workroom and means of livelihood.

Home to tea just in time to catch the Fs and other young ruffians stealing Mr T.'s peas out of his front garden and the poor old man watching them helplessly from the window because he cannot move without help. G. scooted them and said the best cure was cayenne pepper sprinkled on the peas. I was once recommended cayenne to keep dogs out of the shop doorway (no use) but never heard it recommended for the purpose of protecting growing peas. To Ben and Zillah's [in Heckmondwike] after tea. Zillah's sisters not coming [from Hull] after all as E.'s office has been blitzed and A., being a school teacher, is liable for duty after a bad raid. Their letter was sent before the latest and worst blitz on Hull so maybe they won't have saved their furniture after all. Their intention was to take the best bits out of the bungalow at Aldboro' and dispose of the rest and leave Hull for good until after the war, just going in every day to work.* Ben has a week's holiday next

---

* Heavy raids on Hull on 18 July had left some 140 people dead and 108 seriously injured. (T. Geraghty, *A North-East Coast Town, Ordeal and Triumph: The Story of Kingston-upon-Hull in the 1939–1945 Great War* [1951], Appendix.) Most other British cities had not been heavily bombed for over two months, as Germany concentrated its military resources on the Eastern Front.

week. They are undecided whether to spend it at home, [or] go to Blackpool or Aldboro' or Keswick.

While we were at Wakefield this morning young B. came in resplendent in his new uniform, about seven sizes too big. He says he is having a bayonet next week and then in the next breath said his company were dismissed from the Home Guard because they didn't like and wouldn't obey the sergeant. I was puzzled how he got his uniform if he was officially not in the Home Guard any longer. Aggie told a good story of a friend of hers who was so engrossed in deep conversation with a friend in the market she didn't notice she was being enveloped in a queue and was suddenly bustled along in spite of her protests that she wanted to come out, until on the crest of the wave she saw it was a *strawberry* queue, whereupon she 'caird quiet' [fell silent], as we say here, and obtained a basket with no bother at all. There have been riots and rows galore in Dewsbury Market. I would not be a greengrocer at present. Stalls are turned over and the police have to be summoned.

Monday, 21 July

As it is [the annual] Dewsbury Feast holiday and we now have no bread ever on Mondays, Bert said we may as well have the half day. We went to Leeds as he wanted some things from Abe (a Jew he deals with) that he cannot get elsewhere – tinned meat, and fruit and matches, and salmon. But the shop was not open. We spent some time outside and I was amused at the fashions. The Jews all dress well (or should we say flashily) and no matter how shapeless they are (and they are all shapeless after 20 or so) like the latest fashion. I notice they have a particular taste for high heels, not following the prevailing fashion for flat heels and rubber soles.

Listening now to the wireless. A ridiculous song (?) called 'I wish I could fish like Annie can fish'. These words also compose most of the song. Speaking of fish, we are done out of our Monday evening supper as the fish and chip shop people have no potatoes and so have gone off to Morecambe. Now Ronnie Waldmann is conducting his puzzle corner. How that man does gabble! The wireless is a *very* mixed blessing. (1. Flights of the Bumble Bee. 2. Curly Headed Bobby. 3. ——. 4. Someday I'll Find You. 5. British Grenadiers.) Just discovered we have some new green candles on the mantel shelf. Margaret says they have been there days. I say that cannot be because *I* have dusted the shelf every day this week. Margaret says she always knew I went about in a fog. I feel rather hurt at this unkind remark and retort that at any rate it wasn't I who put the clock in the pantry and took the pickles upstairs. (Guessed four out of five tunes correctly.)

Tuesday, 22 July

Have now completed and sorted counterfoils for the Food Office. The last day for registering was Saturday and the counterfoils should have been in to the Food Office today. We have 35 families registered. Out of these 18 people live alone or in lodgings. Thirteen families registered for every rationed thing. Several new people registered for everything save eggs, which they cannot change at present. Two registered part of family for everything and others registered all family for several things. We have Sugar 74 counterfoils, Butter 80 counterfoils, Bacon 80 counterfoils, Cheese 84 counterfoils – last time we had Butter 72, Bacon 50, Cheese 78, Sugar 69 – which will be a good increase when the two large families who have not yet brought in their books are added. One didn't fill up books. (Did not notice this when presented or should have given it back.) I offered to fill [in] for one (a very busy widow with several children and goes out to work). Two filled in with pencil. Seven came and asked advice how to fill in. Nearly everyone studied the huge chart Bert made and hung up telling them just what to do – and what not to do, such as fill [in] our name because we have rubber stamp. Two I made complete their job in the shop. (Both *males*.) Two given back to complete. About six gave in their books confidently without saying 'Will you look and see if they're done right?' Three new [people] thought they could have rations on handing books in. Many seemed to get tired or were interrupted when filling in their books for I had to finish off a good many counterfoils already begun. They had no system in filling up and hopped from one counterfoil to another, leaving bits undone here and there, but surprisingly few had left out their identity number although many omitted the ration book number. At least four old customers had to be nagged at to get in their books. And at least twenty said 'It is a business, isn't it? I wish it were all over.' This last sentence is said at least once every day by someone, generally a woman and generally after discussing food.

Bert has painted the V sign on the shop door. Two people have asked what it meant. Mr G. complains that his allotment has been stripped of peas and his young carrots torn up, Mrs M. that her onions have been rifled, and all the exhibition peas have been pinched from the sidewalks in the park where flowers used to grow. The police only laugh if complaints are made.

Wednesday, 23 July

Took in counterfoils to Food Office today. There are still a few families to come in. The first time I have ever seen the Food Office with no one in.

We spent the half day in the country, taking lobster paste sandwiches and tea and cake. Margaret manages a cake every week as three out of the four of us forgo sugar. She has also made jam, five pounds strawberry, four raspberry and redcurrant, two gooseberry, and we have the extra sugar ration yet to come. Until tomorrow we are without sugar, bacon and marge in the shop. What a good thing most of our customers take their rations weekly and not daily. Our great day for dealing out rations is Friday, although some, especially the pensioners, come on a Thursday. Why this is so I don't know because Old Age pension is paid on a Friday. Our week gradually works up [to a] crescendo, starting quietly on Monday, increasing in tempo on Tuesday, retards Wednesday, accelerando Thursday, furioso Friday, diminuendo from Saturday morning to a quiet finale Saturday evening. Our hours are – 8 o'clock prompt start in a morning, close 7 p.m. Monday and Tuesday, 1 p.m. Wednesday, 8 p.m. Thursday and Friday and 7.30 p.m. Saturday. We are always busier in afternoons than mornings, a contrast from our old Wakefield shop where morning was the busiest period.

The reason we are short of rationed goods this week is because we have supplied a good many soldiers' rations for which we detach coupons and send them in monthly to the Food Office but we only get a permit for replacement every two months. We have two wholesalers, who deliver fortnightly, one from Leeds, one from Wakefield. From one we get butter and marge and fat, and sugar and bacon, from the other the rest of the rationed goods. Of course from each [we get] all else they can let us have. This week we are promised tinned milk, casserole steak and raisins. We shall see! We have had these promises before. When we do get a windfall we have to hide goods skilfully behind show cards and camouflage them generally. Sometimes we have to wait until a certain 'line' accumulates, tinned milk, for instance, generally delivered in dozens. It would not do to supply some and not others of our 'registereds' when they all live in one another's pocket, so to speak, and are eager to compare notes about 'the shop'. Mr D. says Lord Woolton is turning us into a nation of thieves and liars. Conditions are certainly making accomplished liars of all shopkeepers. I now look people firmly in the eye and say 'No, we have no cigarettes left. Isn't [it] a business not having enough to go round?' well aware that in the drawer I am leaning against there are 'thousands'. As for biscuits and chocolate! I begin to recognise certain people and what they are after and open my mouth to say 'No, sorry' before they are well inside the door. Sometimes they merely request an inoffensive loaf or bag of salt, after all, and I have to gulp down the 'tarradiddle' [fib]. Children are the worst. They know when the vans come and tear off home to report.

We have had trouble with the yeast lately, and of course with the customers. It went into a strange dark sticky mess. We put it down to the very hot weather but now the yeast man says it was an experiment of the Government's, which didn't come off. Thousands of bags were spoiled. Yeast is now to be made in the old way, and our customers will be soothed. But we get no recompense for what we had to throw away. Bert says another muddle by the Government. Everything they touch, why don't they leave things alone, etc. etc. Bert thinks these rules and regulations are all made to harass the poor grocer. He thinks they should have grocers at the Food Office. 'What do t'upper class know about it?' He says it's wicked the money that's wasted controlling this, subsidising that. At first when things began to be scarce he went up to the wholesalers every week and had awful rows because he said he wasn't getting his share. When the coupons had to be cut from the ration books and counted it was purgatory every month getting them counted and balanced up with stock. We had rows and rows. We started after tea on Sunday evening and were at it, three of us, until 11 and 12 and in the end got in such a tuck we didn't know what we were doing. This was really unnecessary because if the Food Office have the number of your customers they have a check on what you should be supplied with. The present system is much easier, but it would be better if people had to take so much butter, marge and fat instead of being allowed to choose marge in place of butter and fat.

Thursday, 24 July

Today we have received nine more [ration] books, one just discovered and brought in apologetically, five that were promised for today – the woman goes out to work and the children young – and three were brought in casually with no apology and a shrug of the shoulders when I said they should have been in last Saturday. We have at last got all our extra sugar. Most have taken it gleefully but a few said they could not afford to pay for it all at once. Miss G. C. said she would have a feast. She would put all the lot on the table and have spoonsful in her tea. She went off in high feather with a cake and a tin of baked beans. We have no jam to start the new rationing period. There's another daft idea of the Government's. They have decided to allow jam every four weeks instead of every calendar month as printed in the ration books. There will be endless difficulty and arguments here. Also the ration books start with July. Our customers have already had their July ration of jam on the old books. We have only one bag of potatoes for the weekend. The last one contained 5 pounds of soil, out of 8 stone; out of a box of tomatoes charged and marked 12 pounds we could only weigh 20 half pounds for customers; and the peas had a huge stone planted in the middle that couldn't have got there by accident. Had an argument with Bert that he should charge more for the tinned soups and paste that came in this week to make up for these losses, pointing out that our customers have benefits that people in Dewsbury are queuing daily for, and that when they are controlled he will get little at [*sic*] them. In the end he saw the point but feared he would not get rid of them before August 4th. But there is no danger of that. The wholesalers have mysteriously found a good many things they have hitherto denied having, and are pleased, nay eager, for us to have them. They are anxious to disgorge of course before price control. We have only one tin of biscuits (sweet) and some crackers (from Jacobs) this week. Auntie says she stood half an hour in the Co-op for a quarter pound of biscuits. She is glad she is finishing there and coming to us. Mrs H. reports that things are just as bad to get at Scarboro' as anywhere else. She thought she was going to 'milk and honey' I think. Everywhere is closed and they cannot go on to the Marine Drive or the Beach [access to which was blocked off with barbed wire].

Today is the day Petulengro [astrologer in the *Sunday Chronicle*] prophesied dire things for Hitler. Heard of nothing happening yet but perhaps tomorrow ... Have always had faith in P. in spite of many disappointments, since he foretold danger to Queen Mary and that same week her car overturned [she suffered minor injuries in a collision on 23 May 1939].

Friday, 25 July

The sugar delay has lost us a family of nine for the new rationing year. The Rs are going elsewhere. But we shall abundantly make it up with new customers.

Mr D. called from Wakefield on the off chance of picking something up but it didn't come off. He said he had been lucky at Manchester and got 2 lbs butter. At another place 7 lbs dates because the man said there was not enough to go round his customers. Mr D. said there were only three registered at Marks & Spencer last period for jam, and therefore they did not bother with it. He said that at Wakefield Rag Day this year [a charity event for the Clayton Hospital] 1,000 people were catered for and only 300 turned up to tea. They sold what stuff they could, guessing at the weights because they had no scales, and many people paid for 1 lb tomatoes only to find they had barely ¾ lb. Miss P. back from Manchester reports she could get anything at Lewis's. She brought back 2 tins milk and 2 tins fruit. This news of course brought poor Lord Woolton back again into the conversation. He, it was said, is the head of [David] Lewis's [department store in Leeds] so of course they have plenty of stuff. 'He's making some brass.' Then was reaped up the story told us by a woman that her sister had paid 1s 10d for pilchards at the Leeds branch the week before they were controlled. At this time we were selling the same kind at 1s per tin. Mr S. joined in the talk to the effect that where he had been in London the Woolworths' window was full of treacle and placarded 'Ration here for jam, sugar, butter, marge and fat'. Mr D.

said Wakefield's Woolworths sold cat flowers. All were against these stores cutting in into other lines, Bert of course being particularly bitter.

Mr D. grieved because he could not 'pick up' any petrol anywhere. He has used his August coupons and next week is on holiday. Says he has had no difficulty up to now but cannot raise a drop. Advised Bert to try for extra for the business. Bert says [he] tried before at Wakefield but [it] didn't come off and anyway he has done alright up to now as he has friends here and there on Government work who can spare a drop. But he talks of putting the car up this winter. Abe will have to join up, so he will have no need to go to Leeds (to the Jews). He went today and got salmon for ourselves and salad cream. For the shop tinned vegetables and Ovaltine and Horlicks that the wholesalers dole out in quarter dozens, pilchards and sardines and 2 gross matches.

Margaret and I have got rooms at Blackpool for a day or two the week after next. Was not going away but feel cannot stick another's winter's blackout without a change. This has been a trying year, with removal and rationing and one thing and another. Shall have to see if N. C. [a relative from Northamptonshire] will help Bert for a day or two. That's the worst of a shop. You can't lock the door and leave it, but must make arrangements for its welfare in your absence like leaving livestock. Resolved to have no encumbrances when I am an old maid living alone.

Saturday, 26 July

Have taken in to Food Office last counterfoils I hope. We have now registered 39 families – 84 sugar, 90 butter, 62 bacon, 94 cheese counterfoils. Have made a complete new register with a page for each family so that we can enter any 'extras' with date, such as tinned milk, salmon etc. Tinned milk seems to be the one thing they all crave for. Many of them I think have never had a regular milk man but used that sickly dollop, no doubt straight from the tin, and thus saved both sugar and milk. Now of course they seek it more than ever to supplement their sugar rations. One old Irish lady – she is a perfect pest – asking for tinned milk every week, always seizes the tin and kisses it fervently when one is forthcoming. I see I shall have to look out for my 'odd' folk as I call the ones who live by themselves. Bert says they are not worth bothering about, their rations are all bits and bats, which annoys me because I think all *regular* customers, spending much or little, should be equally considered. After all there should be more in business than handing goods over the counter and getting the money for them. If customers are loyal to you, you should be as generous as possible to them. But Bert, as I often remind him, sees no further than the end of his nose.

Bert read out tonight that we are to have a million cases of salmon from Canada. Margaret says she wonders how many we shall get, and how many will be Lewis's. Sarcasm!

Sunday, 27 July

We picnicked today at Cawthorne by the roadside and had a calm happy four hours. Delighted to see at close quarters a squirrel. We lay discussing our next move, for we are agreed in not wishing to settle at Dewsbury Moor. Bert says if we could get a little shop in a quiet street at Blackpool like that opposite Mrs G.'s and took in about four people for B & B we should be alright, and in the winter and slack season our time would be our own. It would be funny if we *did* sometime go to Blackpool for both Margaret and I have vowed we wouldn't go near, even for a holiday. Well, here we are, booked for a holiday there at any rate. More permanent moves must wait until after the war. What a lot of people think it will be over before Xmas. Am afraid I am not so sanguine.

Called at Mirfield to see if Ma was ready to come home. She was not. Mr D. is rampageous about his eggs. They brought him grade B for the last week with his customers and he didn't find out until too late, so don't know what he would have said. He said enough, according to Ma. I believe she learnt several new terms. Mr D. was a coachman before he was a busman. He had cooled down to calling them 'snotty-nosed swindlers' when we called. He said he would have thrown the b——s (new word for eggs) at them if he'd known they were second grade. Mrs D. says it's surprising how many 'cracked' ones she finds when packing for collection. Cracked of course are not accepted.

Noticed when riding a car – most Vs [for victory] are done with chalk on gateposts and walls. The most popular dogs seem to be black Scotties. About one in four led dogs are that kind. Women do not adapt their faces to suit the perky hats that are prevalent this season. They should – or wear a plain one. A heavy, perplexed expression does not match a disc of straw and a yard of veiling.

Aunt L. went last week to see Great Aunt S., who is recovering from a severe attack of bronchitis and who, at 92, is preparing to live as strenuously as ever. She told me 10 years ago she would live to 100 and she will, too, if she has set her mind on it. Up to quite recently she wrote articles for the *Manchester Guardian*. During the last war she wrote poetry and sold copies for charity, making a considerable sum by this means. Not bad for a woman who has had no schooling. She

lives now by herself and isn't too grateful when kindly neighbours look in to see how she is. 'It's alright, but I've no time
for gossip. I want to get on with my work. I've a lot of writing
to do.'

There seems to be a good deal of fuss about the strong
measures against Japan [the 'freezing' of Japanese assets in
the USA and Britain]. Why weren't these taken years ago?

Monday, 28 July

Ben and Zillah are not going away after all. Ben says he will
be glad of the chance to meet [i.e., experience] his own
home. They have lived there 14 months and he has had no
leisure, working seven days a week until seven at night [in a
munitions works]. They have heard from Hull [where Zillah
was from]. Amy [a sister] wrote to say Zillah need not hope
to see 13 of Franklin Street [the family home] any more.
They had hoped to get their furniture away this week, but
when Edna [another sister] went in the day after the blitz
the police fetched her out as an unexploded bomb lay in the
terrace behind.

And now the *Daily Mail* has started an astrologer ['Archidamus']. Shows what sells newspapers. Or the type of people
who read newspapers. Must admit I read the forecasts myself
and have great fun comparing them. Petulengro usually
threatens me with accidents, through sharp instruments, or
road accidents, or burns. (He has not yet said a fall from an
aeroplane or a tossing by a mad bull. If only these prophets
would be more explicit, and more original.) This week I am
gratified to see that only males should guard against accidents
to hands and arms, though I am to take things easily and not
be rash and extravagant. [Edward] Lindoe [astrologer in the

People] gives misunderstandings on Monday but difficulties overcome by Wednesday.*

Mrs M. has had visitors from Scotland. She says they were 'clammed' [i.e., starved] and did nothing but eat when they were here. She says they have bread and margarine every day to all meals, and ham and meat at the weekend, and a pound of biscuits once a month. That Clydeside gets it awful and there are hundreds buried under the ruins.

Brooke Bond's [a major tea brand] man says he has a friend in London with a wife and one child working who get all their meals in cafes during the week and only have to make their rations spin out for the weekend. He says the friend was quite indignant when Brooke Bond's remonstrated with him and said they could not manage otherwise. Brooke Bond's says there is something wrong with a system that allows a clerical worker to do this and manual workers going short. He also said it was funny how certain large stores were coming out into lines they had never approached before, and having plenty of commodities others were short of. He said, too, that it was no good the Government deciding *now* to rescind the prohibition which disallows shopkeepers to have less than 25 registered because the people will have gone elsewhere, the custom is lost, and it is no use telling the shopkeepers to go on munitions because in most cases they are elderly and incapable of such arduous work.

* Astrologers at this time were a subject of study by Mass Observation's Tom Harrisson in the *New Statesman and Nation*, 16 August 1941, pp. 152–53, and 'What *Did* the Stars Foretell?' *Picture Post*, 6 September 1941, pp. 17–21. Astrology had a large following, especially among women, and interest in it had increased steadily since the start of the war. It may have had a short-term 'steadying influence'. The claim that astrology is a science and, like all sciences imperfect, is a major theme of Edward Lyndoe, *Complete Practical Astrology* (London: Putnam, 1938).

Wednesday, 30 July

Spent the afternoon on Heath Common where soldiers were practising trick motor-cycling, riding on one another's shoulders, between obstacles and being pulled in little trucks. H. and B. were with us. We had lemon cheese made from the four little lemons A. had given Margaret. There was no one else on the Common. H. has succeeded in getting us tickets for a bus for Blackpool on the 11th and a return for me for the Sunday. Margaret said she would not go by train from Thornhill at 8.15 in the morning. I think we are neither of us keen after the fearsome stories in the press but if we get there Mrs J. will board us (we hope) and we also hope the room will not be required for soldiers. One traveller said he would not go away on any account, another that he would and blow Hitler – he was called up in December and meant to have his holiday. Mr L. said Mr Churchill's speech was curious. Did he mean invasion here or in France when he warned us to be ready?* Russia had done far better than anyone had hoped. Miss P. says her sister in Somerset thinks we shan't have to blackout this winter – all will be over. Miss P. says she can hardly believe that. I said if that was the case Hitler would have won,

---

* In a speech the previous day in the House of Commons, which was concerned almost entirely with matters relating to war production, the Prime Minister concluded by declaring that while the nation was now better off than some months ago, it could not let down its guard or relax its efforts. 'It would be madness for us to suppose that Russia or the United States is going to win this war for us. The invasion season is at hand. All the Armed Forces have been warned to be at concert pitch by 1st September, and to retain the utmost vigilance meanwhile. We have to reckon with a gambler's desperation ... If we fail, all fails, and if we fall, all will fall together.' In these concluding words he was, it seems, re-declaring the sort of resolve that he had conveyed so effectively in the spring and summer of 1940. (Robert Rhodes James, ed., *Winston S. Churchill: His Complete Speeches, 1897–1963* [8 vols.; London and New York, 1974], VI, 6471.)

and she went out exclaiming 'We mustn't allow that' with her hands above her head.

Thursday, 31 July

Mr B. says the war will be over next week. On my looking incredulous, he said 'Well, anyway, this winter. Look how t'Russians is sticking up to 'em and pummelling 'em. They're beaten already.' Strange how little reference is made to the war, directly or indirectly, though there is plenty of talk about food. Practically everyone who can remember says the food situation is not so bad as 'last time'. We have had nothing but potatoes this week – no tomatoes or peas – to sell.

Friday, 1 August

Gave our customers a treat today to celebrate the new rationing period. *Fruit salad* (from the Jews), baked beans and sultanas for everyone. It was grand to see their faces when we placed them on the counter without a word. We happened to have plenty of biscuits and sweets too, so made a good 'first impression'. Mr B. grumbled about being docked with cigs and when Bert said we had more customers to supply now he had the cheek to say we shouldn't take on more customers if it meant such as him going short of smokes! He gets six packets per week from us and then has other places, such as the canteen etc.

Saturday, 2 August

Just heard the BBC blandly announcing that the August ration of eggs ran out at 3 per registered customer, a decrease on the

5 to 7 they should have had in July. Then the wireless crackled loudly as if saying 'Gertcha!' Bert and I exchanged glances but were speechless. We have allowed our customers one egg each member of family and no prospect of any next week. This week the Co-op has none. Now Lord Woolton, what about it? A certain salesman in Dewsbury market has been fined for selling perfectly fresh eggs at 3d each, £50. He said he was selling at a loss then.

We sell ours at the controlled price of 2½d for *best eggs*. I blush as I hand these over. *They stink through the shells.* We have only had one returned and no one grumbles but if the subject of eggs is raised they say what bad eggs they have had from us lately. One woman said she would have no more – her last pudding cost her 10d for an egg. Now where is the sense of fining a man for selling a fresh egg at 3d and legalising the sale of bad eggs sold as fresh at 2½d? Regarding the *number*, Lord Woolton, did your spokesman *mean* 5 to 7 per registered *customer* or per registered *family*?

Later. Went to Mirfield to fetch Ma home. Things were quieter since Mr D. has given up retailing. He has nothing to do but pack and wait for the eggs to be collected. He says his eggs will never see this district. They will go to the 'upper ten'. The sorters know an egg when they see one. We shall get the 'battery eggs', he says, and proceeded to describe in detail the process of turning birds into egg making machines until I felt sick and wondered if all this uproar and commotion and cruelty (if any other sort of bird was treated in this horrible way there would be some fining and lectures from the 'bench') was worth the results we are getting. All this for an egg and often a bad 'un at that! Mr D. also had a grievance because the man who collects is a mill worker and also has a fish shop, and yet has the cheek to take on a job like that.

Sunday, 3 August

To brother Ben Rudolph's to tea. Ma said she thought the war would soon be over. Ben Rudolph said it was only just beginning. The war would last just twelve months after the Americans came in. Amy and Edna have salvaged most of their furniture but the day after the roof was blown off there was torrential rain so things were in a pretty mess. But they are lucky to have the bungalow to go to. Their neighbour in Franklin Street is seriously injured and next to that all killed and across the road mother killed, two boys blinded and father disappeared. There have been 17 raids on Hull recently but the press and BBC have not heard of them

Hull was the last city to be seriously damaged by German bombing in 1941. The wreckage shown here is adjacent to Franklin Street, where Kathleen's sisters-in-law's family home had been.

Photograph © The Hull History Centre

[such news was censored]. Ben Rudolph got a new camera, another German. He does not yet know whether so good as the Leica. But the difficulty is films [increasingly hard to obtain].

Monday, 4 August

A rainy depressing Bank Holiday. Hope it is different next week for our Blackpool trip. Have decided to take food with us to be on the safe side. Shall do without midday meal rather than queue for it three hours. A good many round here going to Blackpool last week in August so not bothering about Mr Churchill's warning [about a possible invasion].

Wednesday, 6 August

A letter from Alice P. [a relative from Northamptonshire] to say she is coming on Saturday for ten days. Margaret says it would be so, when we are going away, and thinks the Blackpool venture cannot prosper because of the many setbacks, but I say a poor start may be a good finish and am all set for a good holiday. A. P. must enjoy herself as best she may in our absence. A customer tells me she was short of nothing in Blackpool and brought back loads of stuff last week.

Friday, 8 August

C. L. paid his usual Friday visit to gather anything he could in the way of biscuits, cigs, etc. What with Bert's relations and ours, we could keep stocks moving without customers. C. L.

said General Wavell had not gone to India.* He was planning a move in Russia, and Germany would be invaded from the North of Russia. He said the war would finish this year.

Sunday, 10 August

To Ben Rudolph's to tea. Zillah opened the tinned chicken she got from Bert in February. Amy and Edna were there. Amy looked dreadful. They both dozed most of the time. We listened to that Reynaldo [Hahn, conductor and composer] and thought him fine. Amy said it was futile to wear an identity disc. The only way was to have your number tattooed all over you and then they might find a bit that could be identified [from the corpse].

Monday, 11 August

Here at Blackpool at last after a journey of no mark save a squabble between a man and wife about a forgotten identity card. I think she was disappointed because we were not stopped at the 'Barriers' (like the French Revolution!) for our cards as she could henpeck some more. I was disappointed because *her* card was at the bottom of all her luggage. Mrs J. had relented and promised to board us but was glad we had taken some food all the same. After lunch we walked towards Central [Station] but managed to get completely lost at the back of the town among the gasometers. It was like a Glamour girl caught without makeup. In the evening it was cold as we walked and sat in a shelter and read.

* In fact, General Archibald Wavell (1883–1950) had just gone there as Commander-in-Chief. He was replaced as C-in-C in the Middle East by General Claude Auchinleck (1884–1981).

Tuesday, 12 August

Walked round by Squires Gate Aerodrome this morning. The aeroplanes often fly over the roofs but no one takes any notice. There were queues at all food shops, some serving customers (residents) at one counter and visitors at another. By the time a woman on holiday has shopped for her family the morning will be gone. There are no cigs, sweets or matches though many of the windows are attract-ively dressed with dummy boxes. We have agreeable people in our rooms. An ex-miner, ex-trade union official, now a fish-shop proprietor 'and doing well'. His daughter and son-in-law, both ex-nurses at Wakefield asylum, he now in some sort of naval ambulance. A coal dealer from Manchester is also interesting. He says the officials controlling the coal to them can only tell them what to do but have no power to enforce anyone to do anything. It seems as big a farce as the food business. The ex-miner says he will go back to the pit when they have asked him as many times as he asked for a job when out of work.

From our lodging behind the Pleasure Beach we can see the Big Dipper but it is strange to have it working only till dusk [because of the blackout]. There is a curious flatness and staleness and lack of both colour and noise. Of course these things only get going when the lights are turned on. We lingered outside Madame Aleste's to watch the man plunge a sword through the lady in the box, and then decided to spend 7d (6d + 1d tax) to get out [of] the cold for half an hour. We went in and saw the lady on her throne, all blue satin and silver question marks, and while her assistant in evening dress was waiting for the last seats to be filled, I listened to conversations around me. The ladies in front discussed previous similar 'dos', the girls on my right giggled over a (probably) first cigarette, and the men behind, one a soldier, one a physical trainer perhaps, discussed physical jerks for soldiers who were older and agreed that the physical training was too stiff for nearly 40, although alright for young ones. The physical trainer also said the Air Force wanted to take a leaf out of the Army book and smarten their drill and their men. 'They didn't half drill.' The doors were closed and lights lowered and the usual method of Madame answering assistant's questions was followed. In answer to him Madame stated what page of the book I was reading was reached and what line and chapter. Later she told my birth date. She told one woman that her daughter in America had become engaged and another that she would have five more children. The man behind said, 'Of course it was a fake but clever, dashed clever'. Madame then made her prediction that the war would be over in eighteen months' time, that Britain would have great dangers to face, but that as always she would be finally victorious. We then bought a horoscope and card reading pamphlet including a special lucky charm (a scarab design stamped on a card) and came out into the blackout.

Wednesday, 13 August

A rainy wild day sent me straight off to Marks & Spencer after breakfast to buy a raincoat which cost 11s and 8 coupons. The store was packed already at 9.30. A woman was arguing with the assistant that coupons were not needed for macs. The day we spent walking and sitting in shelters on the South Promenade and the evening at the show on the South Pier. The ex-miner says politics is a dirty game. He knows it from the 'inside'. He says we are not seriously trying to win this war. A letter from Ma. She says a customer hearing Alice talk in the shop gazed for a minute and then said, 'You do talk different from us *English*, don't you?' Poor Alice and her Northants twang.

Thursday, 14 August

A letter today to say N.'s mother had fallen down the cellar stairs, which threw us into consternation for N. was to help Bert on Thursday and Friday with the rations. Debated whether one of us should go home. Decided to send a wire and see about a train for Friday. Had a queue at Central Station to enquire. The station was in complete darkness – the blackout, I suppose – and the crush was terrific. A loud speaker, supposedly to help people, only added to the confusion by indistinctness. We had literally to fight our way out and then couldn't get a breathing space until we were up to Sweeten's bookshop where we dived in for a rest only to find it as bad as the station. I snatched *I, Claudius* (Penguin) [a 1934 novel by Robert Graves] as I was carried along the surge, Margaret got two 3s 6d W. Rileys [a Yorkshire novelist], which I thought extravagant, and I seized the proprietor and demanded [Jane Austen's] *Emma* in a cheap edition. He produced her with such conjuring magic that he must have had her up his sleeve and I paid up but could easily have rooked him for the Penguins. We got out and after a few violent heaves reached the Prom and (comparative) comfort. 'If that is Thursday morning, whatever will it be on Saturday?' I said, skipping out of the way of a tram and into the path of an oncoming part of the RAF. I had to give way as they evidently would not. After, the South Pier pressure eased and we were able to sit and relax and worry about home affairs.

In the afternoon we waited for an answer to the wire and listened to the great announcement by [Deputy Prime Minister Clement] Attlee. Mrs J. said – Was that all? She thought at least America was coming into the war or Turkey. Everyone seemed to think it was a flat finish to our hopes.* Wire came at 6.40 – where on earth had it been all that time? – saying 'Not required – Could manage' – so we set forth to the Ice Drome with minds relieved. Here we could buy half-pound chocolates as we passed through the vestibule. (The first sweets we have seen in Blackpool. Good thing we brought some with us.) The show was fine. The ex-miner made us laugh at supper with his tale of Normanton Urban District Council and the councillor who, asked his opinion on the large overdraft at the bank, proposed they should build more council houses with it. He also gave us some examples of the graft that goes on in these places and when I said it was a pity folk didn't question and take more interest in Local Government, he said that was the whole trouble. Most councils did as they liked without question because no one bothered to question them. He was disappointed with the broadcast too. The son-in-law said, 'Let's get on wi' t'war and never heed t'other stuff'.

Friday, 15 August

A beast of a day. Rain unceasing and after tea a sea mist. Margaret and I wished we were at home. Most of our fellow

---

* Attlee's announcement, which was preceded by some fanfare, was simply to reveal the previously undisclosed meeting off the coast of Newfoundland between President Roosevelt and Prime Minister Churchill. People had been expecting more.

lodgers gone home today instead of tomorrow. After tea we wandered through the Pleasure Beach, pausing to have our character read by the handwriting lady. She looked sorry for us and asked if we were going to the Ice Drome. We said we had been. She said did we like dancing, we said No. She said 'Pictures?' We shook our heads and she gazed disapprovingly at us, thinking no doubt 'What have the fools come to Blackpool for?' We thought the same as the rain streamed from our oilskin bonnets and we paddled about like ducks. (I wonder why the place wasn't properly drained. Didn't the American-something Syndicate 'calculate' it might sometimes rain? Or perhaps they couldn't 'trail' the money.) We watched some people rolling balls into a hole and fondly imagining they were moving the race horses that galloped on the board above. (How people ask to be gulled.) There were 24 sixpences taken at least every five minutes at this stand. The prizes were packets of cigs. This works out at £7 14s less cigs retail (although they will be bought wholesale), £1 6s 6d, equals £6 7s 6d every hour profit. (There is always a crowd. Not much slack time.) Margaret said this was better than having a shop in Blackpool.

We then wandered on to the pier and were surprised at the number of people walking disconsolately there. We looked in a fancy-work shop and then entered the amber shop where I bought Margaret an amber brooch for her birthday. The lady seemed relieved to have someone to talk to and said it wasn't her shop but the proprietor was ill and she was only doing it for kindness. I thought she was very kind to stay there on anyone's account, even her own. We wandered into a postcard shop and enjoyed a free show until the shopman asked pointedly if we wanted anything as it was closing time, so I hurriedly seized a book (*Invitation to the Waltz* – Rosamond Lehmann [1941]) and Margaret bought cards and we fled. We sat on a seat and watched the mist – there was not an inch of view – and ate chocolate and wondered why people ever left home to come to Blackpool. When it was nearly 9 and the mist still closing in we made for home. As we climbed the crossing a car clanged drearily round the Scenic Railway in the gloom, and I thought this was the dismallist scene I had ever struck, in or out of Blackpool, and wondered what imbeciles would ride on a Scenic Railway in such weather.

Saturday, 16 August

The afternoon being promising we ventured to Cleveleys [just north of Blackpool] and sat in the sun some time, then to tea where we were denied cakes because we had toast, a curious reason we thought. Then we wandered into the shopping centre and looked at all the comic cards gratis until I was overcome with compunction and bought four sixpence books right off – *The Century's Poetry*, *Russia*, *The Thought-Reading Machine* [by André Maurois, 1938], and *The Quest for Corvo* [by A. J. A. Symons, 1935]. Then we went and listened to the Pierrots [musical and comedic entertainers] and had the best sixpence march since we came.

Sunday, 17 August

Bitterly cold and wet. Wandered up and down in the rain, waiting for Bert. He arrived at 11.30 but we missed him and never met until lunch. I packed my bag ready for them to bring home on Thursday and counted the books we had bought. *The Century's Poetry*, *Russia*, *Thought-Reading*

Machine, Invitation to the Waltz, Quest for Corva, Claudius for me, two Rileys for Margaret, *Emma* for Ma, besides the several we brought with us and never read. No wonder, for we had knitting and bought the *Daily Mail* and *Manchester Guardian* every day. Bert and Margaret ran me up to the bus station and I departed in a torrential downpour and gladness of heart. As we left St Annes [on the sea, three miles from Blackpool] the sun shone brilliantly. The journey was ordinary, except for me having to pay 6d for a tumbler of orangeade. Was fain and glad to reach home, and a bath and a bed to myself and soft.

Monday, 18 August

Ma saw Alice P. off at the station and then we settled down to an enjoyable day. This is *our real* holiday, just together. On opening shop this morning I found there was no sugar, margarine or potatoes, and of course we had no bread all day, so there has been more paid out than taken. Brooke Bond's said something would have to be done about the tea situation [it had been rationed since July 1940]. Didn't know there was a tea situation but to hear him, it's desperate. He also said – look what seats the Government had had to give Labour to keep them quiet, and there would be such a bust up in this country before long.

Tuesday, 19 August

Margaret writes the weather is lovely since I left [Blackpool]. Went to see Mrs C. She seems well considering her age and the nasty fall she had. N. says Dr S. says we are not putting our back into it. He says Winston Churchill used to be a fighter. He was a fighter when he took office but he's had it all taken out of him by these obstructionists.

Thursday, 21 August

Margaret and Bert came home this afternoon. Ten shillings short in cash when we checked up. Wish people would stay at home and look after their own money and business. Argument with Bert that 8s 6d per day was too much to charge for the sort of accommodation we had. He thought it fine but I don't like having to queue for bathroom and lavatory and expect for that price at least cold if not hot and cold water in bedroom. Of course, we should not go to Blackpool, I know, if we don't want to be cramped, but really when I pay 8s 6d for bed and board I expect at least comfort, if not luxury. I certainly don't *eat* it out.

Friday, 22 August

No biscuits and sweets for anyone. Two eggs per family. Mrs W. took tut [was annoyed] because of this and only bought the rations for her lodger. Not concerned as she has done well here with extras despite the fact her family is registered elsewhere. I should not be so generous to these people who deal at several shops as Bert is. He has no discrimination.

Saturday, 23 August

Bought some flowers at a stall in Dewsbury for Mrs Cox. Three chrysanthemums at 10d and greenery 10d but the woman murmured 3s 5½d altogether and slipped a small bag into my basket. This proved to be ¼ lb tomatoes which

I did not want as we had plenty but took as it seemed to be expected of me. This is the worst part of war, I think, making ordinary decent folk who have always paid up for what they wanted, and wanted the best, into furtive, secret scroungers. I am sure that if I had stolen the things I could not feel more guilty.

Sunday, 24 August

To Ben Rudolph's to tea. Amy and Edna have returned home. Zillah wanted Amy to try for a post around here but she would not consider [it] as she is at her maximum salary and would have much less in this district, besides Hull perhaps not accepting her again after the war. Zillah says someone told her they were killing the teachers at Hull with the strain they were putting them to. Zillah thinks it abominable that teachers at Heckmondwike and similar places should have seven or four weeks holiday when those in the blitz areas are near breaking point. Zillah says when Amy was evacuated first time to some little village she was charged £2 per week and had only porridge for breakfast, no lunch, and cold meat and bread for tea. At this place the children were lined up and the women walked up and down viewing them and saying 'I'll have this one', 'I'll take these two', like a cattle market, picking out all the pretty ones and clean ones first. Amy was so indignant that she said when it was over, 'Now I suppose the teachers are to be lined up and looked over.' The official in charge was shocked and said, 'Miss Nalton, does it appear like that to you?' Whereupon, I understand, Amy told him precisely how it did appear to her. After much shifting about she is back in Hull but her class is sadly depleted.

Listened to Winston tonight. When he finished Margaret said impatiently 'And what has he told us after all?' 'Nothing', I said gloomily. 'Nothing at all.'

Tuesday, 26 August

To-day the police came and asked Bert if he knew how to immobilise his car if necessary [in case of invasion]. Margaret is taking stock of the black-outs to see if she can improve on them.

Friday, 29 August

People coming to register for onions. Bert will not put their names down until he knows what to do from Food Office. Have no faith they will waste paper over onions. What is to prevent a person putting her family's name down at several shops? This is going to be another irritating business and for little profit. Mr G. came in great indignation because someone asked him if he didn't think he ought to go back to the pit. Mr G. says he had enough of the pit before. He says when he came back from Germany in 1920 there was no work for him. When he did get work and lamed himself there was no compensation. He says British miners were out of work while coal was being imported from Germany. He says he would not go back under any consideration. He now works at a soap works until 8 o'clock every night.

Saturday, 30 August

Auntie was here after shop closing. We discussed gas attacks and all agreed that Hitler had something up his sleeve for us – even Bert, who until two months ago thought the war was practically finished. Auntie said in the last war every time there were ill health rumours about the Kaiser he sent us new unpleasantness, and it would be the same now. Hitler and Goering and the rest put rumours about concerning their own health as a blind. We discussed the Scunthorpe squabble over the Councillors and the Gas Practice and all agreed it would have been better for the Councillors to keep quiet or own up manfully they were in the wrong.* We discussed our own gas practices and said what use were they when notice was given and people invited to take part in them at specified times and places. We discussed [Air Raid Precautions] wardens (paid) and said we should have to depend on ourselves only if anything happened. Those we had round here were a pretty sample, one old and fat, one lame and a pensioner of last war. We thought paid wardens should know elementary First Aid and Fire Fighting. And I wanted to know why they got 6s per week food allowance on top of their pay. Bert said some of them wanted the war to go on forever. They were in clover now and didn't care how long it went on. I confessed my war dread was to be in the street with incendiaries falling and one falling right on me and shrivelling me up. Explosives do not cause the same dread. Perhaps because I have not had much experience of them yet.

Auntie remarked that Marks & Spencer were piled with green tomatoes, some of them only as big as a gooseberry. It is evident that growers have been stripping the

---

* Gas had been tested during a civil defence exercise in Scunthorpe's Council Chamber, apparently without providing a means for those present to escape (*Scunthorpe and Frodingham Star*, 30 August 1941, p. 3). The incident seems to have been an instance of a local muddle made into a matter for mockery nationwide.

vines to get them on the market before the price went down on Monday and now it is not to go down and serves them right.

Monday, 1 September

Came a lady into the shop this morning so perturbed that she couldn't remember what she wanted. It seemed she had the jitters because it was September 1st and Mr Churchill said we were to be invaded on that day. Nothing I could say convinced her that we shouldn't have fire and death raining upon us and Jerry on the doorstep before morning. She merely stonewalled with 'Mr Churchill said so...' Two or three (men and women) remarked during the day that we should have to look out for something now.

Tuesday, 2 September

Waiting for the bus a lady started talking to me and said, after remarking on the lovely day and holidays, that she had seen the crash at Blackpool,* that her son worked at [RAF] Squires Gate Aerodrome, that we were never told of all the accidents that happen 'inside', landing etc., that four were killed there landing last week (learners). She then said she'd thought up to a month ago that the war would be over quickly but now she was sure it would go on for a long, long time. She then said she'd a son a gunner on the Scottish coast and that every time there was a raid she had 'stomach ache' for days. Her son says they are often machine gunned

---

* On 27 August 1941 a mid-air accident over the city involving the RAF caused part of one plane to crash on the roof of the Central Railway Station, scattering debris and aviation fuel. Eighteen people died and thirty-nine were injured.

but Jerry can't aim. He said they had shot down a plane over the sea five miles away. All this conversation was uninvited and unsupported by me beyond a few 'Oh's. And all in five minutes.

Wednesday, 3 September

Now some exertion to get customers shepherded into 'onion' department. They don't bother despite the notice on the counter telling what to do to obtain their 2 lbs per head. I believe only one customer has brought in counterfoils without a word from us. We were puzzled ourselves what to do until I went to the Post Office to enquire. The press merely said 'give in your names' and if anything was said on the wireless we'd missed it. I do think that the shop-keeper might be told these little details. All information is directed to the consumer and the shopkeeper has to do the running about to find out the truth of the wonderful talk circulating. To Mirfield this afternoon to fetch Ma home. Mr D. says (yet again) Lord Woolton is the ruination of this country. Everything he touches goes off the market. Now it is blackberries. Who'd want to pick blackberries at 3d a lb. Would he? He ought to be made to pick every berry in the kingdom at that price and see how he liked it. I thought blackberries had hardly gone on the market at the beginning of September but it is no use arguing. Curious how 'het up' everyone gets over food, much more than over the war, or raids or road accidents or America coming, or the blackout. They are resigned about all these latter things, but food really hits the tender spot.

A few weeks earlier, on 28 July 1941, a doctor in Leeds had visited a woman of about sixty who, with her husband, ran a greengrocer's stall in the city's market. Their work, he said, was tiring but had usually provided them with a decent living. War was effecting big changes. 'Now, although they have much less to sell and are without tomatoes and raspberries amongst other things, they are having a dreadful life trying to persuade people that they haven't got the particular fruits and vegetables everybody is short of. "It isn't the men customers," she says, "who are the trouble. They can take No for an answer. But the women are just like wolves, pestering you and arguing with you and cursing you for refusing what they ask for. They tell me 'I hope you get bombed,' and 'You ought to be in gaol'."' (Mass Observation Archive, Diarist no. 5124.) As Kathleen later testified, by the second half of the war food supplies were generally more reliable and aroused less public consternation.

Thursday, 4 September

A lady to register for onions and could she have them now please? 'No, indeed,' I said, 'the Food Controllers don't work that quickly.' 'When then?' she demanded. 'Christmas, perhaps,' I said vaguely, 'or maybe the end of the war.' Exit lady very displeased. Resolved (yet again) to stop nursing customers through these registerings. They must fill in their own coupons in future. The space allowed to write in is ridiculous, Lord Woolton. Why must we be irritated by things being awkward that could just as well be easy. When I have written Elizabeth Littleton, Paradise Buildings, Heckmondwike Road, The Moor, Dewsbury on coupon SC4 and then have to find space for our rubber stamp, I am far from amiable and not in the mood to be confronted with seven ration books and 'Will you fill up our coupons for onions now please, because mother wants to take the books to the butcher?' I calculate I have filled in 80 of the 96 coupons handed in.

A shopkeeper stamps a housewife's ration book.
In the foreground can be seen the tea, sugar, 'national butter',
margarine, cooking fats and bacon she is allowed for one week.
Photograph © IWM D2373

Friday, 5 September

Bert wondering if he will have to register for fire watching as he holds no warrant card from Mr Hobbs [at 35 Heckmondwike Road] to enter any home in case of emergency. He is supposed to be a fire watcher for this district. I said (once again) we should have a stirrup pump for this place and the two cottages adjoining. Mr Hobbs said we should have to buy one, in a scandalised voice. I said it wouldn't be much if three of us joined. Mr Hobbs said Mr S. had one. (Mr S. lives seven houses, two barns and several spaces away.) I said yes and Mr S. will stick to it if incendiaries are falling. 'Oh, you'll be alright,' said Mr Hobbs. 'We shall be round about.' I shut up then. Mr Hobbs is the owner of this three storey building and the two cottages (one of which he lives in) next door. He is a warden and works every other week on nights.

Saturday, 6 September

Wonder what Americans think of Mr [Mackenzie] King's hints?* Bert and another man discussing said that Yanks thought too much of their money and comfort. Both have spent some years in America. I hope this is not a true description of Americans but what are we to think?

* In a speech on Thursday at Mansion House in London, the Canadian Prime Minister had spoken as if the security of Canada (at war since 10 September 1939) and the United States (not yet in the war, but nudging towards it) were inextricably intertwined – in the defence of freedom (*The Times*, 5 September 1941, p. 5). Churchill, who was present, made the extravagant claim that 'Canada is the linchpin of the English-speaking world,' justifying this assertion with the observation that it had intimate and friendly relations with both the United States and Britain. (*Collected Speeches*, VI, 6479–80.) Churchill, of course, was anxious for the Americans to become fully-fledged wartime allies as soon as possible.

Sunday, 7 September

As Margaret still has her jam sugar carefully saved we decided to try for some blackberries and set out with a basket and several paper bags. But the children and birds had beaten us. So we sat in the car and read (Bert slept). Margaret read the Sunday papers (reading out Lyndoe and Petulengro to my annoyance – I like to read them for myself). Ma reads *Emma*, I read *Begin Here* by D[orothy] Sayers and a Pelican *Russia* – Bernard Pares [1940]. Dark at 8.30. Margaret says we should practise our gas masks every night. I think every time the siren goes often enough.

Monday, 8 September

E. brought our 20-year-old cousin from Northants to see us today. N. wishes to join the WAAFs [Women's Auxilliary Air Force] but her employer, a chemist, will not release her. She says Lady B. says she must join the WRENS [Women's Royal Naval Service]. It is the only service and she will get her in [it was the most socially exclusive of the women's auxiliary services]. Mr C. says he will speak for her too. I said I thought there was to be *no* snobbery in this war. N. said she knew a girl who tried to join but gave it up because she was required to state her father's occupation and income and other intimate details which didn't affect *her* suitability.

Wednesday, 10 September

To Harrogate for the half day with E. and N. The shops were closed but we looked in the windows and impressed upon N. the snobbishness and exclusiveness of the place,

telling of the bombs dropped out of the blue one afternoon
[12 September 1940] and Harrogate's indignation. I said
I believed there was a protest letter to Hitler. N. looked
incredulous and then laughed. After wandering in the Valley
Gardens a short time we had to go back to the bus tea-less
and waited hungrily for the last two of our travellers half an
hour. They came eventually and were greeted with pointed
remarks from some of the company for keeping us all waiting. Most of our travellers were middle-aged and elderly
ladies with leatherette bags and paper carriers, doubtless
with food in, and about three oldish men. At Knaresborough
we looked about for a tea-place, the best-looking were
closed for a week's holiday. In the end it was Hobson's
Choice, a frowzy looking tearoom over an empty-windowed
pastry cook's. We had the choice of ham roll and salad or
jam. We chose the former which proved to be a pink mystery tasting of boiled rice, one slice of tomato, one ditto of
cucumber and a teaspoonful of chopped lettuce. This with
homemade bread, margarine and tea cost us 1s 6d per each.
I left 2d for the girl, thinking she had earned it after carrying heavy trays all afternoon up and down two flights. Up by
the Castle the wind was so strong we were glad to go down
to the river but E. would not pay to see the Wishing Well
and Mother Shipton's Cave, 'having seen it once,' so after
looking at the shops we trekked back to the bus 30 minutes
before time. On the way I bought an illustrated paper and
two Penguins – *Russian Short Stories* and *Herodotus* which is
positively my last book-buying this year. Margaret says I am
like Hitler and his territorial claims – always one after the
last. On the way home N. who, I am afraid, had not a very
thrilling day, remarked she had expected to find the sea at
Harrogate!

Friday, 12 September

Margaret said she heard on the wireless that American and English production would equal Germany's in 1943. Bert flew into one of his rages and said it was ridiculous, the war couldn't last another year, all would have to be over by next spring or look at the people who would be bankrupt. Folk weren't going to carry on and lose money, neither Germany nor Britain. It wasn't like the last war when folk were making piles of brass and didn't care how long it lasted. Nobody was making anything out of this. I limited myself to picturing Hitler harassed by the thought of the miseries and worries of the British businessman. Am often amazed by the way people regard it as someone else's war, and talk of 'they' in an 'onlooking' kind of way, instead of 'we' as you would suppose. And many seem to think 'they' will stop it when it suits their purpose. Mr N. at the Post Office says U.I. [Unemployment Insurance] is going up in the New Year, ready to give the out-of-works more brass after the war and keep 'em quiet. As I have never really found my feet after the last slump, and only had third rate and half paid jobs since, this view did nothing to cheer me. I keep considering going on munitions but the thought of afterwards appals me. I think the years of my 'twenties' when out of work and 'unwanted' will never be erased from my memory. They have certainly altered my whole attitude to life and other people. I couldn't risk unemployment again even if 'safety' means poverty all my life.

Saturday, 13 September

Mrs Hobbs (our landlady) announces her novel is nearing completion. She is in no doubt that it will be published – 'Someone who knew' had told her it was good [no novel by Sarah Hobbs is held in the British Library]. When I asked how many thousand words she looked taken aback and then said 'Oh, about 175,000'. Miss P. says weren't the Russians doing well for us? And isn't it a good thing Hitler turned that way instead of this?

2

Grumbles and Groans

September–October 1941

Sunday, 14 September.

To Ben Rudolph's after tea. He has to register next week but a man is going to 'do' them all, so no time will be broken. The London evacuees from the farm cottage have departed mysteriously taking with them O. H.'s sideboard dresser that she had lent them, also numerous other things that various people had lent. Zillah says they managed to obtain *five* bicycles among them during the six months they were there, not to mention such details as pulling up all the farmer's rhubarb and vegs and selling them from door to door. Ben Rudolph says he can't get his hair cut. As fast as he finds a new barber he is called up. B. A. has gone to be a land girl in Sussex. We were discussing all the youngsters we knew who had got married this year, without a home. Zillah says Mrs N. says she hopes G. realises he will have a home to provide when he returns, and looks like having a delicate wife too for she has been in hospital twice this year.

Many of the girls live at home and continue to go to work, going to their husband's people when he has leave.

Monday, 15 September

Had a restless night after listening to the wireless telling of losses of Germans and Russians. Kept waking myself by repeating aloud 'Millions, millions'. The halfpenny carrot season is now in full swing. Carrots are the last thing the children buy when there are no sweets, biscuits or apples. The amount of carrots some of them consume in a day is astounding, and with no apparent ill effects. Mrs L. says her father is selling his home grown pears at 4s per stone at Pickering, the same as we are charged in the shops 1s per lb.

Tuesday, 16 September

Listened last night to *St Joan* [by George Bernard Shaw] for a short time and was becoming interested. So was Margaret but Ma grew restless and said how much longer was that going on and Bert was sarcastic about highbrows, so we shut it off. Here we are four people, all with decided likes and dislikes about wireless fare, and consequently none of us except Bert gets satisfied. He likes variety and light shows and gets them. I have ceased to bother about my preferences because I cannot indulge them. Ma likes the news on four times a day, for fear we miss something, and Margaret would have it on continuously, being one of those who would keep it on even if not interested, ready for the next item she wants to hear. She also reads all the time she is 'listening'. It is curious that Margaret, who is touchy about noises and voices, can stand any amount of wireless. Ben Rudolph is just the same. Zillah used to have it on all day from 8 to 12 midnight when she was first married [in the later 1920s] for company.

Wednesday, 17 September

And now sweets are to be price controlled. Wonder if it will make a difference to our way of selling, so many for 1d. We may have to stop this. Bert cross because we can get much more for them this way and it helps out [with] something we get little on. Sweets and toffee that should be 5d per quarter we get 6d to 8d for by giving the kiddies a few in their hand.

To Mirfield for tea. Mrs D. says they are kept at it selling apples. They have nearly stripped the trees before the fruit was quite ready because the orchard was being robbed every night and the hedges and trees broken down. The kiddies come constantly out of school hours for a 1d apple. Mrs D. says she worries sometimes over the money they bring, 2s or 2s 6d regularly and spend 3d or 4d. She is sure they should not have all that money, such young children. Mr D. says the egg collector says the eggs have dropped off surprisingly. He says people are selling them for high prices on the sly. (This means we shall be eggless next I suppose.) We still get our half dozen per week off the milk girl. She charges 3½d but Margaret says it is worth it as they are new laid. Mr D., struggling for two days with his blackout blind, told Margaret this morning it was perfect but on going to show her how it worked the thing wouldn't work and Mrs D. with many swears had to stand on the table to coax it. The blackout is one of the trying things of the war I think. One is always subconsciously afraid of showing a gleam of light, or forgetting the blinds, or otherwise transgressing. Mr D. thinks the Russians are doing well. He says it must be horrible out there – knee deep in blood.

Today MO papers came and *Clothes Rationing Survey* booklet which greatly intrigued Ma. She refers to it as 'your Prize'. Have no time to look at booklet yet [*Change*, no. 1, August 1941].

Already flustered by trying to read *Clearer Thinking* [by Alfred Ernest Mander, 1936, subtitled *Logic for Everyman*] and *Russia* on the one hand and keep two diaries going on the other.* And knit gloves as well, out of old unravelled jumpers for Xmas presents! Was pleased with my first effort until I found that both gloves were for one hand. To crown it all Bella Hill brought in a book she had borrowed for me to read – *Gone with the Wind* [by Margaret Mitchell, 1936]. 800 pages. Pooh! And the way the story ends threatens a sequel. Taken a dislike to the green eyed, magnolia skinned heroine on the first page. Shall never endure her through 800. Shall have to read one in 20 about so that I can look intelligent if the subject crops up. Sent M. G. a tin of lobster for her birthday which is more sense than the *J. Ireland's Songs* she sent me.

Thursday, 18 September

Glanced through MO papers as I was dressing and am 'floored' straight away. See [I] shall have to put on my thinking cap for questions this week, and it is an ill-fitting garment. My mind flits easily from point to point like a bird on a branch but when a settled opinion is asked for and reasons to be given, particularly about a nebulous idea like 'Progress' I am flummoxed.† As the man said, 'I know enough to know I know nowt'.

---

* This is the only indication that Kathleen was also keeping a private diary. We assume that it has not survived.

† MO's Directive for September asked about 'progress'. 'What do you personally mean by "progress"? Do you think the world has "progressed" in the past 100 years, and if so in what ways do you think it has progressed? If not, explain. Do you normally look on progress as a process which goes on automatically all the time, or do you think it only occurs at certain times?' (MOA, FR 854.1.) Since none of the Responses to the Directives from 1941 has survived, we do not know what Kathleen thought about this topic.

Bert went down to the Food Office in a disturbed frame
of mind to answer the charge of discrepancies in his butter
returns, but he was consoled to find a queue all bent on the
same errand. What with folk fetching their returns in bits
and bats instead of altogether and evacuees and soldiers (two
or three different ration rates for them) I think we do marvellously well. At any rate the Food Office is reasonable and
approachable. We had a lady in for emergency rations whom I
thought very dour until she chanced to remark it was strange
to see glass in shop windows – when it dawned on me she was
an evacuee. She was and living with Mrs M. who told me later
that the woman and two tiny children had been bombed out
of Hull; her husband was on a minesweeper and didn't know,
and they had been living in half a shelter for six months. When
the billeting officer came round Mrs M. offered to take two
children but when they arrived their mother was with them
'and what could I do, I had to take them in. The woman
looked paid out and I am going to give her a rest and look
after the kiddies for her'. They were two nights in hospital at
Bradford before coming here, being examined, and then some
of the people who had promised to have them went back on
their word – one woman saying loudly and cruelly 'I am not
having any children so you can just take them away' – so that
many of them had to be taken back to Hull again. Margaret
says she wishes no one ill but it really would do this district
good to have a small dose of what Hull has had. I think it is
lack of imagination rather than lack of heart that makes people
callous, and many a one has the same attitude to evacuees as
to the unemployed – 'Yes it is a pity, but what can I do? It's
not my business. It's the Government's' – with a little con-
descension in their attitude. Only similar experience will jolt
some of them awake. After all Hull isn't Russia – they cannot

have disaster much nearer their own doorstep and still be able
to turn their back on it. But it makes one wonder – when one
reads how the Russian women are fighting side by side with
the men and everyone joining whole heartedly into what there
is to do.

Friday, 19 September

Listened to Lord Woolton last night and thought him reasonable enough, except for his saying that people will have to get
more meals out. This may be alright for workers and people
at the centre of things but it is useless for our district where
people would have to pay 2d bus fare to reach them. And I
don't think the Yorkshire housewife will ever get into the way
of dining out. Besides you get three or four out of a family
taking meals like that and it's going to cost something in a
week even at 9d a head only. It is cheaper to give them bread
and fish paste or such like. A working class woman cannot
afford 9d per head per meal or anything like it. Though a lot of
them could get better meals if they stayed at home and spent
some time preparing them instead of going out for a low wage
which they have to pay out in other ways to keep things going.
These older married women would do better by their country
to stay at home and look after their families better. But some
of them would much rather go out. Mrs C. has worked all her
life as a 'rag picker' earning good money, her two children
had started working and her husband had a steady job on the
roads. Then she had another child and the family peace was
broken. She could no longer go to work and 'keep her end up'.
She tells me her husband and daughter frequently throw it up
at her that she is not 'bringing anything in' and therefore has
no say in household affairs. 'I held my head as high as anyone

and dressed as well, before I had *him*. Now I'm just a mug for them.'

*In the broadcast under discussion, the Minister of Food did indeed recommend that citizens, especially those unaccompanied by children, could cope better with household rationing if they sometimes ate out at British Restaurants (initially referred to as Communal Feeding Centres), which were then being set up to provide hot, nourishing meals at reasonable prices, usually a shilling or less for a full-course midday meal. No ration coupons were required for these meals, and the service was cafeteria-style, then a novelty. As Lord Woolton put it, 'people can go there to get supplementary food in just the same way as other people can go to clubs, [private] restaurants and hotels'. (BBC Written Archives Centre, p. 4 of the script.) In April that year a British Restaurant, staffed mainly by members of the Women's Voluntary Services, had been opened in Dewsbury at the Wellington Road Methodist Sunday School, not far from the LMS train station. (*Dewsbury District News, *19 April 1941, p. 5 and 22 March 1941, p. 5.) *Kathleen's concern was that since Dewsbury Moor was on the outskirts of the town, its residents would have to pay to take a bus to get to and eat at the new British Restaurant. These restaurants usually worked best when they were located in places where there were lots of daytime workers nearby, which was certainly the case in town centres.*

*The reference to Mrs C., a rag picker, is a reminder that the recycling of woollen garments was a prominent industry in Dewsbury, and that sorting these 'rags' for future 'shoddy' goods demanded considerable skill. As the *Dewsbury Official Handbook *for 1950 observed (p. 71), 'so far, no machine has been invented which can perform the job of a skilled sorter. Indeed, an expert in this trade can command much higher wages than those provided by the Trade Board Acts. Merchants always try to retain in their employ such* *sorters, usually women, whose keen sight and nimble fingers can at once differentiate between various types of cloth rags. Some of these women are able to classify a rag at first glance – quite a feat when one remembers the almost infinite variety of grades, even in the average wardrobe.'*

The work had a significant impact on the profits achieved. 'This process of sorting determines just how much the merchant is to make on any particular batch of rags, for whereas some cloths are relatively valuable, others, which contain a large proportion of cotton or artificial fibres, may be worth very little. When the rags have been sorted, they are baled and labelled by various trade names. Some of these grades may not be wanted for years, but they are always potentially valuable to the merchant.' During the war Dewsbury was a receiving depot for most of the Forces' discarded clothing. 'A special Government department was set up to deal with the vast quantity of uniforms which had become unwearable. Thousands of tons were stored in the town, and from time to time amounts were released to rag merchants and after treatment [for purification] much of the material was re-made into uniform cloth.' (Ibid., pp. 71–72.)

The evening's talk at 37 Heckmondwike Road had not yet ended.

We then discussed (going back to Lord Woolton) fairness of rationing and agreed that it was hard that a little more couldn't be given to the old folk who live by themselves and less to young children. For instance, a woman with a baby in arms and a toddler does not need ½ lb bacon and ¼ lb of tea for them every week but these would be grand for the old folk who cannot get out to seek delicacies for themselves. But we agreed a lot of the grumbling about being short was not for essentials but for luxuries which in the years before the war had come to mean essentials to many. When we were at

Wakefield shop it was not unusual to sell customers 5 to 7 lbs cheap sweet biscuits per week (in ¼d and ½d). The children who come for them at this rate were always the poorest clad, and they always spent most on sweets too. Frequently women would say 'Our so-and-so will not eat any breakfast. All he wants is cream biscuits.' As for the miner who said he had to take dry bread five days a week – well, he should roust his wife round for that. Margaret said you know what miners are. He'd probably drunk all his wage.

Saturday, 20 September

Bert to Food Office and straightened out his butter tangle. He says the Food Office said 'That's another cleared up' in relieved tones. I suppose they have their troubles too. Maybe he had been getting into trouble because there was too much butter melting away in Dewsbury. At any rate Bert said there was a rare queue of worried looking shopkeepers. The milk business is going to be awkward. We have about 18 gallons allocated according to registrations but our present amount dealt with is only 36 pints per week. I fear a good many of those registered are the sort who don't have a regular milk man and are only counting on getting an occasional tin. The Medical Officer should have made clear if tinned milk was to be rationed. We look like having gallons of milk on our hands when we begin.

Monday, 22 September

Discussing refugees in the shop today Mrs L. said all her neighbours were in fear and trembling that they would be forced to take some. Several people, however, have already taken some. Old Mrs H. took in a mother and two young children and on hearing there were two older boys at Batley she said they could come as well so as all to be together. Mrs L. says her brother and sister at York each have children and they manage very well but it is the parents and other relations visiting at weekends and expecting 'Yorkshire pudding and such-like' that upset things and if protest is made they are told they are well paid for it. Another friend of Mrs L.'s had four boys but she soon got rid of them for dirty habits but not before they ruined her two beds [by bed-wetting]. Mrs H. said her mother had had a packet [trouble] with evacuees and wouldn't have another if she went to prison for refusing.* The first one she had, a girl, had only the clothes she stood up in; they rigged her out and kept her until her parents sent for her back and sent her home with two suitcases full of clothes, but there was neither any acknowledgement or return of suitcases. The next attempt was with a boy of eleven whose habits were filthy. They struggled on however until he went home for Christmas and then told him not to come back. On Christmas Eve, however, he returned, late at night and said his parents had sent him. But they refused to let him in and dispatched him to the Billeting Officer who fixed him with more suitable accommodation, that is, with people more his own stamp.

Tuesday, 23 September

Switched off the wireless after the 9 [o'clock] news when that tedious Mr Brown began to talk Polish horrors. I think we are having too much war and war talk shoved down our

---

* Householders could be forced to take in one or more evacuees. However, billeting officers tried to avoid coercion since it usually led to unhappy results.

throats. We should be given a more bracing atmosphere to help us through dark winter days. Surely there are some good speakers somewhere in Britain who won't treat us like school children. Anyway, haven't we horror enough without piling on the agony?

Wednesday, 24 September

The question about shelter plans prompted me to look at ours. I had to scramble over new dug ground and then knee deep into high grass and weeds, and found its doorway tastefully decorated with a tall seeding plant, and its interior filled with bricks, about three cartloads. Whatever possessed Mrs Hobbs to have the thing there for in the first place, and why did she permit the Council to put an extension to it if it was never meant to be used? I believe she had some high notion about it being a refuge for strangers passing but they would break their necks in any attempt to reach it in the dark, even if they knew it was there, which they could not possibly [know] – it is not seen from the road. Mr and Mrs Hobbs, our landlady and lord, have ceased to be wardens, and handed all their traps in. It will be strange when next we have a siren not to have Mrs Hobbs tearing round the estate blowing her whistle and again at 'all clear' ringing the handbell vigorously; in between times she sits in her shelter all the time. N. says their wardens used to ring and rattle and blow all at one and the same time, until people complained they didn't know whether they had to go to shelter or bed or put on their masks. Our raids at Dewsbury Moor are comic opera ones. If something *did* happen I dread to think how we should fare. Mrs J. says all the surface shelters are disgraceful, the children use them as lavatories, and Mrs G. says the ones near her house are the same and have only been completed a month. She says she wouldn't go in them on any account. I said I should ask for them to be locked.

N. and Bella Hill were going blackberrying today so Mr Hobbs decided to take a day off from work and go. He said there were plenty of men standing about doing nothing without his help. For this 'government' job he gets £3 per week.

Monday, 29 September

Had afternoon off to see [George Bernard Shaw's] *Major Barbara* [at the Pioneer Cinema] which is only the second time to pictures this year.

Wednesday, 1 October

Bella Hill says there are fifty evacuees coming on the Moor on Friday. She says it is about time some of those big houses up Birkdale and Oxford Roads has someone; they had more room and had as much right to be put about as poor folk. What about H. S. and his brother, both ex-mayors and both houses with only two occupants? I said Yes, there was a letter [from 'Share and Share Alike'] in the *Reporter* last week from Bennett Lane complaining that besides having the [anti-aircraft] 'gun' they had soldiers and evacuees ever since the war began and it was time things were faired up, and this letter mentioned Birkdale and Oxford Roads. Margaret said it was the fault of the Government for appointing local Billeting Officers. They knew all the local Bigwigs and were thinking of their jobs after the war. Bella Hill said, 'They'll not have any, lass, whoever writes to t'papers. Money gets away with it every time.'

To Mirfield for tea. Mr D. said he'd been talking to a man at Ossett who never got up if in bed when there was an alert.

But said Mr D. 'If I was your neighbour and my house got on fire you couldn't get dressed and out to help me in two minutes. And neither could I help if I was in bed and had to dress. I always dress and put on my boots on "alert".' This reply impressed the man who said he had never considered having to help anyone else and he would in future get up. Such is the power of suggestion coupled with Mr D.'s voice and presence. I said it was funny how Germany had got all those men trained and armaments before the war and everyone in this country who knew kept quiet about it. Mr D. said no one kept quiet. Baldwin, Chamberlain, Churchill, Lord Lloyd all warned us Germany was preparing but [Clement] Attlee [leader of the Labour Party] and his crush wouldn't have rearmament at any price. They would have all those houses built and social services and of course the public supported those who had the most to offer, and that was how we got into this mess. He said Germany had often boasted she could turn any of her mills on to armament work in 24 hours.

Thursday, 2 October

Listened to *Brains Trust* recording at dinnertime [1.15] which recalled our experiment on Sunday at M. S.'s 'after Joad'.* The lifting was a success in the first instance, [with] K. M. who is very slight, but with M. S. about 14 stone a complete failure. On hearing Joad's full story today I said no wonder we failed – we'd had no beer!

We had an 'alert' [for] about half an hour last night. I remained in bed and should have slept but for Bert continuously

---

* Philosopher Cyril Joad was a regular member of the vastly popular BBC question-and-answer programme, *Brains Trust*.

opening the shop door. Mrs Hobbs our landlady does not make the night resound with her whistle now as she has resigned voluntary ARP [Air Raid Precautions], and Mr Hobbs too, having taken tut [disapproval] because their best girl furrier had had to change her job to something more essential than renovating fur coats. Formerly Mrs Hobbs used to whistle round the neighbourhood running at breakneck speed and then burrow in her shelter until the 'all clear'.

Friday, 3 October

Mrs Hobbs informs me rather spitefully it will soon be my turn [to be called up for national service] and I shall not be exempt because I am not on food 'production' and in any case not a 'key' worker. I nearly said 'Is your assistant a "key" worker?' but refrained. Bella Hill says the Labour Exchange told the girl it did not matter how many letters Mrs Hobbs wrote or how many influential people Mrs Hobbs 'enlisted' to speak for her, she would have to go on war work and that was the end of it. We seem to have several new faces among the children seeking sweets. They ask for 'goodies' instead of 'spice' [sweets] so conclude they are 'Hull-ites', evacuees. The 'spice' department will be sold-out earlier than ever.

Sunday, 5 October

To Mirfield to see Ma. Discussed evacuees. Mrs D. said her sister in Lincolnshire had a little girl whom she wanted to leave as she felt too old (nearly seventy) to bother, and besides the mother (unmarried) seemed to think she'd found a permanent home for the child. Mrs D. says her sister complains to the Vicar frequently but a fresh home has not been found for the poor child yet. Mrs D. said Mrs W. (a lady magistrate) had been round Mirfield to see about billeting. At one house she was confronted by 'Are you having some bairns yoursen?' Mrs W. said 'no'. 'I'll have some when you do. As many as you do. And my house isn't so big as yours.' There is surprisingly little resentment, really, that the 'better class' folk are getting off having 'lodgers'. Most folk seem to regard it as something to be avoided if possible, if not they must be resigned. The only willing ones I have talked to are women who have got several children, either small or grown up.

Monday, 6 October

Mrs W. was telling me her troubles with the Public Assistance Officer [in charge of poor relief]. Her husband is in the institution as a result of the last war, incurable. She said she had so much to put up with from the Public Assistance Officer that as soon as the lads started working she gave up having relief at all and they have all three lived on 38s per week for some time. Now John has got a better job and immediately she had a letter from the Public Assistance Officer to ask how much she proposed paying towards her husband's keep. She said she was not grumbling but she did think she ought to have a chance to get on her feet. The boys had no new clothes for two years apart from working boots and her household things were getting done [i.e., worn out]. I said she ought to live at Wakefield which is a scrounger's paradise if ever there was one. They are not stingy with Public Assistance there. She said well, she hoped she had finished with Public Assistance. They would manage somehow now the lads were getting older.

We had had no tea for three days. This must be the crisis that Brooke Bond's man threatened so long.

Tuesday, 7 October

Ulkew, our best sweet traveller, came today. (He is also my cousin and favours us very much so that I think sometimes someone will grumble at 'short allowance'.) I asked him what about serving the canteens. He said they would have to do it whether they wanted or not and it was a silly order because it simply meant the bosses and top-dogs would have their pickings of all the sweets and chocolate to the canteens and the workers would have the leavings if any. He said it would be much better to let it out to the shopkeepers who know their own customers and could be trusted to share it as they knew best. I said, 'Hear, hear,' but considering everything we don't do so badly here though we are very careful with our rations, keeping them first for the children and second for customers.

Bert had had occasion to warn Mrs C. about leaving some of her weekly bill on. She is the only one of our dozen tick customers who ever does. The others who spend anything from 12s to £2 always 'pay on the nail' and rarely vary from week to week more than 2s. They are much more straight than at Wakefield, especially about paying odd coppers owing, and seldom quibble about their bills. Our landlady, Mrs Hobbs, who had the shop before, used to add sixpence per customer for 'book keeping trouble' but we stopped this unfair practice, though we could if we were disposed add shillings, as only three of our customers keep an account to check up by.

Reading *Claudius* but find it a strain rather, what with keeping track of all the characters and reading [H. G.] Wells' *History* to explain what the book doesn't. Ma looks with disfavour on 'Penguins and Pelicans', thinking no good can be got from any book costing only *six pence*. But she succumbed to *Pygmalion* [by George Bernard Shaw, 1912], saying 'I don't know what sort of book you've bought me – but it's true what it says, all the same.'

Wednesday, 8 October

As N.'s employer will now have to release her, E. has written for her to live with her and go on munitions, so E. won't have room for evacuees. But N. will not do that, I think. She will join the Forces as she has wished to for some time.

Thursday, 9 October

The black news from Russia [concerning the German assault on Moscow] has stirred people to talk about the war when they come in the shop. Three people asked if we had heard the news at 8 o'clock. Several said things looked bad for Russia. *Men* spoke in sort of admiration of the Germans. 'He must have some stuff. It doesn't seem to make any difference how much he loses, he just goes on.' 'They're clever, you know, whatever you say about them. They have been getting ready for years.' 'They can show us points.' Mrs M., evacuated from Hull, came in with her little boy of three. I said when was he going to school? She said would the war be over when he was old enough. I said I didn't know, but not this winter. She said, no, nor next, and seemed gloomy. Her husband is on a minesweeper. A traveller said what did we think now of the war. Bert said they were trying to get dug in before winter. Traveller said yes, and then it would be a job dislodging them. The difficulty was getting supplies to them. He knew Persia personally from last war, and what transport would be like. What a good thing Hitler had gone there first instead of here. He must have unlimited men and stuff.

Saturday, 11 October

Mr C. in today said that people were making a tremendous fuss about Russia but that they would hold out. The Germans were still 200 miles from Moscow. The Russians would trap them. But Mr C. would not have it that France would collapse right up to the last day, nor that we should ever be bombed, although he's an old soldier. Tonight M. G. came and then N. G. We had a real 'war' talk. M. G. led up by saying how unfairly the voluntary Fire Service are treated. Her brother, who has served voluntary since spring 1938 and has 100% record for attendance, was given no option when he was of age but put on regular service, and was divested of his stripes (like cashiering, M. G. says), as if he'd done something wrong, and now he has to kick his heels all day and polish the fire engine, when he is a trained wireless expert and keen to go on radio location. M. G. says contrast this with her second brother's treatment. He, a Grammar school University-trained teacher, never did anything for the war until he was called up. He was greeted with open arms. The Colonel gave him the choicest of England's Army work to choose from and talked to him like a father. M. G. says it is unfair that the willing ones who have helped from the beginning should be penalised and the hangers-back made much of.

Then we discussed Mrs Hobbs's business, which seems to haunt us just now. Bert, as usual on the wrong tack, said who was Mrs Hobbs anyhow that her assistants shouldn't go, and what importance was a furrier's business? N. said, when she could be heard, that the point was that a girl at the Labour Exchange should have the sole decision about a business that had taken years to build, and why wasn't there a tribunal to hear and discuss these things? I said that the *Daily Mail* [which now favoured the conscription of young single women] said women were pampered about these things and given unlimited time to make their minds up. I'd always understood there was a tribunal. M. G. said no, it wasn't like that. She knew a girl who was called up, and said she would like to join ATS [Auxiliary Territorial Service] or WAAFs. The girl clerk looked her up and down scornfully and told her, 'You'd better go on munitions, my girl,' whereupon the girl marched out saying 'B——you, I'll do nowt'. 'You will be sent for,' said the clerk. 'Yes, send,' said the girl, 'and won't I tell them something.' This was months ago and she has never heard a word. Bert, still on the subject, said why shouldn't Mrs Hobbs do her own furrying if it came to that? N. said, fair was fair, and there should be more than one person to hear her side. Even Bert had to admit that was right. M. G. said of course there was bound to be unfairness in dealing with millions and millions. There was bound to be grievances and squabbles. But I wondered if the Russians wasted their time trying to get out of service and sacrifice. We talked of all the married women we knew, too old for service but young enough to have a darn good time and enjoy life. Margaret said there would probably be older folk drawn in yet, the way things were shaping. I said I hoped I didn't have to go on munitions. Margaret said she thought not, I was a food assistant, but cheer up, it's no use trying to stop things; we shall have to accept things as they come.

Then it was evacuees. Margaret said why were they all being brought to poor homes? N. said because they were suitable for the type of evacuee. (She's helped to billet.) The town was plotted into districts and it was Dewsbury Moor's turn. I was not convinced and said, well what about a better type, like us, for instance? Surely we should be good enough for Oxford Road district [a prosperous part of town]. To my surprise both N. and M. G. jumped on me and said there was no better type; it was always the same kind who had to be found homes – the other sort found their own billets. We should if we were bombed out.* 'That depends—' I began, but was shouted down before I could say what if we lost all our money, what if our friends were in similar plight, or already full up? So I fell to considering where we could go about here to lodge and apart from Ma going to Mirfield couldn't think of anywhere for us.

Monday, 13 October

Lord Beaverbrook's talk last night was clearly to ginger us up to work harder [the newspaper magnate had headed a recent high-level mission to Moscow]. The Russian business is a puzzle. After being warned of the nasty Bolshies so long we're now asked to embrace them as brothers and Allies. Before they were never mentioned on the wireless or press other than derisively; now their praises are sung to the skies. Well, all the praises are deserved and something more substantial too. I never did believe all they said about Russia anyway; it may have been true – but only half the truth I think. But we needn't skit any more at the Germans for turning somersaults.† And I wonder what's going to be the 'Big Pots'' attitude to Russia after the war.

* People of financial means usually relocated by means of private billets, perhaps with relatives or friends. Official billeting was used mainly by those who were not well off, including the wives of men in the Forces (who were poorly paid).

† Kathleen is referring to the Nazi-Soviet Non-Aggression Pact of 24 August 1939. Now, as she saw it, Britain was engaged in a major about-face concerning the Soviet Union, which for years had been denounced by British leaders.

Tuesday, October 14

Brooke Bond's man says what the dickens are the Government thinking of? There need be no shortage of tea at all if they would only bring it into the country, instead of shiploads of other useless goods. 'Take these,' seizing a packet of Corn Flakes and brandishing it. 'A ton of these things fills a ship. Now how much tea couldn't you bring instead of those?' 'Ah,' I said, 'but we are now at the mercy of the American Business Man and if he wants us to have Corn Flakes instead, Corn Flakes we must have.'

Wednesday, 15 October

To Wakefield. Saw Mrs V. She says she has had a new fireplace in her (Corporation) house and has papered and decorated it all through herself. But when they wanted to billet a woman and young baby on her she told them she couldn't have anyone – her health wouldn't stand it. This is pretty good, I think, as she is occupying a three-bedroomed house and receiving Public Assistance. I told her she wouldn't get away with it like that at Dewsbury, but she merely smiled and said to avoid further such risk she had put her name down for the ARP as a cook, but was hoping she'd hear nothing further!

Saturday, 18 October

Had weekly row with Mr B., who says how is it other folk can get stuff and he can't? How is it other shops have plenty of stuff? 'We have plenty too,' I retorted, waving at the shelves. 'Only we can't sell you it. Look at all that jam, for instance.

Six months' supply at the rate we can sell it and it's all paid for. When are we going to get our money back for that?' He gaped round and said nothing. 'Now you come seeking milk,' I said, 'and we've got dozens of bottles and can't sell you one. If you want milk go where you are registered and if you want a tin of milk you must wait till your milkman's cows run dry; then you'll have plenty, but not sweetened.' He said who ever heard of a milkman delivering tinned milk? I said we shall hear of queerer things before this war's over. He went out mollified but will have forgotten and come ranting in next week, saying he's going to find another shop, he can't get nowt here.

Sunday, 19 October

As Bert has no petrol and we cannot go out, spent the morning repacking my emergency bag [for possible evacuation at short notice]. This time included a list of Savings Certificates and a few Penguins. This lives in the cellar kitchen. Bert says the war will be over by spring – no country can stand the pace. I think now it will be two years at the earliest, and then there will be no definite conclusion, just a petering out from exhaustion.

Later. To Mirfield to bring Ma home. Mr D. said why weren't we doing more, why weren't we ready, why didn't we land in Norway? Now was our chance. What had the Government been doing these two years? Mr Churchill made a fine First Lord [of the Admiralty] but he didn't think he was doing the thing now. Bert said he didn't think the Government were pulling – something was holding them back. Mr D. said they were trying to save British blood but it would have to be spent some time – we should have to meet them at the last. When announcements of War Efforts Week [to raise money for the Forces] started, Mrs D. shut it off hastily, saying she'd no patience, they were always begging for something and what did they do with it – just chuck it away and waste it. Mr D. said what about these poor devils who were putting their money in War Savings (I'm one but I didn't let on) – they wouldn't get a penny of it back because there would be none to pay with; they'd be working for a pound a week if that. He didn't like to think about what it would like after the war – it was bad enough last time – but this ...! God help the youngsters who were growing up, they'd have to face the music.

Monday, 20 October

When I asked a customer 1s ½d for a half stone of flour she wanted to know why flour was up as she'd paid ½d less for a loaf today. I said I didn't know but it was so. But I could see she didn't believe me and her face if not her tongue was accusing as she went out. We have apples today at 9d and cannot convince the kiddies their pennies or even halfpennies will [not] buy one. They look so bewildered as if to say, there are the apples, here is the money, why are we denied them? Carrots are a poor substitute to offer them. I should hate to be offered a carrot when my mind was set on apples. Long ago when I was a food faddist I ate grated carrots and everyone thought me peculiar. Now they are fashionable I seem to have lost my taste for them.

The siren sounded as we were finishing supper. Bert, who had a cold, took himself off to bed, leaving the womenfolk to keep guard. He said we could call him if the guns went. Margaret has just announced that she thinks it was not our siren, to Ma's indignation – to think she might have gone to bed hours ago.

Fifteen minutes later. Ma just retired still wearing her raid regalia – tweed hat and bright blue dressing gown – when guns caused her to hurry down again. Margaret and I patrolled outside. Nothing doing.

Tuesday, 21 October

12 o'clock before the All Clear went. Only one person mentioned the alarm in the shop today. Bert said he was awake ready to get up but strange to relate he never heard either guns or plane. Mrs Hobbs has written to Mr [Ernest] Bevin [Minister of Labour and National Service] *personally* about her assistant who has not yet left, although she has had six green cards to go to different jobs.

Wednesday, 22 October

The wireless news seems gloomy tonight with Lord Beaverbrook saying we must prepare for invasion – our turn will surely come; and then in the *Postscript* that Mr [Douglas] Jay telling us we were not in earnest about the war, that we should have to have shorter rations and less clothes and (if we had them) do with less servants, that we had years of grim struggle ahead of us even if things went well. I do wish we could be told right out things are bad and will be, instead of being on this perpetual see-saw. The Government tells us nothing, the wireless tells us even less, and the newspapers are either written in seventh Heaven or deepest pit of gloom.

Thursday, 23 October

Oranges today. Spent my time turning a deaf ear to those women who had children 'just over age – it doesn't seem fair,'* those who had invalids who longed for oranges, and old Mrs H. who said tartly 'It didn't matter about us old 'uns. We mud (may) clam to death. We shall only be fit for t'tannery soon.' 'And tough bit of leather *you'll* make,' I thought, but I only said, 'Oh, you'll see two or three more wars yet, in your time.

A display of fruit and vegetables in a greengrocer's shop includes a sign stating that the oranges on sale are intended only for children.
Photograph © IWM D7966

* Oranges were reserved for children under the age of six – at least during the first seven days a retailer displayed them.

This isn't your last by any means.' And she was so surprised she forgot herself and smiled.

Bert got his food permits for next month, and is puzzled because cheese allowance has dropped to 1 oz and butter risen to 4 oz. Have no information about this. Hope it is true. The butter shortage hurts me more than anything in this war. Bert will not allow us an ounce over rations. Margaret grumbles sometimes because he expects homemade cake every day and she says she cannot manage it on the rations. Good thing we are all small eaters and only Bert takes sugar. We never take our full bacon rations (as there is never enough left when everyone is supplied), seldom take eggs (our milk girl brings us fresh ones) and never take cheese. Therefore it is annoying when the knowing ones say, 'You are alright. Nothing to do but help yourself.'

Reading Beatrice Webb's *My Apprenticeship* [1926] and feeling thankful I live now, even in the middle of my second war, and not fifty years before. I bought Ma *The Good Soldier Schweik* [by Jaroslav Hasek, 1923] and she grumbles that it is daft on every page, but I tell her she must persevere and not have 6d wasted.

Sunday, 26 October

Thought the *Variety Show* last night poor and [comedian] Oliver Wakefield disgusting. His concluding remarks were the limit. If Oliver Wakefield and his circle like this rubbish they should indulge in private and not force it on folk who are not in a position to retaliate with a good telling off [see below, 27 October 1941]. The news came on at once and anyone who tuned in for 9 o'clock would catch that exquisite sample of British Humour. (I wonder if our foreign listeners think it worthwhile risking their lives when that's what they hear.) If the BBC cannot get good comedians every week let them say so right out and put on gramophone records. We shall appreciate real humour all the more when we do hear it. [Actress] Jeanne de Casalis was broadcasting two consecutive nights last week, one at short notice, but her humour was humour, and entirely fresh each time. Besides I dislike the subtle insult the BBC hands us that this much is good enough for us.

Later. Bert having a windfall of petrol from his doctor in return for all the biscuits and cigs he keeps taking him, we set out on a round of visits. First to M. S.'s where I was soon in hot water because I said H. had done right to have a baby. M. S.'s mother was indignant and said wartime was no time to have one, and anyway what was there to bring any child into the world for – look what suffering there would be after this upheaval. I said people were a jolly sight better off after the last war in spite of everything and in any case the children would be looked after if no one else [was]. 'Who is going to pay all these taxes and war debts?' she went on. 'There won't be any debts,' I said. 'There'll have to be a different straightening up this time. And as for taxes – you get it back one way or another. Do you mean to tell me young mothers today are not better off in every way, in spite of bombs and rationing, than you were when your children were little?' She was bound to confess that was true. 'And do you honestly wish you had never been born yourself?' She said well, there had been plenty of times when life wasn't worth living – but then H.'s entrance changed the subject. I have no patience with these arguments about not having children. They are all selfish ones however high falutin they are made to sound.

It was a treat to go and see the new parents. They were delighted with their offspring and said it was a planned and wanted baby. (Planning now being fashionable, even for families.) H. is 35 and his wife a year younger, and have been married seven years. He said he wasn't too keen at first but M. said she wanted a family and was getting older. So little Hazel makes her debut to a somewhat disapproving world but her parents love her and that's all that matters.

3

A Shopkeeper's World

October–November 1941

Monday, 27 October

Miss F. came in greatly put about because her evacuees had left suddenly last night. The woman and child have been for a fortnight, the man three days. They had got their permanent ration books and registered also here for free milk only on Saturday. Miss F. said they thought the wife and child would be kept by the Government and if the man got a job here all would be lovely. When he found he would have to support his own family, he sheered them back to Hull, where he'd chucked up one job at £4 10s per week. I said I wondered how much time and money and how many people have been involved on their behalf from first to last. Miss F. said he counted £39 notes in front of her.

Greatly interested in Beatrice Webb's views on Co-operative movement as one or another of us have been employees at some time, but cannot share her enthusiasm for Co-ops (retail). Think they have had their day. The ones I am familiar with are certainly not so smart in appearance or service as private shops of the same size. And they get the wrong type on committees. But I do not think they harm ordinary shops so much as Woolworths and Marks & Spencer are shaping to do. At Wakefield, Woolworths, next door to an old established chemist's shop, sells all kinds of 'chemistry' at prices so high as 5s 6d.

Glad to see Oliver Wakefield is banned by BBC. Not before time, too.

Oliver Wakefield's comedy sketch on Music Hall, *25 October 1941, provoked immediate consternation in the BBC as well as outrage among the general public on the grounds that his concluding joke was too vulgar for broadcast. The Director General ordered the comedian banned from the airwaves for six months and the entire sketch to be replaced by music when the show was rebroadcast. Subsequent enquiries revealed that the offending material drew its humour from innuendo, incomplete sentences, and pregnant pauses that left much to the listener's imagination. Such routines were commonplace in music hall performances and would no doubt have seemed harmless a couple of generations later.*

The BBC had several concerns. First, as the nation's public and only broadcaster, its programmes were held to a higher standard than performances in private venues, such as popular theatre. As one listener said of another offending show, 'Me and my mates don't mind that sort of thing among ourselves but the BBC's different.' Second, many programmes were live and thus offered little opportunity to control a performer's pacing and delivery (the scripts were vetted beforehand). Third, material suitable for members of the Forces was liable to be deemed offensive

*when also delivered to people's homes, where listeners were not
pre-selected.*

Wednesday, 29 October

To Mirfield to fetch Ma. Piercing cold and snowy. Mr D. on
his favourite subject, waste that goes on in this country. Mrs
D. set him off, telling of her friend's girl (20), who is in some
service – couldn't make out which – and has just come home
and shocked her mother by the clothes she has brought. Two
uniforms, stacks of silken underwear, three pairs shoes, etc.
etc. Her outfit has done the country in for £60. She comes of a
poor family and has had no sort of job before. Mrs D. says she
will never settle down at home again. I grew impatient and
said wasn't it about time the Government stopped bribing girls
to do their duty in this daft way, and tell them plainly what
the alternative will be, if they don't buckle to, under Hitler.[†]

Mr D. then got on about the waste of food. There are two
large houses nearby, one sheltering refugees, one an orphan-
age. He says a man told him of the scandalous waste that
comes from here, half eaten joints of meat, loaves of bread,
and other perfectly good food, thrown in the swill tub. I said
I couldn't credit it; where did they get it from, to waste? Mr
D. said it was true; the man was feeding twelve pigs of his
own and two of his brother's off the refuse from a small area
around there. I said it ought to be reported but of course this

* BBC Written Archives Centre, R34/292/2, and Broadcasting Press Cuttings, Book
3 (i), Box 1, *Daily Express*, 3 February 1941.

† The lavishness of this girl's outfit seems implausible, notably the silken underwear and total cost of £60. Complaints that certain individuals were doing much
better from the war than they deserved were commonplace, as this diary and many
other sources attest. Since the children of poor families were often ill-clad, a fully
kitted-out uniform might seem comparatively lavish.

man would not say anything if he was doing so well out of the waste.[*]

The fisherman offered Mr D. a bag of fish heads for his poultry. Mr D. demurred on account of flavouring the eggs whereupon the fisherman said, 'They're not for your customers now, are they? What have you to worry about?' Mr D. agreed they were not and took the fish and boiled it, and if the eggs are flavoured he will keep a few poultry apart for his own use.

Thursday, 30 October

More oranges. I proposed we sell them singly to the kiddies going to school so we shall be sure they get them. People getting ratty because we have yet no onions. Also, false deductions about butter ration. Still only 2 oz.

Monday, 3 November

We have had various opinions expressed regarding the rationing of tinned goods, some customers saying it would be better to register at one's own shop for them, seemingly having little faith supplies will be as ample as Lord Woolton says. I cannot see the point made by the *Daily Mail* [p. 2] that this new rationing will stop large multiple stores from monopolising trade; presumably they will still have their own large sources of supply and the advantage of being at the centre of things.

---

[*] Small-scale pig-keeping was actively promoted during the war, and kitchen waste, which householders were encouraged to set aside in special buckets for collection, was a major source of pig food.

E. called to see us and we turned to the current topic of women and war work. E. said she could easily do part time work, preferably three whole days per week, if she knew where anyone wanted part timers. She said employers didn't favour part timers because of double clerical work but why couldn't wages be drawn once a fortnight? I said there was plenty of odd moments when we could do something if there was any kind of work that could be given out to be done at home, as they used to do shoe work in Northants.*

Tuesday, 4 November

After the two-months turmoil which has raged about us regarding Mrs Hobbs's chief assistant, who was called up for war work and who did not go, the problem is solved by her going to have a family, so neither the country nor Mrs Hobbs will have her services henceforth. (Wonder if Mrs Hobbs will write Mr Bevin again and explain his intervention is no longer necessary.) Feeling depressed and convinced that this war will not be 'won' by anyone. It seems to me that only half our people have the 'winning' spirit. I wonder if it is a good thing that we are so well-fed, after two years of war. Doesn't this help to [foster] complacency?

Thursday, 6 November

Most people seem pleased about the new rationing [changes designed to improve the distribution of some rationed produce]. Most say that 'we are not doing so badly' regarding

* She is thinking of the putting-out system, when material was distributed to be worked up in people's homes. Northamptonshire was a centre of the boot and shoe industry.

food, 'a lot better than last war'. I am becoming more and more sure we are doing far too well; we are being made too comfortable, one way or another. Same old argument with Mr B. regarding rations which he says we defraud him of. Tea again this week. He says he should have ½ lb for two of them, and he is going to the Food Office about it. I said I wished to goodness he would. The tea question would be simplified if people had to register at one shop. Our supply is based on our sugar requirements and is not nearly enough for our regular customers. And we have no allowance for soldiers and extras.

Friday, 7 November

Mrs L. says she 'stayed at home' this morning to go shopping, and says she will not work Saturdays any more because there is nothing left when she gets to the shops and anyway she has housework to do besides. She is not the only married woman who comes in the shop and tells me this. But would single women get away with it? Not likely. Married women are the most pampered class in the country.* And married women with young children should be barred from going out to work until all single and childless women (of any age if capable) are doing national work.

Sunday, 9 November

Now Lyndoe [astrologist in the *People*] is predicting until 1953! Whether it is to be war and crisis all the way he doesn't

---

* She may, in part, have been thinking of the fact that married women with no children, if their husbands were in the Forces, were exempt from being called up for national service.

make very clear. Anyway it's safe to fix on eleven years away. Everyone will have forgotten by then.

Monday, 10 November

Lyons' tea man says they use 2 lbs tea per three weeks and 1 lb coffee per week for three people. Apparently he doesn't ration himself, whether customers go short or not.

Discussing woodwork in houses (because Margaret is trying to make us draught proof – a hopeless job here), we fell to wondering why doorknobs should be put at such an inconvenient height instead of opposite the arm when bent from the elbow. And that led me off thinking that it must be far easier to build and make ugly things rather than beautiful or why we are surrounded and steeped in ugliness. Considering Dewsbury and Heckmondwike, with not a redeeming feature in them, one can but conclude that a sense of beauty does *not* 'come natural' but can only be acquired with training and time, and there is room for neither in a manufacturing district. The awful thing is that most folk don't *know* they live in ugly (or just drab) surroundings and therefore of course don't care about it.

Another Mass Observation diarist (no. 5380), a woman from Glasgow in her mid twenties, had similar feelings about nearby Leeds, on which she elaborated after a visit there on 21 January 1944. 'Leeds is a depressing town, although it has a lovely position and one or two fine buildings well laid-out. But the squalor of all this part of England makes one appalled at the thought of all these hideous buildings being put up once all over these industrial counties. What horrors the Industrial Revolution is responsible for and what a mentality those people must have had who caused all this to be perpetrated.' Then she wrote more benignly: 'But in spite of the buildings, I feel at home in this country with its hills, grey skies and damp sweeping wind. Even the grimy stone houses have a homelike and familiar look after all the brick houses of the south [she was then residing in St Albans]. The people are surprisingly pleasant' – 'charming and helpful,' she found.

Tuesday, 11 November

Got our new ration cards. Also a sheet from the Food Office with instructions. Glad I have not to pass an exam on all the food rules and regulations that are showered on us. It is getting to be a case of 'let's do it this way and hope for the best – no time to look it up'. I flatter myself I shall be a 'skilled worker' by the end of the war. Oranges again this week. Wish they would give them out at school or clinics. Our customers with bigger children get upset and it's 'what a to-do' all round.

I thought the PM's speech good on the whole [Churchill warned Japan against attacking the United States]. Refreshing after the 'cumbersome' ones we get from America [*American Commentary*, no doubt]. (We are going to sing China's praises too, now. After five years of passing by.) Only two people voluntarily mentioned hearing it. Also, no one mentioned Armistice Day. A few people were wearing poppies.

Wednesday, 12 November

Margaret has written all her friends to say she is not buying Xmas presents this year, and hopes they will agree to do the same as she proposes, put the money in War Savings – strength of mind which I wish I could emulate. The tea situation waxes more and more vexatious. Our customers are annoyed when we have not their full rations, and rightly, because, although there is supposed to be no registering, no one will take on strangers when they cannot supply 'regulars'. If tea is really short why can't we be told and have the ration lowered? Bert has decided not to supply soldiers with tea [it was felt they could readily get supplies elsewhere], after ignoring my suggestion to do this a month ago.

What effect will the new Shop Order have on Woolworths etc.? None, I suppose. They are already well in.

Some confusion over the new rationing [the rules frequently changed]. Several people have asked if they may register here and are dubious when we tell them they may go anywhere for tinned goods. Apparently they feel 'safer' when 'tied' to a shop. And what a number of people did not know or had forgotten there will be extra sugar and fat next week!

Sunday, 16 November

Spending day in bed as think have earned holiday after two heavy days. Friday 'took the biscuit'. Think I shall write Lord Woolton a detailed account of one of our Fridays for him to consider how he would tackle it. It will run so:

Friday – thick fog and bitterly cold in shop. Started with knowledge supplies had not arrived. No bacon or sugar. Prepare rations as far as possible in little piles for each customer with any 'treat' there is (choc, fruit etc.) to save time later on. About 9.40 Bert says what time is the bus to town as we have no copper. (If fine he'd have gone himself in car. In bad weather I go!) Hastily donning hat and coat run across road, catching bus by miracle. (On time because foggy – otherwise ten minutes late.) Conscious not looking best in knitted cap, overall peeping under coat and dirty stockings. Arrive back 10.20 starved through [chilled to the bone]. Margaret comforts with rum and coffee. Mrs S. (ex-Mayoress) trying to wheedle extra butter from Bert. 'Are there no poor folk who take all margarine?' 'No, madame, afraid all take the full ration of butter.' 'Is it time for jam?' (She says this every week.) Bert and I strain lungs explaining not yet. (She is stone deaf.) Supplies not yet here. Continue weighing rations. Our landlord in to say PC Riley died suddenly. Long and involved explanation to Bert who says does not know PC Riley. Landlord says, yes, [he] helped Bert start car last week. Bert remembers and says good thing [he] did not die when pushing car. During this various small boys seeking ½d carrots. I have to break off and serve while Bert ponders on PC Riley. Shut door nine times after small boys. Several [people] for rations. Explain about sugar and bacon. All very nice about it. Will call later. Old Mrs H. in to see if anything has come. Got *her* rations yesterday. Lingers in case of missing something. Bert retires into background, as usual, when Mr H. appears. No baker. 11.30. Yeast man with mint imperials. Bless him! Customers come and go. Mrs H. remains. Bert says suggestively 'Yes, Mrs H.' but Mrs H. ignores him. Several customers seeking pies and bread. Neither. All say, Isn't it sudden about Bobby Riley? Mrs H. whispers – Can she have biscuits and matches? Knows she had her allowance yesterday but anything to get rid [of her]. Goes at last. 12 o'clock. Baker. Also forgot flock of kiddies for mint imperials. Controlled at 5d per quarter. Bert says sell at 6d and say nowt. Pandemonium begins. Do bread orders (always my job!) in and between whiles. Hope [we] have saved buns for everyone who wants them.

Hasty lunch of fried kidney (no bacon!) and spice (Xmas) cake. Greengrocer unexpectedly appears with cases of apples and oranges. (The latter are entered on special card we had to keep for purpose.) Bert says [they] *would* come on Friday. Puts out oranges with 'Under 6' notice but does not prevent all who come in trying to get some. Bert very honest about oranges and does save them for the kiddies. Special [constable] on this beat calls for a warm. Has heard nothing of PC Riley only that he is retiring. Woman joins in that blinds are not down [at his house]. (All afternoon controversy rages – is he dead or not?) 4 o'clock. Rush, rush. Everyone for rations. Not sat 10 minutes since 8 o'clock. Bert says take pay[ment] for sugar and bacon, then we shall be safe. Bert selling apples right and left to all comers. Beg he will think of 'registereds'. Says there's plenty. Try to rescue some (including 2 lbs for us). Know he is letting too many cigs go. They'll not last out. Folk saying there is no dried fruit – it said on wireless etc. etc. (Drat the wireless!) And can they have tinned milk with 'points' coupons? Go to tea and listen to Ma's adventures. She's been out all day. Interrupted by arrival of rations at last. (5 o'clock.) Leave tea and help Margaret serve while Bert weighs incoming supplies and enters them in record book. Shop packed. Margaret not good shopkeeper. *Will* argue with complaining customers and lecture kiddies when they come in for 'second helping' of 'spice'. Bobby Riley argument reaching new intensity when little Norman W. suddenly drops bombshell by saying his father was speaking to Bobby Riley at dinnertime and therefore he is not dead. Everyone looks daggers at young W. for being able to cause this sensation. Kiddies coming for oranges with and without book. Little boy to say given him 6d short change. Deny this strenuously. Women trying to get oranges and failing. Apples dwindling alarmingly. Bert stops sale except to registereds. Fear too late! Cigs finished. Shop still packed. Have to pause to black out.

6 o'clock. If another child asks for ½d carrot shall upend him into sack. Trying to reckon up large order when Mrs J. (Bert's customer) asks if her husband has got a pie and cigs last Tuesday on her 'tick'. Bert says can I remember? Tear myself from my own job and plunge into dimness of 'Last Tuesday'. After some groping emerge with Mr J. and cigs and *two* pies. Mrs J.'s chin bodes ill for Mr J. Little boy back again with aggressive note demanding 6d change forthwith. Write on bottom, "Must have lost it" and return.

7 o'clock breathing space. Bert says extra rations for next week's increase have not been sent. We are both unusually amiable for Friday night. Relieved apples went round. Last customer Mrs C. to pay weekly bill. Bert says must wipe off balance owing. Says 'Ay, lad. It'll be alright.' Bert points out she said that before. 'Ay, lad.' Bert gives it up.

We close 7.45. Take last two oranges into house. Sink into chair with buzzing head (wishing I dare switch off Tommy Handley [star of *ITMA – It's That Man Again*] – drat the wireless!) and dreamingly anticipate tripe and onions preparing by Ma. Realisation better still. Climb wearily to bed 9.30 and read consoling chapter on the tribulations of Early Christians! Last thought is that have forgotten to save apples for Mrs V., our second best customer!

Even when customers were 'difficult', according to Kathleen in March 1943 (MOA, Directive Response), they 'bring new interests and we hear tales and gossip and laugh. This is a big advantage, being in a local shop instead of a multiple store – our customers are also our neighbours. We are interested in them as people, not just as customers.'

4

Matters Large and Small

November 1941–March 1942

Monday, 17 November

Bert down to Food Office this morning about missing supplies. Food Office sympathetic, surprised (said we should
have at least fortnight's in advance), plaintive (hadn't known
which way to turn for work for week), but *not* helpful. (Gave
no advice how we were to get supplies before next delivery
day, a week on Thursday.) Bert and Margaret to Wakefield.
Saw our late 'char' resplendent in new pink satin blouse, quite
recovered since threat of evacuees has faded. She missed her
rent last week in order to buy a dress length, put a bob on a
horse and 'recouped' this week. Brooke Bond's says tea will
have to be rationed in the end. It was the silliest and unfairest
system for shopkeepers they could invent. And it would be
the same with tinned goods. Of course shopkeepers would
save best kinds of meat for 'regulars', the people who gave
them their living. I said I thought we should be obliged to do

[so], because so many of our customers shopped only here and never went in town; a good many worked all day, and we had got in the habit of saving them anything that was going.

A. told Margaret that she knew a man who had traced the whole course of the war in the Bible. The Germans would meet their fate in the Caucasus, on Mt Ararat, which though *not a volcano*, would *explode* and wipe them all out. Our forces would be safe, being nowhere near at the time. (What about the poor Russians?)

Tuesday, 18 November

Bert raging about the tinned meats delivered today. Two dozen 1½ lb tins sausage meat seem to be the main items. Have reckoned up points we have in stock – 558 for tins which require 24 points each, 853 for smaller, 'reasonably' sized tins (this excluding sardines). Not a fair proportion. We cannot sell such large tins about here. It will require very large households for 24 points to be spent on one tin. We have only quarters [of] salmon and no steak or tongue. Bert going to Wakefield tomorrow to see about it. I foresee endless difficulties with customers, and general dissatisfaction all round. We always get into hot water regularly over eggs, oranges, milk and dried fruit, all of which (except oranges) are always considerably under quantities given over wireless. As for onions!! We have yet to see our first in this shop. When I asked the greengrocer yesterday he pretended to be insulted and said they had not seen one at the warehouse for twelve months. 'But what am I to tell customers? When the wireless says ——' But what the greengrocer said then! Customers think either we or the wireless (and press) is lying and favour the latter. I believe they think we have secret onion orgies at dead of night and use them all up.

Wednesday, 19 November

Bert went to wholesalers but they referred him to traveller next week to arrange for exchange of large tinned meat. They said we should be lucky to have rest of stuff in by December. Their van men are working twelve hours a day, and they are awfully behind. The blackout hinders. One van man told me of a woman who asked why a big strong man like him wasn't in the army. 'Missis,' he replied, 'I b——well wish I was. It'd be a rest cure after what I do now.' Being half-day went down to town to join Free Library and came away with three books. This after vowing to stop reading and abstaining from book-buying for a full month!

Thursday, 20 November

Got nicely ahead with preparing rations for tomorrow. Currants and raisins have come in but no extra sugar for increased ration and no eggs. This means some customers waiting for extra sugar until next week. I dislike these 'back reckonings'; there is usually a tussle with one or two customers.

Friday, 21 November

Friday over, thank goodness. Bert went to Leeds to 'Abie's' and came back with heaps of things he couldn't get from ordinary wholesalers. Health Salts, Bovril, Rowntree's Cocoa, dried milk and several tins of salmon and steak, besides a box of chocs. Funny how these Jews get hold of stuff. 'Abie's' have been established years, running both wholesale and retail business (cut-price in peace time) and have always dealt fairly with Bert. I don't say they are black marketers – but it *is* funny how Jews get hold of things.

Sunday, 23 November

Reading *Change* [probably no. 2 on Home Propaganda]. I blushed at the reference to knowledge (or non-knowledge) of constituent MP and hastily inquired of the family who our MP was, but drew a blank; no one knew. Margaret said she always knew when we lived at Heck because it was always Sir John Simon, but she didn't take any notice otherwise. I said, 'Surely you knew it was Arthur Greenwood at Wakefield,' but she repeated she didn't bother. Shall have to make inquiries in the morning and remedy my remissness. Afraid am altogether lacking in interest in local affairs. The War Ship Week [1–8 November, designed to raise money for war bonds and other forms of saving] has come and gone, and caused not a flutter in my life nor prised from me a penny. Beyond seeing the bills posted outside the Town Hall and oh yes, buying a concert ticket from a schoolgirl, I have never given it a thought. (On the other hand War Ship Week organisers have apparently never given us a thought. I suppose we are too far away on Dewsbury Moor to be canvassed.) Anyhow, like the boy from Irthlingboro', I just keep on taking no notice of all these Weeks and what not, but just plod on buying my 2s 6d Savings Stamps each week, more if I can afford it, and pride myself I do as well as most folk.

Wednesday, 26 November

Cheers for Wilfred! If we have many News Readings like this I shall really *listen* instead of letting the news flow over me. And to confess he didn't know how to pronounce a word – even if it was a Proper Noun! I'll bet there was a lot of map reading this evening. Next we shall be told to keep a pronouncing dictionary handy. Oh, it as a grand change, lad! We need folk like this to breeten [brighten] us up a bit.

The broadcaster Wilfred Pickles (1904–1978) was the first Northerner chosen to read the national news, and his regional accent attracted much notice, favourable and unfavourable, not to mention his informal style, which included wishing listeners 'good neet'. His voice was a great contrast to the usual Oxbridge accents on the BBC, and he and others thought that his Yorkshire voice helped people from the North to identify with the nation at war – it was seen as an acknowledgement that linguistic diversity was a good thing. Letters to the BBC from later years show how effectively Pickles connected with listeners.[*]

Friday, 28 November

Onions at last. People very sarcastic about same. Also oranges. These cause much trouble with mothers of older children and those with old folk and invalids; all think we could stretch a point in their favour, particularly when they are registered customers. Also last instructions from Food Office regarding points coupons. We are told not to serve anyone who has not filled up the front page of their pink books. Acting on that we shall not sell many 'points' goods for I doubt if three of our customers have done so.

Saturday, 29 November

Auntie came to tea. We discussed the Staffordshire recruiting business. Auntie said her loom-mate would have to go after

---

* Wilfred Pickles, *Between You and Me* (London: Werner Laurie, 1949), chap. 13; and BBC Written Archives Centre, R30/3,699/1.

Xmas. She said a good many in the mill would have to go but the majority seemed to take the attitude that they would go when fetched. She says there is much resentment among the girls that they should be interviewed at the Labour Exchange by girls the same age or even younger than themselves. This is *wrong*. It is wrong that young girls like that should have the decision about anyone's removal [to work elsewhere]. There should be older men and women with experience and sympathy. In any case apart altogether from wartime considerations, these youngsters should *not* be at the Labour Exchange counters. Older people resent having to be directed by them. If they are so indispensable (?) they should be given work in the background. I can see no reason why the Exchanges should be recruiting offices. Why cannot there be proper places for the job?

The Ministry of Labour was becoming aware of the delicacy of young women interviewing and having the power to give directions to older women, and after 1941 there were changes. Various documents from a 1941 file in the National Archives (LAB 8/380) testify to the sensitivity connected with the interviewing process, which the Ministry certainly acknowledged, and its desire to make it as humane and flexible as possible.

The diary of an office worker in her mid-twenties living in Manchester gives a sense of both the delicacy of this interviewing process and also the caution needed in coming to general conclusions (MO Diarist no. 5261). 'Heard another story today about the interviewers of women,' she wrote on 7 November 1941. 'It seems they are only young girls themselves, and I should imagine they thoroughly enjoy the power they have over the girls who come before them. How can such young people have the necessary tact, knowledge of home difficulties and patience which this job requires? Why isn't the job given to much older women, and why aren't

*these girls themselves put into the munitions factories? The actual
registration is a very easy job requiring no special skill or knowledge
and I am sure could have been given as a part-time job to ex-clerical
workers who are unable, on account of domestic reasons etc., to take
on a full-time job. Yet at the Labour Exchange where I registered, all
the registrars were girls under 30 years of age.'*

*Some weeks later she found reasons to moderate her views. 'In
fairness' she wished to 'record the other side of the story. A friend
who is a hairdresser has just had an interview and could not have
been treated better. The interviewer even put excuses into her
mouth for her not leaving home' (16 December 1941). The diarist
herself was interviewed on 1 January 1942 – and found little cause
for complaint. 'I encountered no nastiness at the interviews, though
there were no smiles or "Good-mornings", and the interviewer was
about 32, businesslike and efficient.'*

*During November and December of 1941 a vigorous campaign
was being run in Dewsbury to recruit women to work in a new
munitions factory in Staffordshire. The Government's broad objec-
tive was to release by the end of January 12,000 women from their
jobs in the region's woollen textile industry so that they could shift
their labour to the crucial munitions industry in another county. The
Heavy Woollen District, which employed large numbers of women
in factories, was targeted for recruitment, especially 'girls' aged 18
to 25, and the press was actively enlisted to promote a policy that
was thought to be a national priority. Significantly, much of the
advertising and commentary was cast in terms of aiding Russia,
Britain's new ally, in its hour of need. 'If Russia fails we fail. If we
fail Russia, Hitler wins, and it will be our turn next. We must not fail
Russia' (Dewsbury Reporter, 22 November 1941, p. 5). The workers
in Britain now had a timely opportunity to lend a hand to (it was
implied, though not stated) Europe's only workers' state, as it cour-
ageously confronted the Nazi juggernaut. An advertisement from*

the Ministry of Labour and National Service and the Ministry of Supply (Dewsbury Reporter, *29 November 1941, p. 3) was headlined in a fashion to highlight this priority of aiding Russia. 'This Empty Workshop [it was pictured] in a new Royal Ordnance Factory in Staffordshire should be making Tens of Thousands of Shells a day for Russia. Yorkshire Women of the West Riding, you can help Britain keep her pledge to Russia – 11,500 of you can start work at once!'*

As well as appealing as usual to patriotic duty, the promotional language stressed the adventures that might be expected and the comforts that would be enjoyed in connection with the new and distant workplace – these were important considerations, for most young factory women lived lives that were deeply rooted in this part of the West Riding and had rarely if ever ventured as far as Staffordshire. They had, then, to be reassured. They had to be convinced that they would benefit personally from behaving patriotically. 'The girls will find in their new environment a real home. They will be housed in a new residential club, with separate bedrooms, including a wardrobe and cupboard, a good dining-room working on the cafeteria system. There are recreation rooms, a theatre, a laundry with drying arrangements, hairdressing rooms, plenty of opportunity for personal shopping. Boy friends will be welcome, and everything done to secure the comfort and happiness of the workers. Wages will be on a generous scale. Girls will be encouraged to join in groups, to form savings groups, and to enter into a cordial and social relationship.' (Dewsbury Reporter, 15 November 1941, p. 5.) Only the best, apparently, would be provided for these heretofore not especially valued factory workers.

More exuberance in the same vein was evident in the following weeks. Further details were reported on the residential comforts available in Staffordshire, some supported by pictures. Women who agreed to migrate in the interest of service to the nation would live well – probably (it was implied) at a higher standard than

Women workers played a vital role in making munitions.
While Kathleen writes about the recruitment drive for Staffordshire,
these women are making parts for the Royal Ordnance Factory,
Leeds, which was just a few miles from Dewsbury.
Photograph © IWM MH19651

*they enjoyed in Yorkshire. Free cosmetics were even mentioned
(Dewsbury Reporter, 29 November 1941, p. 8). Newspapers were
keen to report on how the recruitment was going, sometimes
with details concerning individual volunteers. By 12 December
Dewsbury was credited with 210 recruits, Batley with 'only' 100
(said to be disappointing). Some weeks later, in February, stories
were appearing in the press testifying to the local girls' content-
ment and usefulness in their Staffordshire surroundings.**

* *Dewsbury District News*, 13 December 1941, p. 8; *Dewsbury Reporter*, 7 February
1942, p. 8, and 21 February 1942, p. 1. By contrast, Kathleen told MO a few weeks
later that 'Girls home on leave from Staffordshire complain of skin trouble – break-
ings out on hands and face' (DR, January 1942).

Wednesday, 3 December

The 'points' scheme is getting well underway. Most people are taking all 'points value' at one time saying, 'Then we shall know we have finished until December 15.' We have had several to 'look round' and plan what to spend coupons on but up to now all buyers have been our own customers, most of them registered customers. Only one has had to be denied on account of unfilled name and address. We have had two price lists for the tinned goods this morning, making four communications in all for 'points' up to now.

We have now pinned up on our own notice board the following leaflets:

1 price list Pickles and Sauces, 24 page
1 supplement to same
4 leaflets instructions for eggs
6 leaflets instructions and copy permit for milk
1 copy permit and 2 instructions for tea
3 instructions for cheese
1 instructions for onions
2 instructions for dried fruit
6 instructions and 4 stock sheets for preserves
9 'General Instructions', which include altered instructions for ordinary rations (fats, sugar, tea, jam, cheese, eggs, milk etc.) [and] how to adjust same; instructions for emergencies, soldiers, seamen, travellers, invalids, priorities, orthodox Jews' and vegetarians' rations. Most of these are anything from 300/1000 words and some are extremely tiresome to read, being needlessly complicated I think, but perhaps it is difficult to put such involved matters simply. This is not counting our Schedule of Maximum Prices from the Chamber of Commerce, a 11 inch by 8 inch 26 page booklet of which we get a new one about once

a month. Then we have the longstanding lists showing how to charge fractions of a pound for oranges etc.

All this which you might call 'office work' is only one side of the worry. There is the 'customer-side'. Serving these days is not a matter of weighing a certain amount of rations for each customer and there's an end to it. There are the little things of which they expect their share, matches, their own kind of cigs, pastries and pies and cakes, apples, sauces, chocolate and sweets, and cereals. Oh, all kind of things which are scarce and which they expect by reason of being rationed at a certain place. I suppose the big shops don't have this difficulty of 'saving and squaring'; it will be first come, first served with unrationed goods. But small shops, whose customers are in and out several times a day, must share things round the 'family' [i.e., the local customers]. And only right, too. The difficulty is to keep the cheeky ones from getting above their due and seeing that the shy ones have their share. Then there are the very good customers who are not rationed for anything and plague of all, those who are rationed for only some things, and those who rationed only part of the family. This last should be stopped, if it is possible to do so. All members of one family should be registered at one shop.

Friday, 5 December

Mr D., the paper traveller, says he has lost custom at the tripe works since they were compelled to close down and divide their business with a firm at Heck and one at Morley. They can carry on the soap making side but the fat refining has gone. They are promised it back after the war but have no hopes of recovering their trade. The firm are very bitter, Mr

D. says, because they say it is presenting someone else with their customers and giving away the result of years of work. There are 67 similar places closing down. The Morley place is having to build new machinery to accommodate the new business. The firm say it is only the thin end of the wedge, that Unilever will aim at complete control after the war. This of course set Bert off on his favourite hobby horse, Lord Woolton, and he reaped up all about the canned pilchards that were for sale at Lewis's [in Leeds] at 1s 10d the week before controlled price at 11d. Mr D. said his daughter works in M&S and said they have had stacks of chocolate in the well known makes and sweets of all kinds. I said they never sold those good brands before. Mr D. said it was rotten, altogether, and the Jews were behind all this 'big business' [casual anti-Semitism was then commonplace in Britain].

Saturday, 6 December

No eggs again, for the third week. Bert in obedience to instructions had returned all egg powder to be relabelled, so we came in for some grumbling when people came for rations.* 'Points' goods are going very well. Salmon is first favourite, with galantine, which we have had before, second. There is a marked preference for things that are familiar, and the American strange names cause much hesitation. Most folk say 'We shall have to try that' but are waiting for more points. Tongue is in constant demand but we have none yet. To my surprise have only had to warn three people about not filling

* The winter of 1941–42 was a time of severe egg shortage, in whatever form. Dried egg from abroad, mainly the United States, began to supplant shelled eggs; the former needed only about a quarter of the space on a merchant shipping vessel that was required for whole eggs.

in their new books. One lady I knew would not fill them in so we did it for her, as she is a good customer.

*The points scheme referred to in this passage started on 1 December and was later seen by the Ministry of Food as 'perhaps the biggest event of all in the history of rationing during these four years' (*The Market Square: The Story of the Food Ration Book 1940–1944 *[March 1944; reprinted by the Imperial War Museum, 1997], p. 26). The scheme was prompted by shortages of unrationed foods. 'Not only were the available quantities of many of them so small as to offer only a derisory individual entitlement, but in general the desire for any one such food was so erratic that a comparatively normal scheme would have wasted on some people what others were clamouring for. The possibilities of lumping several foods into a points scheme was in many ways attractive.' The scheme depended on vast numbers of cut coupons and 'an adequate backing of stocks', the latter of which was much helped by the arrival of such foods as Spam. With their points coupons, most commonly 20 points for a four-week period, consumers could choose to purchase at any shop whatever unrationed food happened to be available on a given day. Initially the only items covered were canned meats, canned fish and canned beans. Later other foods were added, such as condensed milk, rice, dried fruits, and biscuits (Ibid., pp. 26–29 and 57–58).*

Sunday, 7 December

We had a strange affair yesterday. A man brought in a ration book to register with us and said he had never possessed one before nor yet an identity card. What he has lived on for two years I don't know, but apparently he has no home and sleeps in a barn at the tripe works. Which set me wondering if there are many like him, folk who have been overlooked.

Mrs M. has asked her evacuees to leave. She says she did not mind while there was just Mrs N. and the two children but when two more were brought in (making four kiddies under seven) and the brother took to coming every other weekend, she thought the bit she was doing for the country too big a bit and has demanded new arrangements. So Mrs N. and the babies are leaving and Mrs M. will look after the schoolgirls. She says city folks' ways are not ours. They take no interest in their homes and would rather be outside walking than doing household duties.

Auntie says she is considering giving up work now as the new taxation [which created some four million new taxpayers] will take all her pension. She will have to continue until she has saved the money for the first instalment. I think it hard a person of 62 should be taxed on meagre savings. Auntie says it is laughable the persons who have suddenly developed thought for their parents and claim they are helping support them. She says she does not mind the tax if it is to help the country and if we are all going short together, but it makes her think when in the *Yorkshire Post* are adverts for gloves from 3 guineas to 6 guineas per pair. She says it is abominable to put such adverts in the press if we are in the straits they say we are in.

Monday, 8 December

America has been pushed in at last [Pearl Harbor was attacked the day before]. What a splash! First thoughts were of relief, as when we first entered the war, 'Now we shall do something.' Second thoughts – 'Well, why shouldn't *they* have a dose, too?' And then a conviction, which I try to push back, that this war will never be won, it will come to a standstill from sheer exhaustion. Realise I enjoy this war at periods like these when excitement is intense. After all, what is there to look forward to in the 'Peace' if it is anything like the last. A dreary business of watching other people get the best of life, of insecurity and tawdriness, and cheapness, and toiling and 'tewing' [constantly working and worrying]. This is a purely selfish view and proves the war has not yet affected me personally. That is, I have no relations near or distant in danger, no air raid experiences, have not suffered from it *personally*, though in a general way I am sickened. It troubles me that I should get a sort of 'pleasure' from war but it is the truth. I wonder if others are the same. They say so little, folk about here, but latest events have loosened their tongues a bit. There is a pretty general belief that the war will go on for a long time, and also we shall not do as well as we have done in the matter of food as America will be occupied with her own affairs. Most seem to be resigned to the idea of some kind of war work.

Tuesday, 9 December

Walking into a shop this morning I landed in the middle of a discussion between the shopman and a motherly smart middle-aged lady, on what we must do to prevent 'it' happening again. The lady said quite unheatedly that we must exterminate all Germans under 25; we shall never be able to do anything with them. The shopman, an old soldier, said he would take steps to prevent them ever breeding again, any of them. The lady said she wouldn't go as far as that (apparently seeing no irrelevancy in that). The shopman said he would do as he said – they would do it to us. And he drew an unpleasant and lurid picture of what would happen to our women with the

German soldiers. The lady went out saying again she would exterminate them – there would be 'no more Germans'. And she was such a mild-faced comfortable-looking woman. But she meant what she said.

Wednesday, 10 December

A wretched half holiday. Bert took us for a ride to Hartshead Church and we spent half an hour in a north east wind looking at gravestones; then sat in the car and gloomily discussed the latest news, and wondered what on earth had happened to make us lose two battleships at one blow.* Bert said we should show them now America had come in. I said maybe, but I would believe it when it came off. America seemed to be pretty rattled, for a start anyway, and why wasn't she ready for attack. Japan wasn't on the door step; surely scouts could have warned of approaching raiders. The people after my own heart are the Russians who are getting on with the job without so much talk.

Friday, 12 December

Apples, but still no eggs. The 'points' scheme seems to be causing confusion; people are coming for a second supply this week, under the impression it is a weekly rather than a monthly allowance. The 'single' householders are grumbling because there is no small stuff except sardines. Mrs L. in to display her new teeth. I duly admired especially the *gold one* which her husband has bought her for a Christmas present. She returned later with her income-tax troubles but Bert

---

* That day two British warships, the battleship *Prince of Wales* and battle cruiser *Repulse*, were sunk by Japanese aircraft off the coast of Malaya, greatly weakening the British presence in the Far East.

referred her to the Collector. He said he had enough worry with his own without shouldering other peoples'. The tax is a staggerer for those who have never had to pay before.

Sunday, 14 December

[Astrologists] Lyndoe and Petulengro both claim to have prophesied Japan's entry. I *will* start keeping their forecasts. They say one thing one week and another the next and rely on people having short memories. More and more irritated with the attitude taken up by most people that now America is in we shall get things going, she'll show Japan. I don't believe they think in terms of what it means to themselves in the way of going without things. I said to Reckett's [wholesale] traveller yesterday that we couldn't expect so much stuff in the shops. He said, Oh, he didn't know. Look at all the stuff on our shelves. Most of it was brought across the sea. I said, Yes, but in the future ... He said, Oh, he didn't know. He didn't see why not. Mr Hobbs our landlord says we shall split Germany up this time. It's the only way to keep them under.

Saturday, 20 December

Points going well. As they cannot get salmon people are venturing to try the new American meats [e.g., Spam]. Eggs this week for first time for month. Thank the Lord we made them go round. Bert decided to close two days.

Tuesday, 23 December

Bert went to Leeds to the Jews and got salmon and matches and tinned fruit! This may be last time as 'Abe' has to join up. People seeking eggs again, in spite of my impressing upon them last week it was a monthly ration. Great confusion over holidays, some works closing until Monday, some not closing at all. B. B. Biscuits said he was having one day. I said, 'Oh, you are obeying Government orders, then.' Bert said, 'Yes, and weren't they setting us an example, the Government?' Biscuits said, 'They are, but they would damned well have something to say if we followed it.' Have heard several references to the Government having a 'long holiday' at a time like this.

Wednesday, 24 December

There seems to be a general agreement to leave 'rations' until Saturday, in case they are used up too soon, but we have been busy none the less, principally with 'points'. Every customer comments that it must make a lot of work for us, cutting coupons out, and about one in three confesses complete mystification with the whole business and throws herself on our mercy to help her spend her coupons. The most difficult to fix up are the 'singles' for there are no small things except sardines and they are reluctant to spend all their coupons on something which will take days to eat up. A great fire at [nearby] Ravensthorpe about 5.30 caused a diversion.* Then Mrs C. came in breathless after a struggle to free her cat from a salmon tin. Then our landlord's dog was killed by a car down the road. And finally an old lady knocked down by a car. A

---

* According to the press, the fire broke out in industrial premises and 'Within a few minutes a three storey building was blazing and the glow in the sky could be seen for miles around. Messages were flashed on the screens of all the cinemas in Dewsbury asking soldiers to report to their headquarters at once. They were used effectively to divert traffic on the Huddersfield main road.' (*Dewsbury District News*, 27 December 1941, p. 5).

lively Christmas Eve if not a merry one. Finished the day with a glass and a half of beer and a mince pie, in spite of Ma looking over her 'specs'.

Wednesday, 25 December, Christmas Day

After a late breakfast (pork pie made with American 'canned' and very nice too) we rode round visiting friends and relations until mid-afternoon when we returned in time to receive our visitors, Mr and Mrs Hill from next door, but one, and Auntie, who lives alone. We dined on tinned Irish chicken, water cress, apple jelly and forcemeat, followed by jelly and cream (tinned) and Christmas cake and crackers (containing parlour fireworks but couldn't make them do anything but smell). Which I do not deem to be too bad for a third War-Christmas. Afterwards we played darts and talked until midnight. Henry Hill had to be up at 4.30 next morning or we should have prolonged the party. Auntie said that following the news in the local press that all mills were closing until Monday, there was much anger when they were ordered to close only for a day, and she said there was much sarcastic reference to Parliament's length of holiday. We also discussed the young girls we know who were hurriedly marrying. Auntie said she didn't think it should save them from going away. I said, 'Well, whether it does or not, they will draw their allowance, and that is all going to cost the country something. It will end up as usual in the single lasses having to take the mucky end of the stick. If there is a pampered class in the community it is married women.' But I had no chance to ride a favourite steed further because of 'Old Ebeneezer' ['Christmas at the Old Town Hall' at 9.30 on the BBC Forces Programme].

Saturday, 27 December

Many women chucked up and walked out of work yesterday
in the middle of the morning, Auntie says. Mrs M. reports
her husband had to 'play' off night work because the women
had not worked during the day. She says the Belgians and
other foreigners who work there hate the English and call
them pigs and will not work if someone doesn't stand over
them.

Wednesday, 31 December

Sitting waiting for the Old Year to finish, just Margaret and
I. Have said that tomorrow in ordinary times we should be
flinging handfuls of 'spice' [sweets] into the road for the
kiddies to scramble for. They used to go round in crowds
and do mischief if not served. They also went to pubs and
scrambled for hot pennies. 'Winnie' seemed in great fettle.
How he does drop his aitches, and anyone could tell who was
speaking whatever language he spoke in. I wonder if he will
go to Russia.*

Making no resolutions.

---

* This speech on 30 December to a joint session of the Canadian Parliament in
Ottawa did indeed show Churchill in robust form – and for a minute or so speaking
French. The speech included a soon-to-be famous metaphor. He criticised the government of France for unnecessarily capitulating to Germany in June 1940: 'When I
warned them that Britain would fight on alone whatever they did, their generals told
their Prime Minister and his divided Cabinet, "In three weeks England will have
her neck wrung like a chicken." Some chicken! Some neck!' (The roars of approval
were nearly deafening.) (*Collected Speeches*, VI, 6544.) Churchill first travelled to
Moscow the following August.

Tuesday, 6 January, 1942

Received another ream of paper from the Food Office regarding milk. It finishes as follows: Regulation 82 of the Defence (General) Regulations, 1939, as amended provides *inter alia* as follows: 'If, in furnishing any information for the purposes of any of these Regulations or of any order, rule or bylaw made under any of these Regulations, any person makes any statement which he knows to be false in any material particular, or recklessly makes any statement which is false in a material particular, he shall be guilty of an offence, against that Regulation.' Instead of saying briefly, 'Anyone giving false returns will be punished heavily'. There is a footnote:

(a) Note: The week preceding the week during which this declaration and return is required to be furnished.

(b) Note: The week following the week during which this declaration and return is required to be furnished. (What means *inter alia*?)

'All for 2s 6d per week,' Bert says. 'It damn well isn't worth it for what we get out of it.' Then occasionally we have communications from the Fuel Control Board, because we sell a few coal bricks, telling us all about miners' wages and so on. 'It's scandalous,' says Bert. 'The waste that's going on in this country. Talk about being short of paper!'

On Sunday we were at Mirfield and Mrs D. was telling us about a warehouse by the river that was stuffed with grain and the rats got in. 'And how many Inspectors did they have down to that place in a week? Six! There they was and Rat Week going on at the same time. And another lot of officials telling you we must keep the rats down. And they have these places a-harbouring of 'em. And me, can't [find] a bit of grain for my poor fowl. And they wonder why there is no eggs to collect at the weekend. It's wicked, the goings on in this country. Shameful!'

Wednesday, 7 January

Went to the pictures to see the *Pacific* film but owing to two dense or dishonest doorkeepers, sat through two programmes (at different houses) without success. There was, however, a good film of a Norwegian raid, that seemed so unreal with the wooden houses and snow-covered rocks that I had to keep reminding myself it was not an American 'far North' thriller.

Friday, 9 January

People coming into shop all day long to ask if they had any 'points' left or to try and 'sub' some on next month's starting on Monday. At least eight out of ten say 'I can't understand them. They get me beat.' I patiently explain the value of the coupons and then they say 'Oh, yes, I know that but how do we know when we have used [them] up?' I explain each are dated. Then, 'Oh, yes, I can't be bothered. I leave it to you. I don't understand them. Tell me what I can have.' Sometimes, in slack moments, I ponder. There doesn't seem to me anything so very difficult to understand about the 'points' system. It seems anyone, even a child, could grasp it in five minutes if they really gave their mind to it. And then I think of the Russians and how they are putting their backs into their jobs and going all out to win. Then I ponder again. If anyone told these women they were shirkers and time wasters they would be indignant. But after all shopping is part of their job, and surely it is up to them, just as much as anyone else, to *do* their job, not half do it. I do not think (in spite of the *Daily Mail*) that the Government is the only section of the community that doesn't realise what 'total war' means.

Sunday, 11 January

To Mirfield where we had three babies to entertain us, twins and a singlet. We were all entranced. Babies are such a novelty to us, having none in the immediate family and none in our circle of friends. I thought what a waste as I looked round that room, in which there were three women who would have made good mothers, and two who had been cheated of grandchildren.

Monday 12 January

Sound of prolonged groans because the rations are cut, particularly sugar, which seems even more than tea to be the thing people would like more of. 'They like so much in their tea' is a general complaint. 'Two and three spoonsful. We can't make a bit of sweet stuff. It all goes for their tea.' 'They' usually meaning menfolk, who it seems are the sugar devourers.

Another long epistle from Food Office regarding milk, this time correcting and amending previous instructions. Rations came this morning which should have been here last Thursday. Half our customers had to go without sugar and marge.

Tuesday, 13 January

A letter from the Food Office asking us to 'state our grounds' for selling milk and accepting registered customers for same, as we hold no licence to do so. Hasty scurry to find list of things we are allowed to sell. Of course 'fresh milk' is not on it. Bert (easily impressed by forms and regulations) becomes flurried. I draft out 'written explanation' as requested, saying we were under the impression 'fresh milk' was included on licence and naturally we accepted registrations for same. Took [it] down to Food Office. Then to Rate Office, also in Town Hall. Got lost as usual in Town Hall. Why on earth they cannot be planned as a school is planned with a large hall and rooms all round, instead of so many dark and dreary passages. Get out at last with relief and wish for the thousandth time I was an architect with millions of pounds and a free hand in Dewsbury and Heckmondwike.

Wednesday, 14 January

Our free supply of Aspros [aspirin] (formerly sent to pay the Patent Medicine Licence, now rescinded) arrived today. They send us 5s worth per annum. With the free supply was a huge thick cardboard showpiece and a smaller one of beautifully white 'pre-war' cardboard, all enclosed in a strong brown-paper wrapping. The van man said he was sick of them, delivering to almost every shop. I should have whanged [thrown] the lot into the waste collection but Bert was pleased and put them in a prominent place. Mrs S. from the fried fish shop came in just then. She said she had received a monster poster with 'Fry Frozen Cod' printed on it, nothing else. I begin to wonder if I am a 'grumph' to spend my time dogging Bert not to burn his envelopes and rescuing paper from the rubbish box. (The shareholders of Aspros certainly are *not* 'grumphs'.)

Tuesday, 20 January

Get another letter from Food Office saying he is bringing the question of Milk Licence before his committee and in the meantime we may continue to supply our customers. (What have we been doing during the intervening week, does he think?)

Wednesday, 21 January

'I wonder why the MPs are so against broadcasting themselves?' I remarked. 'Because they don't want us to know what fools they are in Parliament,' snapped Ma. So that's that! To the pictures. Had to sit through the whole programmme before the [merchant mariner Frank] Laskier came on. All American features. Do they really dash about so much in cars and propose at 60–100 miles an hour and pull up with such a whining of brakes *every* time? I have seen this in every American film so far and begin to wonder if it [is] the natural way of going on, just as it seems that American life is dominated by gabbling 'swinging' youth. They should let us have more knowledge of other phases of their life, if there are any.

Friday, 23 January

A beautiful burst in the bathroom and no plumber (therefore no water) till Monday. Rations overdue again, also 'points'. Mr L. the wholesaler says the 'points' system is ridiculous, having every order to go to London to be checked. It certainly does not seem to be running smoothly at the moment, unless stuff is being held up on purpose for further rationing.

Saturday 24 January

Margarine, sugar, soda, Quaker oats, and rice, all now in bulk (not to mention cigs unwrapped), and we are threatened with soap powder loose, too. All these things must be wrapped, paper shortage or not, and there seems to be a general conspiracy to push the cost of wrapping onto the shopkeeper. A little thing, maybe, but there are so many little things. Our last lot of greaseproof paper, used for butter, bacon, marge, lard and cheese, cost 1s 2d per lb.

Tuesday, 27 January

E. was here and related how Reggie had been stranded in Glasgow a fortnight. It appears he set off on the Tuesday for Scotland with a load of guns. When nearing Glasgow on the moors some small thing broke in his engine. He got a tow to the nearest garage and explained his trouble and that he was a 'priority'. 'They all tell that tale,' was the reply. And he kicked his heels from Tuesday to a week the following Friday, not daring to leave his load, and desperate to find the gadget he wanted. There appeared not to be one in Scotland. At last, however, he risked it and came down to Leeds, got his piece and went back and practically did the work of fixing himself. The job was done in a quarter of an hour. Thereupon the garage presented him with a bill for £17 4s and said he couldn't take his lorry out until it was paid. He paid, having an open cheque from his employer, and delivered his load and returned. He reckons the episode will have cost his employer £50 for expenses, lost carrying jobs, etc. The firm he was carrying for are taking it up with some Government department.

Thursday, 29 January

An amusing sequel to the milk controversy. Brooke Bond's informs us that Mr H. at the shop down the road, having had a similar letter from Food Office, answered that his licence covered the kind of milk he was selling, that is, bottled milk, and he did not sell fresh milk, and proceeded to give a definition from the dictionary of what fresh milk was. Brooke Bond's says he has had a sheaf of correspondence from Food Office but they have not contradicted him, and now we are wondering how Food Office will proceed. Of course sterilised bottled milk *is not* fresh milk, whichever way you look. For one thing it is only delivered once per week.

Sunday, 1 February

Stock-taking all morning. Bert says he has a larger stock than he has ever carried. And yet little that isn't moving. Are now doing far above twice the turnover we were when we came a year ago. Rommel seems to have us on the hop *again* [in North Africa].

Wednesday, 4 February

To the pictures. Bella Hill and Margaret insisted on accompanying me and grumbled because both star pictures were American. One, about Alaska [*Mutiny in the Arctic*], would have made a fine picture if there had been any sort of plot, but it was as feeble a story as ever I've seen. In fact it seemed as though having taken the shots of icebergs and snowlands they didn't know quite what to do with them. A deal of time and trouble and skill and money must have been spent. What a pity to waste all on a paltry story.

Sunday, 8 February

Thought Sir Stafford Cripps [now a member of the War Cabinet] spoke well tonight, and truly. Enjoyed his speech as much as any of Winston's although he was not as 'heroic', and he gave us some pretty plain speaking.

Monday 9 February

The soap rationing [which came into force this day] has caused nearly as much commotion as the cigarette crisis a few months back, and far more than any food rationing yet. We are all at sea, and do not know No. 1 powders and No. 2 powders so are classing all as No. 1s and trusting to luck. Bar soap weighs 14 oz at present, which is awkward. We are charging one coupon for toilet soap whatever the size at present. Why couldn't we use a page out of the other ration book instead of these footling little squares to be cancelled. Whose idea is it to make things so tiny and so difficult? There is enough margin to make them considerably bigger; though why not treat all rationed goods by the same method? The muckiest folk are making the most fuss. The biggest demand is for 'Fairy' soap which can be used for either cleaning or toilet purposes.

Wednesday, 11 February

To the pictures, making seven times and twice to the theatre since the New Year. More and more depressed by the war news. My thoughts go round and round but achieve no satisfaction. It is as if someone had flung me into a bath of treacle and told me to swim for it. Believe I am getting the jitters.

Saturday, 14 February

Great indignation among customers at escape of German battleships.* More comments than over Pearl Harbour and [the sinking of the] *Prince of Wales*. Customers voluntarily speak of it without my prompting, a sure sign they are disturbed. The first we knew about it was when Mr B. said 'What have they been doing to let them ships escape? They've made fools of us, haven't they?' Old Mrs Mac – 'Making us into a laughing stock.' Another woman, 'It's been a black week and right. As if t'Japs weren't bad enough. And right on t'door step.' (This seems to be a sore point with many, that it happened 'under our noses'.) Another man, 'By gow, it's time we bucked up, what with one thing or another. There's only t'Russians doing owt. They wouldn't have let them slip, you can bet.' (Notice an increasing tendency to disgust with our part in the war and admiration for the Russians – though many acknowledge they owe thanks to us for supplies. Also many seem to admire the cleverness of the Japs as they formerly admired Hitler's successes.) Various rumours during this week that articles of food were to be short, principally sugar, coffee, rice and salt, but not noticed any move to buy more supplies.

---

* On 12 February the German battle cruisers *Scharnhorst* and *Geneisenau* and the heavy cruiser *Prinz Eugen* succeeded in sailing from Brest through the English Channel to home ports, more or less under the noses of the RAF. While the warships did sustain some damage, the British were embarrassed by their escape – and by the loss of over thirty planes in trying to stop them. This bold German initiative was another blow to British morale at the same time as Singapore was about to fall to the Japanese.

Sunday, 15 February

Spent the day generally straightening myself ready to start tomorrow on my task of self-discipline. The decision to make this mighty effort is the result of reasoning as follows:

The world in general is in fearful state, and we, in particular, are in a hell of a mess, whichever way you view our situation. This situation has not come upon us like the Flood. Our actions and inactions made it and they are caused by our muddled and selfish thinking and refusal to think at all. I mean our actions and thinking, and not just our leaders', but those of each of us, including my own. Therefore, acknowledging I have a share in making the world what it is, if I am honest, I cannot dodge my duty, which is to atone by helping make the world what it should be. The first step seems obviously to be to clear from my mind muddle and self-centredness and set it to work, and this I shall attempt.

Monday, 16 February

Everyone gloomy over [the loss of] Singapore [the previous day]. The policeman and Mr Hobbs and Bert discussed it at intervals all morning. The police constable said we were too slow, Bert said it was always alike, we were always too late, and who was [it that] started this disarming business anyway? Police constable said it was [Ramsay] Macdonald first, then [Stanley] Baldwin [Prime Ministers in the 1930s]. That set them off discussing where Baldwin was now. Bert said in America out of the way. *He* knew where to go to.*

---

* Stanley Baldwin, now Lord Baldwin and living in retirement on his estate in Astley, Worcestershire, was deeply unpopular, even despised. His most recent trip to the United States had been in 1939.

Mr Hobbs said his wife had right upset him that morning. She knew a thing or two about this Far East business. She had studied the question, and she said we were in an awful mess. Police constable said his father-in-law (86) studied the news and yesterday (Sunday) when he came to read the papers (being against buying one of his own owing to his principles!) he said he had been right about Singapore. He had said all along it wouldn't stand. The Old Man also said we hadn't the brains in the Government we used to have! 'Look at Ben Riley (Dewsbury MP [Labour, 1935–1945]). What good was he? A well meaning chap, no doubt, but nowt for times like these. Look at Gladstone and Disraeli, and the PM's father. What they said was done.' 'Yes,' said Bert. 'That's the whole trouble. There's too much argument and falling out in our Parliament. They don't do it in Germany or Russia. They get on wi' t'job.'* Mr Hobbs said, 'Well, he didn't know what we could do about it, except keep our heads and keep going on.'

Later. Winston spoke well but hardly convincingly. He never mentioned the escape of the ships. Feel as perplexed as before and full of foreboding. Margaret says 'He never told us a thing we didn't know. There is someone up at the top holding us back. Someone who doesn't want us to win this war.' She says this regularly whenever the war comes up in conversation.

The Prime Minister in this broadcast presented an overall assessment of the progress of the war. 'Let us take the rough with the smooth, let us put the good and bad side by side, and let us try to see exactly where we are.' While acknowledging the humiliating loss of Singapore ('a heavy and far-reaching military defeat'), he

---

* Many frustrated Britons at this time expressed a desire for a tougher and more authoritarian leadership from Westminster.

argued that on balance Britain was in a better position now than in the previous year, mainly because the United States was now an Allied combatant and Russia had so far successfully defended itself. 'We must remember that we are no longer alone. We are in the midst of great company. Three-quarters of the human race are now moving with us.' (Collected Speeches, VI, 6583–87). The following day he spoke in the Commons about the escape of the German warships (Ibid., 6588–89). As for the remarks of Kathleen's sister, conspiracy theories were commonplace during the war, largely, of course, when things went wrong; and this month witnessed probably the lowest morale in Britain during the entire war. Diaries from the time are replete with pessimism.

Tuesday, 17 February

Today a woman sent up at different times for four pounds of oranges. Then she came up herself and rowed because she said there was short weight on the four pounds. We explained oranges could not be weighed so close. She said she didn't care about that, she wanted her full four pounds, with a few swear words and banging on the counter with her fist. She was a large woman and Bert, the silly fool, gave her another orange, charging her, of course. I was so mad I told her not to come in the shop again. She said 'I shall not'. I said, 'No doubt. You'll get nothing if you do.' Then she went after telling Margaret she would push her b——nose in. Then we both berated Bert for pandering to her and giving another orange. This orange business is sickening. Why on earth can't they give them out at clinics or schools if children must have them? Though I cannot for the life of me see what good oranges do taken so infrequently. Oranges, eggs and onions cause more upsets than anything we sell. We are having a run on salt. A traveller reports they are queuing for it in Castleford [about ten miles to the east].

Wednesday, 18 February

Today asked old Mr K. what he thought about it all. 'What *can* we think?' he said, and after a bit burst out, 'We're too busy providing for everybody else to look to oursens. Sending arms to all and sundry. And keeping all these foreigners here.' I laughed at that, but then he said shrewdly 'No, it isn't that. It's them b——s up at t'top, a lot on 'em 'ats thinking more about saving their estates in foreign parts nor fighting. They don't want to have them damaged.' Margaret said 'Yes, but they wouldn't be any good even undamaged if the enemy had them'. He said 'Some on 'em would come to terms if they dared'. Mother says this war is far worse than the last because then we didn't know what was happening until sometime after the event, but now we were looking on, so to speak, and watching the war practically, and it was more of a strain. Margaret said, well, one couldn't resist if one had a wireless, listening in to every news bulletin for fear something was happening.

Saturday, 21 February

Fruit distribution starts on Monday and we have not a tin in. Our wholesaler, one of the largest firms in Yorkshire, reports they have only 214 cases allocated to them, which will not run to anything like one tin per shop. And yet people say (I have not been into Dewsbury this week) that Woolworths and Marks & Spencer are chockfull, windows and all. Woolworths are displaying Smedleys' goods (they never sold this class of goods pre-war). And Bert cannot get his peas from them [the wholesalers] that he paid for last May (£12). But everything is well with the fruit distribution! The wireless assures us that if we have not got it we shall do! Some Hopes! We are nearly sold out of salt. Strangely enough we have only sold 2 oz pepper all week, which is more likely to be scarce.

Monday, 23 February

Several customers report that there were queues everywhere in town this morning for tinned fruit. One said there was a fight in one of the shops. Another said her neighbour had got a month's points' family ration of tinned fruit, coming home with a basket full. We have had several strangers in for tinned fruit and one or two customers who said they would wait and see what we got and if we didn't have any they wouldn't bother. A good many of our customers seem more concerned about tomatoes and have requested some saving.

Tuesday, 24 February

As requested by the Borough engineer, Bert attended a meeting at the Town Hall to discuss salvage arrangements and mutual aid if we should be bombed in Dewsbury. He said there were about a hundred attended, chiefly members of the Chamber of Trade. One suggested that accommodation should be made in shops for those bombed out, that is storage room and counter room. A jeweller stood up and protested it was impracticable to work the scheme that way – what could he do with a grocer in his shop? In the end the meeting was adjourned for further proposals to be drawn up. Bert said there were protests about multiple businesses taking trade in the town. The chairman said that was not the place for that but the Secretary of the Chamber of Commerce took notes for their next meeting. Bert is going as he has applied to be a member.

Wednesday, 25 February

Bella Hill went to her friends at Bradford. They keep a shop. They are unable to get fruit either. Their traveller told them the Jews had cornered it all. There were scrimmages in Bradford Woolworths and Marks & Spencer and the police had to be called in.

Thursday, 26 February

Our fortnight's goods have arrived from wholesalers. No fruit, no tomatoes, no nowt that customers will expect.

Bert has received invitation to annual meeting of Chamber of Trade, which points out that No. 4 on the Agenda will be of interest to all traders – 'The Future of the Small Trader'. I wish I could go. Bert has written Smedleys pointing out that various shops in the town (Woolworths really) are displaying and selling their goods and he would be glad to have his five cases of peas paid for last May, and also some fruit (if there is any left). Margaret says it is disgraceful of the women to stand and brawl over unnecessary luxuries. Why aren't they on war work if they have all that spare time? I said it is disgraceful of the Government to allow the stuff to be concentrated in a few places, encouraging the idle and the brazen, and making discontent all round. Our faithful customers who get everything except meat from us are left high and dry; we have nothing for

them, and those who spend their time queuing and walking the town every day get the prizes. What of the poor
shopkeepers explaining, explaining, apologising, hoping,
and most often, I fear, cursing, cursing. George Little's man
came today. They are a large Manchester wholesaler. He
said they had no fruit whatever to offer their customers. He
said this business was all cut and dried and arranged long
ago. The big firms had practically got a monopoly. Bert had
a letter today forbidding him selling milk after next week as
he has no licence. The letter says just 'milk' not 'fresh milk'
as previously. Bert says he is glad; he won't have as many
blooming forms to fill in.

As Kathleen makes clear, neither shopkeepers nor customers could be
sure what foodstuffs would be available and when.
Here window shoppers gather in the street outside a grocer's
to see what might have come in that week.
Photograph © IWM D2372

Saturday, 28 February

An exhausting week, explaining this and that; why we have no tinned fruit and tomatoes, why we are forbidden to sell milk. Our customers, with touching faith, are saving their points for another week in case we should get any fruit. Our milk customers are indignant and wholly sympathetic.

Monday, 2 March

Bert came away from the Chamber of Trade meeting disgusted with the small attendance, 25 out of membership [of] 150. He said the 'Small Trader' question was gone into and a note is to be sent to B. Riley, MP. One man with a large business in town said he had 300 cases of peas and fruit on order and had not received one. This man said it was the Corporation's fault in the first place for allowing large multiple stores to be in the town. He said he saw no hope for the small shopkeepers after the war unless they pulled themselves up and got together to defend themselves. Bert said he was glad he was outside town [i.e., doing business in Dewsbury Moor, where no chain store was likely to locate].

Tuesday, 3 March

When I brought the new Trading License from Food Office we discovered eggs were not included. Bert flurried down to Food Office to enquire why and was told eggs were not on previous licences – those held by our predecessor in this shop. We shall not be able to sell after the present permit runs out. Bert asked why they issued permits if he was not licensed. They admitted oversight but stuck to it – he cannot sell eggs. Bert said what was the blooming point of licensing if there was no system of checking them with food permits?

This controversy brought again to my mind the conviction that people are getting slacker and slacker about their daily jobs, in giving their mind to what is their plain duty to do and know. Thinking over only the events of the last few days which bear on this I remember:

1. The egg business. Slackness on the part of Mr Hobbs our predecessor here and the Food Office people have resulted in our unwittingly breaking the law.
2. The policeman who told me the Borough Engineering office was on the top floor of the Town Hall. After climbing two long flights with a sprained foot I was not pleased to find the place I wanted was at the Municipal Buildings half a mile away. Surely a 'guard' at the most important public building in the town should 'know his ground'.
3. The gentleman who kept me waiting three weeks for receipt for my insurance premium, which I had sent by post.
4. Various customers coming in for soap, points, or other rationed goods with the wrong books or no books at all, saying in a complacent voice, 'I never can understand the things'. This means extra work for me, making notes of what they take. As I can't go around keeping everyone up to scratch I can only make up for their deficiencies by being extra scrupulous myself that I do not fall into slackness – a sort of atonement for their sins. No doubt in other days I should have gone into a convent and prayed for them.

5

Perils of War

March–July 1942

Saturday, 7 March

Registered today.* Had only to show my identity card and give date of birth, the whole business taking two minutes. Am puzzled how I could prove quickly if challenged that the card is mine. There is no means of proving the connection between my card and me *quickly* if I was among strangers.

Monday, 9 March

Hot argument which Margaret started by saying we should have a stirrup pump [for fire-fighting]. Bert said it was not necessary; there were plenty round about, at so and so's and someone else's. Margaret said what is going to happen to the

* Women born in 1906, Kathleen's year of birth, were now being registered for possible national service. Women born between 1907 and 1921 had already been registered.

incendiary while we are running for one? Bert said he should put sand on it. I said I thought they were too hot to approach near. Bert said the firemen would see and come at once. Margaret said, yes, if an incendiary hadn't dropped on their own house, when they would naturally stick to the stirrup pump. She said there was nothing like having things of your own and being independent of others as far as possible. I said it was the landlord's job really but he took no interest in protecting his own property. It will be a poor do for us if ever we have to depend on the men round here. Ma said it made you wonder if all England was no more prepared than Dewsbury Moor. It ended in Bert grumpily saying 'Get one if you like but how are you going to use the thing?' Previously he has pooh-poohed the idea.

Wednesday, 11 March

E. came, said knitting wool was going to be unobtainable, so we went into town and got some, I spending my last coupons. Several customers say flour is to be rationed and black [i.e., whole wheat]. Heard several say we shall be hard put to for food next winter, one saying she thought we should have enough but no variety, one going so far as to forecast a diet of dried peas and porridge. But only two have said they were putting aside their 'points' for later. Most people seem to spend them when they want something for a meal immediately.

Thursday, 12 March

Quite a number of people mentioned the bayoneting of the men in Hong Kong [by the Japanese], expressing indignation, and gloomily saying the war would not be over yet, and most of them finished up as usual with, 'I wish t'war was over, I do'. Old Mrs H., our inveterate grumbler, said (for the first time) 'We ought to be thankful. We don't know how well off we are here.'

Saturday, 14 March

Decided not to have a 'perm' as think it self-indulgence when so many are struggling and suffering. Have the feeling we are living inside a bubble or glass globe which may be shattered at any moment. Reading in the *Listener* [12 March 1942, pp. 331–32] an article on Japan makes me wonder if eventually Germany too will be helping fight them. (There seem to be plenty of people *now* who can tell us what the Japs are, to judge by the press. Why didn't they speak up before?) I said about Germany being on our side and the policeman said, 'Well, lots of people thought in the last war they should have been instead of the French. Our soldiers didn't like the French then. You can never trust them. When the Germans say they will do a thing they do it. But it's a job to straighten it out; it's all mixed up this time.' The policeman also said the Government should have stopped the sale of clothes altogether unless people could give a very good reason for needing a garment. I said I couldn't see but this Utility business was a farce when luxury clothes were still allowed to be made. He said, 'No, if clothes must be sold we should all wear a uniform like soldiers. We are all supposed to be equally at war.' I said, 'It's the same with other things like allowing that firm to make liqueur chocolates. There is always a protected, privileged few and the Government's appeals for everyone to sacrifice lose a good deal of "pull".'

The Board of Trade had introduced the Utility Clothing Scheme as a way of ensuring that an adequate quantity and quality of new clothes were produced and 'wasteful' practices eliminated. London fashion designers were asked to make outfits of simple design, with few buttons, of narrow cut and without pleats or flounces, and lacking such superfluous trimming as lace or appliqué. While most members of the elite actually gave up wearing evening dress as a patriotic gesture, garments in their well-stocked wardrobes could be refashioned into stylish and new-looking items – an option that would not have been available to most of Dewsbury's citizens – or simply worn in comfort until wartime restrictions were eventually lifted. The response to clothes rationing of one rich Conservative Member of Parliament exemplifies the resilience enjoyed by privilege. As he wrote in his private diary on 1 June 1941, 'The big news this morning is clothes rationing. Oliver Lyttleton [President of the Board of Trade] is only going to allow us 66 coupons per annum. A suit takes 26. Luckily I have 40 or more. Socks will be the shortage. Apart from these, if I am not bombed, I have enough clothes to last me for years.' Later that year (14 November 1941), after spending a day in his constituency, Southend, he remarked on 'the cold, the black-out, the unhappiness, dislocation and misery of the people,' and concluded 'I fear I live in a gilded world'. (Robert Rhodes James, ed., Chips: The Diaries of Sir Henry Channon *[London: Phoenix, 1996; first published 1967], pp. 307 and 313.)*

Kathleen's writing for this day concluded with the following passage.

Cleared out of flour a week before usual time. This comes of the Government's daft way of talking of what they are going to do instead of doing it. Everyone has been rushing to get a stock of white flour in. Have only heard two persons besides myself say they liked brown bread and didn't mind the change. Most women say with dismay 'How can we make puddings, now?' apparently considering brown flour impossible for the job. The flour traveller says the flour should have been gradually darkened and no one would have said anything.

Monday, 16 March

B. B. Biscuits said it is not worth his while to travel; he doesn't know why the firm expects it when he has nothing to offer. Bert said, 'Well, after the war they will have a boom'. B. B. Biscuits said there *would* probably be a boom while they were building the houses up again and straightening up, and then what a slump! He said it was bad enough last time but nothing to what this time would be.

Thursday, 19 March

Bert, having written three times to Smedleys asking for his cases of peas or his money returning and receiving no reply, has now got the Secretary of the Chamber of Commerce to write for him. If that fails he doesn't know what to do as going to law over the matter is hardly worthwhile and yet such high handed methods should be exposed. There may be many small shopkeepers served in similar fashion.

Saturday, 21 March

Auntie came and we had a war argument over supper. It began with food hoarding and how provident folk were penalised and improvident ones encouraged; got on to distribution, when we all agreed people who lived by themselves should have extra rations and extra 'points', and babies should *not* have bacon, meat and tea rations. From that we went to discussing how well we had done generally in food and how we should feel the pinch from now on. I said people didn't realise what we had lost in the Far East; they didn't understand; we should never have the same sway there. Auntie said no, they could say as they liked about the natives having equal rights, it was all bunkum. We had got the profit, and why *should* the natives fight for our interests? If they were not to have their own lands, one set of rulers was the same as another to them. She said she thought this Empire would go down. She had not thought [this] until Singapore but that disgusting business had convinced her. She said it wasn't that people weren't willing or not working but it was the leaders, one thing after another. She had nothing against Churchill – she admired him. (We all agreed that Churchill had not promised us anything.) But as for some of these others, saying everything was alright and then... Margaret said the PM was overseen in his friends; instead of sacking them when they made mistakes he glossed it over. Auntie said he had been betrayed time and again. Mother said, 'We should take a pattern from Russia. They were doing the job.' Margaret said, Yes, with our stuff that should have been in the Far East. Russia was fighting for *Russia* not for *us* as well or she would have declared war on Japan. What was going to happen when Russia had pushed the Germans out? Russia would probably give up and leave us to our fate. Say what you like, we were the only ones who were not fighting solely for ourselves. Both Russia and America came in solely from self-interest; they didn't care about us. We had held the fort for two years. She knew we had made mistakes but considering everything, we had done magnificently.

Tuesday, 24 March

Peas from Smedleys here at last with apologetic note. Bert says he would not have got them if it hadn't been for Chamber of Commerce. Brooke Bond's Tea says he can only come fortnightly in future owing to lack of petrol. He says the petrol business is disgustingly controlled. He says when he went the other night to help entertain soldiers in camp at Swillington (near Wakefield) there were 200 cars parked outside the local pub. He said the landlord said he bet not one of the men was with his own wife. Bert said he expected they would be Jews from Leeds most of them. Brooke Bond's said that the blackout had 'made' many of these country pubs. Folk could steal away and enjoy themselves 'under cover' as it were. He said he knew several similar places – there was one at Tadcaster – a rendezvous for York and Leeds people. And folk whose livelihood depended on getting petrol to do their business were pushed on one side.

Saturday, 28 March

Long argument with Bert and Margaret as to what luggage I must take on my fire watching expedition with M. G. tonight.[*] M. G. said on SOS postcard, 'Bring two sheets and pillow case, also supper and respirator'. Bert said 'Whoever heard of fire watchers going to bed?' Margaret said 'And you don't know who has been sleeping in it. I should lie on the top, dressed.'

---

[*] Fire-watching, which was organised on a rota system, became a requirement of civilians – of men between the ages of 18 and 60, women between 20 and 45 – and kept many of them up at night when they were on duty. The maximum service required was set at 48 hours per four-week period. Some people succeeded in getting exemptions.

Think [I] shall compromise by taking dressing gown only and hope for best regarding bed. All family greatly perturbed at my promising to go and protest at intervals until I rise wrathfully and shout 'Is there a war on, or isn't there?'

Saturday, 4 April

Women, protesting against the inevitable, are making a last minute dash round the shops for white bread and flour. Most are now fairly resigned but determined to eat white bread until the last minute, although some have grumbled that the Government is trying to starve them and they will not eat brown bread for anyone. It is the colour rather than the taste of 'war bread' that upsets them, and there is a general fear that bread will gradually become as it was in the last war when 'it ran out of the oven'.

Sunday, 5 April

Fire watching with M. G. We sat up discussing:

1. *Education*. M. G., a Secondary School teacher, was puzzled to know why her Young Ladies' Class, twenty-year olds, was not a success and why they seemed indifferent when they attended, and [were] irregular in attendance. She taxed one pupil with this and the girl said 'Well, Miss G., I have come for nine months and during that time I have not understood a word you were saying'. Considerably flattered, M. G. sought the advice of another teacher, Bella Hill, who said it was no use using words of more than two syllables because the girls could not or would not

bother to understand. Bella Hill instanced three of her 'Young Ladies' who had joined the forces and said their letters to her were so bad that you may as well call them illiterates. M. G. said she had tried in vain to raise in her 'flock' a sense of responsibility and made first one and then another responsible for various collections and funds, but not one troubled even to count the money, and simply passively resisted any attempt to make them interested, seemingly taking the view that those were her jobs.

2. *Smoking.* We both agreed that we could see nothing in this and wondered how anyone could become a slave to the habit. I instanced F. S. saying indignantly, when I suggested people would have to do without tobacco as there were more important things to bring into the country, that the war would stop if there were no smokes. No one would be able to carry on. M. G. said, Yes, her brothers and all men friends took the same attitude. They looked as if something had been desecrated if such a thing was mentioned as stopping smoking. I said I only knew of one person who had given up smoking this last year and he was never a heavy smoker, and I didn't know whether his motives were patriotic or whether he was merely fed up with trying to get cigs.

3. *The immediate future.* We agreed that things would get much worse for us and we should suffer spiritually and physically as we had not done yet. M. G. thinks we shall have epidemics of various diseases. She also thinks after the war things will be in such a state that we shall have no comfort in our time, no peace of mind. (We are in our thirties.)

4. We discussed what we were fighting for and M. G. said it was sad but she believed true that so many youngsters were giving their lives and rushing into battle not for any particular cause but from sheer animal spirits and excitement. She knew there was a more thoughtful sort too and honoured them still more, because they went into things wide awake, but, to revert to our old discussion, she thought most of us didn't think enough – if we thought at all. I said, Yes, it was one of the things that boded ill for after the war. It would be strange if we spent everything in fighting Dictatorships and then succumbed to one ourselves.

Wednesday, 8 April

To Mirfield where Mr D., when I asked him what India was going to do, said they would not come to terms and then said – astoundingly for a Conservative of the old-fashioned sort – 'You know, this country has never given India a fair deal. They have not been treated right. So what can we expect?'

Thursday, 9 April

Down at the sub-Post Office four women discussing the war. One said it was disgraceful the way our boys and girls were being taken. (This arose from our Postmistress telling of her daughter's dislike of her war job in a foundry.) Another said, Yes, why didn't some of them at t'top go and see how they liked it. They had as much right to go as anyone else instead of wasting their time arguing in Parliament. It made you sick, every time you put t'wireless on, to hear Mr this arguing with Mr that. They should be sent where they were sending our lads and see how they liked it. Third woman said, Well, it made her poorly to hear about the goings on in the East, torturing and so on. It was awful. Fourth said her husband said this war would go on like the last one to a certain point and when it pleased them that was running it and they had made their pile it would stop. Postmistress said she had heard several say the same thing, that when the armament manufacturers said so there would be a finish. Third woman said you would never get India to agree among themselves. They weren't like us; they were mostly wild like savages. Her husband had spent six years in India; they had to chain their rifles to the ground and then the Indians stole them, and no one could catch them because they had no clothes and their bodies were greased and slippery.

Saturday, 11 April

Listened to Cripps' speech [concerning his negotiations with political leaders in India to grant it more autonomy]. Bert said he never expected anything else when they started putting announcement off. They would never get them to agree. Auntie said well, we really in the past hadn't treated India fair so what could we expect. We had exploited the country for our own profit, at least for the benefit of a certain few, and borne down the Indians who were a very cultured people. What right had we ordering them about? Margaret said the sort of folk we sent to India wouldn't improve things, public schoolboys, etc. I said it was why Malaya and other places were lost. From the natives' point of view why should they fight to protect our rubber plantations? No wonder when the Japs promised this and that they thought they couldn't change for the worse. They might find out they had but you couldn't blame them for trying a change. Auntie said you never knew where you were with these vested interests. Look at them paying [Marshal Philippe] Pétain [1856–1951, leader of Vichy France] his income from London. Bert said we were too blooming soft in this country, as he'd always said. Honouring this and that and others were knifing us in the back. As for vested interests, it was vested interests that had poured money into Germany something scandalous, our money, and what had we got for it? Another blooming war.

Thursday, 16 April

The rise in tobacco and cigs has been received calmly, people saying resignedly or sarcastically that the war had to be paid for they supposed. Old-age pensioners chief grumblers. No falling off in sales, people coming for their 'rations' as usual. Only one man said he would get his at the NAAFI* in future – he wasn't paying that price. Wives of soldiers grumble because their menfolk can only get thirty at canteen and have to pay full price otherwise. But general attitude seems to be 'I can't do without a smoke. I shall have to have one whatever the cost.'

But grumbles about National Bread obscure all other grievances this week. It seems it is making everyone ill (but myself, who always eats brown anyway). Symptoms range from slight indigestion to real sickness and diarrhoea, and many have had to go to bed for a few days. (My sister is one of these.) If I suggest the sudden heat wave may have something to do with it I am shouted down. No, it is the bread; the Government is

---

* The Navy, Army and Air Force Institutes ran canteens and refreshment centres for members of the Forces.

trying to pine [i.e., starve] us t'death. In any case who can eat brown bread to bacon and what do puddings and pastry look like? It is a real grievance the *colour*. My remarks that the Greeks and others wouldn't care if bread was sky blue pink if they could get some are received lukewarmly. 'Yes, it is awful for them – they're starving, they say. But just think of having this to eat till the war ends.' There has been an increase in the sale of bread, however, and a falling off in flour sales, because the National is said to be unpleasant and sticky to knead, and also a good many have stocked with white flour this last few weeks and will not have used it up.

Tuesday, 21 April

Sales of flour practically ceased, and Bert with four sacks on hand. Everyone buying bread. They say they cannot knead the National flour.

Thursday, 30 April

Listened to new feature *Marching On* [a dramatisation of outstanding news stories]. All upset in our various ways at description of German children being sent away to work. Ma said Hitler wanted hanging up by one ear. Bert violently broke out, as usual, that this war would never have happened if Britain hadn't been so soft, letting Germany do everything she wanted. Margaret never spoke for half an hour. I wouldn't eat my supper. What a pity programmes like this wouldn't have been devised long ago. I am sure they will make more impression than all the pep talks and newspaper leaders put together.

Wednesday, 6 May

To the Empire to see a play 'straight from the Garrick Theatre, London' called *The Rotters* [by H. F. Maltby] which should have been called 'Rotten'. People in London are easily pleased if they liked it. Some women behind me were discussing theatre versus pictures and plumping for the latter every time because 'you had more change of scenery and no intervals and a far longer programme for your money'. Not a picture-goer myself, I could yet sympathise with them, for this play starting at 7.05 was over by 8.45 and there were two long intervals, and *no* change of scenery.

Sunday, 10 May

Thought Winston in good fettle tonight. Really believe he would sway me whatever he said when he is in form – he certainly can ring the bell. I wonder if we are turning the corner at last.* Shall have to practise wearing gas mask.

Monday or Tuesday, 11 or 12 May

Was amused when old Mrs Wood said we were to have white flour again on Monday – it said so after the news. 'Not on our

---

* This broadcast marked Churchill's second anniversary as Prime Minister, and he proposed to reflect on the past, the present, and the probable future. 'As in the last war, so in this, we are moving through many reverses and defeats to complete and final victory. We have only to endure and to persevere, to conquer ... There can be only one end. When it will come, or how it will come, I cannot tell. But, when we survey the overwhelming resources which are at our disposal, once they are fully marshalled and developed – as they can be, as they will be – we may stride forward into the unknown with growing confidence.' (*Collected Speeches*, VI, 6635 and 6629–30.)

wireless. It said nothing like that,' said Bert. 'Didn't it?' said the old lady, pityingly. 'Oh, but it did on ours.'

Wednesday, 13 May

To Mirfield where Mr D. expressed his opinion that the Russians would work their way round the 'top', and we should invade Norway and then, with Sweden making us munitions, we should come down and crush Germany, but it would take some doing. Then we got on to Chamberlain again, discussing the mystery as to whether he did or did not save the country. Mrs D. said he died a broken-hearted man. I said maybe, but that was better than a broken-hearted country. Mr D. repeated his theory that the Labour Party had led us into this with their 'Peace at any price', high wages, fine houses. Churchill and Eden and others had continually warned us of this.

Thursday, 14 May

To T—— to Bella Hill's father. Liked the village very well, especially as we got six cauliflowers for 2s. In Dewsbury they were 2s each last week. On the way we saw bombers being loaded quite openly on the roadside. It seemed strange to see the lads and lasses of the village strolling uninterestedly by as if the sight were too common for notice. Bella Hill's father said young Tate (16 years) brought home £4 10s last week, nearly twice as much as he earned. We all agreed it was wrong.

From this spring Kathleen usually wrote her diary less often. Several days, even a week or more, might pass when she did not write at all. In contrast to the summer and autumn of 1941, when she was writing almost daily, she was now more likely to be keeping up with her diary on perhaps only six or eight or ten days a month. Still, while frequency declined, many of her entries remained lengthy, informative, spirited, and sometimes colourful.

* * *

After a break of eight days, Kathleen's next diary entry introduces for the first time another major group of Yorkshire workers – the discontented coal miners. They were demanding from the coal-owners increased pay and a minimum was of £4 5s a week, arguing that they were paid significantly less than other industrial workers whose conditions of labour were much less demanding. (Complaints about the high wages paid to those employed in munitions factories were commonplace, among miners and many others.) The miners also wanted to eliminate or greatly reduce the power of private ownership in the industry, and while this did not happen during the war, their real wages were substantially increased.

Saturday, 23 May

Auntie came up and we discussed the miners' point of view and sympathised with them. Margaret said there wasn't as much disparity as there appeared when you reckoned munition workers' overtime and Sundays, but for all that she didn't agree with paying high wages. Bert said he thought it was all going to be different this war; everyone was going to be equal; instead of that, things were worse than ever. Margaret said the mistake was cajoling these unskilled people instead of telling them that was their job and they had to do it. It would be a pretty thing if our soldiers and sailors and airmen stopped fighting to argue about wages. Auntie said she didn't mind how hard she worked, though she was 65, if she was certain others were working equally hard and getting no more pay. It was this unfairness that stuck in her throat. Bert said yes, it was the same in business. Small shopkeepers had to take all the slaver [drivel, nonsense] and were worried and badgered to death and their profits were pared to the bone and the big firms got away with it. It was all a tale that they were not making big profits this war. Look at the Imperial Tobacco Company, what profits they had made again, and he wasn't allowed a halfpenny on 2s 2d worth [of] tobacco. No wonder half the population didn't want to see an end to the war. They were making too good a thing out of it.

Wednesday, 27 May

To Mirfield where of course we had the war to sort out. Principal theme was wages. Mr D.'s granddaughter at Barnoldswick [on the border between Lancashire and the West Riding of Yorkshire] had written to say she liked her war job – it was a change from hairdressing – and she had taken home over five pounds that week. (This after a month's training.) Mr D. of course blamed the Labour Party for squandering the nation's money. I said it wasn't only the Labour Party. It was the whole silly half-baked principle of the Government persuading and cajoling people to do what they should have been *expected* to do. The silly pampering of young women was the most glaring example of this. Mr D. said no wonder the miners were kicking up when a girl could go and draw wages like that and has no responsibility and they had to work as they had for what they got. E. said it would break up family life, wives and daughters going home with half as much again or twice as much as father. Mr D. said, talk about fairness in wartime, you'd never get it. When he was on the buses in the last war he got sixpence an hour for driving to London and back, and other long distances. He never had a day off or a Sunday at home for months. Sixty hours a week was nothing. And his young seventeen-year-old conductress many a time came out with more money than he had.

Friday, 29 May

Still some hopeful ones seeking white flour. There are many grumbles among the few who do bake that the National bread goes dry, they have to bake less quantity more frequently. Our dustman told me they had counted ten whole slices (buttered) in our street's bins. I wonder how much more bread is wasted now than before. Guess Lord Woolton wouldn't be so complacent if he guessed what was wasted. I know several people who have two or three stones of white flour yet in stock. They use it only for puddings etc.

Sunday, 31 May

Someone must be smoking less. We are selling no tobacco except twist and can now spare cigs for anyone where before we had to keep them for customers. How few men use a case. Now they are sent loose – we have to provide no end of bags. They will not save a cigarette packet if they get one. Yet another expense for the poor old shopkeeper.

Sunday, 14 June

We rode out for nearly the last time before putting up the car [petrol for private motoring was about to be banned], to see if we could see anything of All Nations Day celebrations [representing the twenty-eight Allied nations] but saw only one flag put out from a bedroom window and none on the churches, which was surprising for they do have flags. We missed the service in Dewsbury [held at the Town Hall], starting out late. As we had no flag we adorned the car inside with a bow of red, white and blue and I fastened a Jubilee handkerchief at the back window, but we did not feel like flag wagging. As Margaret remarked, it would be better to wait until there is something to cheer about. Not a single customer mentioned anything about today's doings in the shop yesterday, except one who asked if I were going to the service.

Tuesday, 16 June

To Cousin H.'s to see the baby bathed, babies being a novelty in our family. We all sat round in an admiring circle. M. is methodical and thorough with it, taking advantage of all the help now given young mothers. What a pity all are not of the same mind. Most of our customers seem to treat Clinics as something to be laughed at and flatly refuse to give their children cod liver oil, saying 'I couldn't drink that beastly stuff myself'. It makes you wonder if a good deal of all this social welfare business isn't just money thrown down the drain. M.'s baby sleeps from 7 o'clock until 9.30 next morning. Ma says enviously she wished she'd had one like that, but as I tell her they weren't made that way 40 years ago. Perhaps it's Nature adapting itself. Tougher world – tougher kids.

    H. and Bert had a long argument whether gas or high explosive bombs were worst – Bert says gas, because he knew chaps who were suffering from effects of last war yet. H. said no, bombs, because there was little chance of escape from them. He was not afraid of gas and didn't think there was much chance of gas doing damage about here though they might have a try at big cities but that would be a failure. He said all the Wardens in his sector except himself (not old enough) had served in the last war and pooh-poohed the gas scare. They said they had fought in gas attacks and their protection was not so good as civilians' is now, and they came to little harm. H. said he thought there would only be one more blackout.

Wednesday, 17 June

No biscuits for second week in succession. Customers loud in their complaints so that it might be bread they were deprived of [bread was not rationed]. They have had at least half a pound per family per week since we came here and [you would] think the sky has fallen because they are not there as usual. Sometimes think we live in a bubble or glass case in this part of the world – the war makes so little *apparent* deep impression on us. The Japanese horrors, the starving people abroad, the fact that we are outclassed in Libya and are having ships sunk galore is nothing to us so that we get our 'extras' regularly, our cigs and matches and 'points' goods, our eggs and tomatoes. Perhaps if we were told the *whole* truth occasionally instead of one-sided truth or given the pill without the pain we might get the War deeper 'under our skins'.

Sunday, 21 June

Margaret said on hearing the news tonight about Tobruk, 'I *said* something would happen. All that fuss last week about waving flags. Ridiculous in the middle of a war. *Now* don't we look daft?' 'It's happened pretty quick,' I said. 'Goodness, only these few days and we've come to this pass. There's something jolly rotten somewhere or we should have put up more of a show than this. What must the Russians think now? What's the good of all this blah-blah about a second front when we can't cope with what we have on our plates now?' There seems to be no doubt that we're seriously outclassed in Africa. Can see no end to this awful nightmare or only one – compromise. Exhaustion will finish this war and there will be no 'decisive victories'.*

Monday, 22 June

Our landlord said he had stomach ache all night thinking of Tobruk. Everybody flabbergasted. Everyone saying this will lengthen the war.

Tuesday, 23 June

Tobruk is on most people's tongues. General opinion [that] there is something wrong somewhere. Mr L. says he doesn't often talk for talking's sake or venture an opinion but he is convinced that these things are manipulated or why the sudden change when everything is in our favour. This war will end when certain people have made their money and there *is* some money being made on the Q.T. [quiet]. This had developed into a capitalist war. If it was not, why was everyone not put on an equal war footing and all treated like soldiers? Mr S., who lost a leg at Dunkirk, said 'They've made a mess of it again. What we need is old Nelson and Wellington back again. They'd put some pep into us.' Bert, who never reads the paper except racing and anything pertaining to rationing – he

* The Germans had just captured Tobruk in Libya and taken more than 30,000 prisoners and large quantities of stores. This was yet another humiliating defeat in 1942.

says newspapers tell you what suits them whether true or not – read it through, even the *Daily Mail*'s War Correspondent's long article saying our men were badly led. Then he went sky high and was bad tempered all morning. Ma was impressed with the fact that Rommel was a bricklayer's son and said 'Yes, if our working lads had a say instead of all these damned old school ties, things would not be at this pass'. Margaret, when she'd had her turn at the paper, said well we couldn't fight on so many fronts and help all the Empire and raid Germany and help Russia and do all successfully – all on our own. 'Yes,' said Bert. 'What the devil is America doing except talk and criticise. What fighting have they done for any but themselves. It's time they took a share in things.' I said 'The shame isn't that we've been just defeated. It's that we have allowed ourselves to be defeated when we had the advantage and were well armed.' Margaret said you couldn't wonder our war workers grew restless when they were working half their time to equip Germany [because of captured munitions]. I said 'Yes, a Tobruk would be worth two Coventrys [a city heavily damaged by German raids in mid-November 1940] to Hitler any day for he got booty out of it that way'. Depressed all day and very angry. Feel there is a great big row brewing up in this country.

Wednesday 24 June

Ma said there was not a single cheerful item in the news-paper and gloomily wondered if we were going to win the war after all. I said she should read Archidamus [astrologist in the *Daily Mail*, p. 4] and that should cheer her up – all the wonderful things the Allies are *about* to do and what a smack in the eye Hitler is *going* to get. I remarked it was wonderful where Archidamus gets his supply of soothing syrup – it never fails.[*]

Having told the dustman to ask the salvage collector to call as we had piles of cardboard in the cellar, was gratified at his prompt arrival with the cart after dinner, whereupon this conversation ensued. Myself, going out of shop to direct him down the steps to back door: 'The stuff is all ready in the cellar at the back'. Salvage Collector, staring dumbfounded down the steps: 'He said it was in t'shop'. Myself, pleasantly: 'No, round the back, down these steps. It's all the same building, you know.' Salvage Collector, still gazing incredulously: 'He said in t'shop'. Thinking the man was very dense, I patiently explained again that the salvage was at the back. He let out a roar. 'He said in t'shop. Nowt about going round t'back for t'stuff.' It dawned on me that he was standing on some sort of 'rights' and I fetched Bert, who flew in a rage and demanded to know what the devil he thought he was paid for and get the stuff away pretty quick or he'd report him, on which the man said sulkily he'd nowt wrong with us but it was the dustman's job to put the salvage out. In the meantime my sister had done most of his work and he unwillingly finished it, Bert standing over him. Margaret said afterwards she found a lot of tins which he jibbed at taking but she insisted he should as it was salvage. 'Well,' said old Mrs Mac, an interested spectator, 'What's he paid for?' 'The Lord knows,' I said irritably, 'but I doubt if the Corporation does.' 'What some of these chaps want,' she said, 'is Hitler standing over them for six months. It's the only thing that will ever alter them. Talk about self-respect and doing what they're paid to do.'

---

[*] Archimadus predicted, among other things, 'underground feelers from former Nazi enthusiasts and a first rate scandal in the Third Reich'.

I felt more depressed than ever and wondered again if whatever we *are* fighting for is worth all the misery. Perhaps after all Hitler is right – most people would maybe rather be ordered about and clouted than do a job willingly and with pride. Mr D. says this war will end when the money folk have made their pile. Getting tired of hearing this; it seems to be the only contribution most folk can make to war discussions. They probably don't quite mean that but there is a sort of resentment and the Tobruk business has disgusted everyone so much. Mrs D. says it is ridiculous the wages that are being paid to war workers. She knows a girl who went on munitions and the first week she handed her uncle her pay packet saying 'Here you are, Uncle, I haven't *earned* 10s but this is what I've *got*.' Her wages were £8 10s and she said herself it was abominable.

Thursday, 2 July

Mr D. thinks the Generals are not to blame for the Tobruk disaster, but lack of equipment. Margaret says we send Russia all the best stuff and they get the praise for doing the fighting and we keep the worst ourselves and when things go wrong everyone is blaming us. Mr G. thinks we shall go back to trench warfare. He says we are not in such a bad case as 1917–18. He was only trained three weeks before going abroad and had only half a day on a gun before being sent out with one. Mrs F. says why don't we send bombers to Africa instead of bombing Germany? Mr G. does not think we shall invade France but Norway or Northern Italy. Margaret says it makes you wonder if [Douglas] Ritchie [BBC's 'Colonel Britton'] is a fifth columnist when everybody is so mystified by the fall of Tobruk; something fishy somewhere. Have a feeling myself that 'vested interests' are to blame – that the right stuff is not being made because it pays 'someone' better to make inferior.

Saturday, 4 July

Margaret says Mr Churchill has not told us *now* what caused the loss of Tobruk. I had noticed the same thing.*

Sunday, 5 July

Strange that we can find more troops and reinforcements and better tanks *now* for Libya. Why not before? Margaret says we could do with a few less dogs and cats, never mind killing off the poultry. Hear, hear!

Wednesday, 8 July

Auntie and O. and Bella Hill were here. We discussed war wages and waste, when we are not discussing food. I remarked that people were getting excited about the powdered meat which is to be our next 'austerity', saying they would not eat that much. Margaret said she was sick of hearing after three years' war, 'I only like so and so. I cannot eat this. Mine won't touch that.' Auntie said it was disgusting what food people waste, especially bread. The children next to her eat nothing but crumb and throw their crusts to the birds. Another neighbour with grown up family cuts off all the crusts and gives them to the next door dog. We talked of wages and agreed that all present company and most of our relations were worse

---

* The Prime Minister's optimism of a couple of months earlier seemed to be contradicted by the unexpected and yet-to-be-explained defeat at Tobruk, and triggered a vote of no confidence in the Commons (which he won handily, 475 votes to 25).

off than before the war owing to increased cost of living and little or no increase in wages. Bella Hill told of a friend who admitted she and her husband, both working, had spent £300 solely on pleasure since the war started. Bella Hill told her she should be ashamed. She said she was, had not realised their spendings. A party of them went to fashionable pubs and, I suppose, 'drinks all round' was the rule. I wonder if it is any use struggling to save a constant 5s per week out of my 12s for-all-personal-expenses. I said we were promised such things should not be in this war and everything was just as bad. Auntie said, 'Worse'. The Government should have said from the start, '*Your* job's to fight, *your* job's to work. *We* shall plan. And no waste of either time, money or effort from anyone.' Instead of which it was sickening the 'hickling about' that went on. Mr L. thinks Rommel has been *enticed* into Egypt so that [General Sir Claude] Auchinleck [British Commander-in-Chief in the Middle East] can smash him. 'Tis well that *someone* can see good in our reverses.

E. H. says she hopes our prisoners are being treated well but she is afraid for them, especially those in Jap hands, and repeated a tale I had heard previously about a woman getting a letter from her son, a Japanese prisoner, in which he asked her to put the stamp in his collection. On removing it she read the words 'They have cut my tongue out'.

Sunday, 12 July

Bert went off to Blackpool yesterday. He says if the Government really meant us to stay at home they would stop the trains but, he says, there are too many of them [who are] shareholders in the Railways to do that. Sooner he had gone than myself. Have no wish to travel twenty in a railway carriage and queue for permission to come home again. My way of holidaying is to lie in a deck chair in our little garden and read *Moby Dick* [by Herman Melville, 1851] and forget the war. Sometimes I cannot so escape and so have to give myself up to pondering on things I usually have no time to think about. Tobruk – is it really true that vested interests went on making out-of-date tanks for our boys? Are we really, as the Russians tell us, half-hearted about this war? Are we too well fed? Wouldn't more short commons jerk us up a bit? If we should be victorious anything like soon, won't there be an enormous gulf between ourselves who have not yet suffered as a *whole nation* (only *some* here and there) and those whose sufferings are so ghastly? Can there be understanding between us? And sympathy – not pity? Is it because this district and we personally as a family have been so little touched by war that I feel people are complacent and selfish?

These problems have no answer in my mind – *there* is only confusion and doubt and a great foreboding of worse to come. I suppose similar thoughts are passing through thousands of minds every minute of every day.

PART TWO

1942–1945

6

Hardships, and Hopes, at Home

July–November 1942

Monday, 13 July

Bert came home this morning after we had received two post-cards by the first post, one to say he had arrived and the weather was lovely, the other still praising the weather but saying he was coming back. As we surmised, the landlady, as is customary at Blackpool, had put him to sleep in the dining room, being an odd one, and he disliked the idea of going to bed last and rising first so decided to return to comfort. Margaret and I both chortled, particularly myself, who had spent a long, luxurious Sunday sitting in the garden. Margaret said she hoped to goodness that would settle him and he'd be content to stay at home. I thought of the crowds and crowds of daft folk there at Blackpool and then of the Russians, fighting, fighting, giving way step by step, inch by inch, and I wished that all those who can think of enjoyment at this hour would be at least uncomfortable enough to have it impressed on them that there *is* a war on.

Tuesday, 14 July

Bert had a stiff tussle with Mrs C., in arrears with her weekly
bill and rationing elsewhere this next period. Bert refused her
her rations and down she went to the Food Office but got little
help there for they sent her back to try us again. So there was
Mrs C. alternating between the sulks and 'acting gawmless'
[gormless, i.e., slow-witted] and Bert outraged because she has
a husband working and a daughter getting a man's wage. Her
lame excuse for rationing elsewhere was that her daughter had
to join up. 'And,' she burst out aggressively, 'you never asked
me if I weren't rationing with you or where my books were or
anything.' 'Don't want to know,' said Bert grimly. 'I want my
brass and if it's not forthcoming I shall sue you.' In the end he
relented and allowed her rations for cash. But evidently he had
put some fear into her for she turned up during the week with
10s off [her] account.

Sunday, 19 July

Disheartened by the news and lack of faith in the Government, which has told us so many times that the tide would
turn in 1942 and now we are told we are in peril again and the
outlook is grim. We have a 'save the bones' campaign now. But
why wasn't it just as essential to save bones and shipping space
two years ago?* Auntie says there is the feeling that something
is wrong somewhere and that we are not extending to the full.
But there is nothing to come to grips with. One is just baffled
and unquiet.

* Salvage was actively promoted in wartime, and was often carried out by members
of the Women's Voluntary Services, sometimes aided by children. Bones could be
used to make explosives, soap, and fertiliser.

In the early hours the three young Murray girls caroused with soldiers outside my window, all slightly tipsy. This because the previous night I asked them to go away at 1 o'clock. However their father heard them and bade them be quiet and led the youngest away, still laughing and singing. This was not the end for their mother came up and was introduced to the soldiers. Then when the mother had gone there was more unseemly laughter and noise until Margaret went down and opened the shop door and told them to go, which they did quietly. But what kind of parents are they to condone such conduct in girls under 18? By day they are all respectable, pleasant, well behaved people.

Monday, 20 July

A long printed leaflet of 1200 words concerning rationing of sweets [to start at the end of this month] and what we have and have not to do. Bert says it will be worse than all the damned rationing together. Spent two hours with him tonight trying to trace tea mistake for Food Office.

Thursday, 23 July

G. E. says she is going to look for a job after the holidays; she wants about two afternoons a week, something easy – just to get in before she has to register. She has a husband out of the house 12 hours every day and a boy of 14 also out all day and she has never done a stitch or hand's stir of war work. But she is only one of many such that I know and aren't they getting the wind up.

Friday, 24 July

The salvage man jibbed at taking the large box of tins we had collected and said they should go in the dustbin. I said so long as we knew what we *were* expected to do. Previously and in the newspaper we were told putting salvage in the dustbin was a punishable offence. Mr C., a Corporation labourer, says he saves nothing – he has seen how many tins are picked out by the men specially employed at the tip for this job and how many are buried to save themselves the trouble. I sometimes think this salvage chase is as futile as the Mad Hatter's tea party.

Saturday, 25 July

Another tussle with Mrs C. who, having drawn her rations for the last time on Monday, came today to pay 2s 6d off her bill and demand rations for next week. She said her new shop was shut for two days, Monday and Tuesday, and she would be without rations. In vain we tried to convince her she had had all she could have from us. She went out vowing vengeance.

Bert had another spell at the Food Office. He and other waiting tradesmen discussed the desirability of having a special room for their interviews instead of being mixed up with Mothers and Milk Farms, and Removers, and Lost Ration Bookers, and so forth. Bella Hill, O. S., and Auntie came to supper. We didn't discuss the war much. Only that interviewers at Labour Exchanges should be older. Bilberry pie and cow pie [i.e. custard; see 31 July 1942] for supper!

Sunday, 26 July

Finished *Short Stories* by [Alexander] Pushkin [1799–1837]. Very disappointed to find them so ordinary. Annoyed to be blundering on wrong track in my reading. Life is short enough without these wastes of time. Lyndoe more mysterious and sillier than ever today. Nothing daunts him. The best is always just within our grasp ['Believe in Britain's destiny!' he had declared this day in the *People*, p. 6].

Monday, 27 July

Holiday for the [annual] Feast*. Took one look at the weather when Margaret brought my tea and decided bed was the best place. Started to cheer myself with [Anton] Chekhov but at 8.30 the sirens blew and up we all scrambled, astounded as never [before]. Pottered about all day, slept all afternoon, walked to Mirfield with Bella and Henry Hill across the fields. Stood on a wall and waved my open brolly so Ma could see us from the house [easily visible, a mile or so to the east].

Later at two in the morning. The siren has just gone again. I sit writing with my gas mask on for a bit of practice. My nose itches 'somethink awful' but I am strong minded – not childish – as per ARP Lecturer's instructions and refrain from snatching the thing off. Do not talk as the strange hollow sound of my own voice distresses me, and do not walk about much as my 'snout' becomes entangled in things if I bend my head – have already had it trapped in the cupboard door. Bert says he will put his on when necessary and not before. Have

* There were numerous 'Holidays-at-Home' events arranged for Dewsbury and many other places to deter people from travelling.

written a birthday letter and had a look outside. The streets
are brilliant in the moonlight and Jerry will need no flares. A
contrast to the weather when the alarm went previously. Not
a soul in sight or sound of any kind. Bert keeps ejaculating
'Well, fancy them coming here again after all this time. I never
thought we should have them so far inland again.' (Fifteen
months since last warning.) Ma is wandering about looking
for her purse. She says she does not want to be 'parted from
it' tonight as she has a bill to pay in the morning.

3 o'clock. All clear. Shall not undress, only remove dress and
shoes for fear 'he' comes back. Glad to cast my 'snout'. Truly
feel a different person without it.

Thursday, 30 July

Siren again at 2 o'clock this morning. We were up an hour and
a half. Was not asleep when the blame thing went but I was
tired and got up with an effort – it took me ages to dress in
the moonlight – and on going downstairs laid my head on the
table and closed my eyes and was thankful for July and not
December for I was shivering as it was. Bert and Margaret
paraded outside. Bert never heard them when we used to have
sirens before – slept all through and said we were silly to get
up. *Now* he is up first. Must be taking the war more seriously.
He even looks at the newspaper in a morning, a thing he never
used to do, saying the press was all rubbish.

Felt far from a good day's work after our bad night but, as
it proved, it was the heaviest of the week. There were new
registered customers to get used to, and several of them, with
large families to buy for, came at once. Then we had the kiddies with their sweet cards. All our little customers have spent
their month's coupons already (a penny a time!) and the state

of their [ration] cards – oh, dear me! I try to impress upon them that they have to last a year but the only result is to make them screw them up tighter (for safety!). Incidentally, the D. coupons [for personal points] are very badly printed – with all those lines on them there is no clear line to cut on. A trifling thing but how irritating when in a hurry. Apart from cutting out a few children's tea coupons by mistake, we did not do so badly in such a rush.

The points were and remain a mystery to a good many customers but the sweet cards are much more confusing – to the grown-ups, I mean; the kiddies soon know what they can get with them although one or two thought they could be used instead of money! Most grown-ups take a month's ration of sweets and chocolate at once – if they have plenty of cards in the family – getting them with their other rations. If only two in family they seem to take a quarter pound sweets at a time. The kiddies mostly bring their own cards and ask for chocolate in preference to sweets.

Friday, 31 July

Another rush day. Bert has impressed upon all old customers they must take all their rations at once and not come in for 'bits and bobs' as he calls it. Mrs C. came in with 2s off account. 'You promised to straighten this off before you left us,' expostulated Bert. 'I haven't left,' says Mrs C. indignantly. 'I come in every day.' And so the old girl does – sometimes eight or nine times. I have a wager with Bert she will be wanting to 'tick' [buy on credit] again before the old account is wiped off. He says he will not let her but he is so soft that way. When we came here 18 months ago there were only five weekly customers – now we have about twenty ranging from

The corner shop was a hive of activity, especially when fresh goods came in. This particular store is in Sussex, but the scene in Bert's shop on the sort of busy day Kathleen describes would have been much like this one.
Photograph © IWM D13245

our real 'good' ones who spend from £2 to £3 every week and pay prompt to the minute to those irritating ones who live on the doorstep and run in with coppers in their hands and are always a few short. Notes are taken of these trifles (which mount to a considerable sum in the course of the week) and a gentle reminder given if the money is not forthcoming by the weekend. But this is seldom necessary – most of our customers are scrupulously honest. They are many of them dirty and poorly dressed – but probably better off than they look. A large proportion of them are Irish and Scottish and there are a few Italians.

Margaret started baking at 9 p.m. and dropped the rhubarb pie and smashed dish and pie into a rare mess. She went next door to fetch more rhubarb so she could make another first thing in the morning without Bert's knowing of the catastrophe. Ma said what could she expect, baking at midnight. I said it was a good thing she wasn't scalded and a jolly good thing it wasn't the 'cow pie' (custard).

Wednesday, 5 August

Things are quieter this week than last, the kiddies having spent their sweet coupons and their mothers have used up their 'points'. We cannot get enough bread. We are selling no flour or yeast; even those who formerly thought it disgraceful to buy bread are beaten with the national flour. Henry Hill was telling us of meeting a family in the bus all bandaged up who had gone for a holiday to York and had not been there many hours when an aeroplane dived out of nowhere and dropped bombs, injuring them all slightly, so that they were speeding for home first bus.

Saturday, 8 August

Usual supper crowd. All doleful because of putting the clock back and dreading the coming of winter and the dark [double summer time was ending]. We discussed whether E. H. was right to keep from her aged mother the fact that her other daughter had again been bombed out, at Birmingham. The old lady found out anyhow and there was a row. We all agreed that it was better to know bad news right out than be in a state of suspense. Then we went on to whether there was any virtue in anyone sacrificing their whole life and prospects for another, especially unmarried daughters. Margaret and Auntie said flat out that there was nothing to be proud of, and no one should give up everything, however strong the family ties. I wondered why it is glorious for a young man to give up his life and future for his King and Country, but only irritating when a woman gives up her youth and strength in the service of someone or several people [unmarried daughters were often expected to care for aged and infirm relatives and not have lives of their own].

Sunday, 9 August

Gone to bed and enjoying G[ranville] Barker's *Hamlet* [1937] when there was gunfire and distant sirens. Ma and I dressed, she somewhat laboriously. I always feel most sickened for the old folk when raids are on. They cannot hurry and adapt themselves, and in any case, there is a sense of injustice (however daft it may seem as if wars were ever just) that they who have lived 70 or 80 years should have to face this horrible business at the end. My heart aches for the old ones in Russia and the occupied countries.

Monday, 10 August

The firewood dealer says [Soviet Marshal Semyon] Timo-shenko is leading the Germans into a trap. There is about to be a bust-up and then Jerry will crack up. Christmas will about see the end of the fighting. Mrs Hobbs says a girl who works in Woolworths told her they were selling no sweets under the rationing. The first day the manager put four of them on the sweet stall, no doubt expecting a rush, but at the end of an hour moved them off again. Jolly well serves them right.

Wednesday, 12 August

Mr P. says he offered to take any sort of a bet at the Club that the war will last seven years. Auntie says someone told her of having her fortune told at Blackpool and they said the war would be over in February. Germany would collapse and Hitler commit suicide. Some hopes! Sirens again last night for an hour. Eight times in a fortnight. We all got up. I knitted gloves. No eggs again this week. A match famine. People are having to keep their gas jets burning all day to get a light, with being without fires.

Margaret and I had a row with Bert because he sneered at us for saying we were going to practise stirrup pump. He says he'll know what to do if there is any need. He'll use his common sense. As he displays so little in ordinary times I can't see him suddenly having any in an emergency. Everyone seems to think we are in for a tough winter.

Monday, 17 August

A fire fighting practice at our WVS [Women's Voluntary Services] at the Chapel. Mostly middle aged stout ladies who, like myself, had never handled a stirrup pump before. They pumped and sprayed energetically if not to much purpose.

Mrs Hobbs, our landlady, washed the Chapel windows with her pump. Bella Hill said it was a perfect farce. On the way home Margaret lectured Mr Hobbs yet again on the need for a stirrup pump of his own, with all his property.

Tuesday, 18 August

Margaret's seed has at last fallen on fruitful ground. Mr Hobbs bought a stirrup pump today. Everyone I talk to seems to think that women are going to be treated unfairly over fire watching and those who work will have too much put on them while those who scrape out of it (principally married women [claiming exemption]), who could rest in the day-time, get off. And then there is the unfairness of the compensation for injury. Several people have remarked to me today that it would be a long war – one quoting her husband as saying ten years. Several seem to think there is something 'brewing'.

Wednesday, 19 August

Cheered by news of the raid [at Dieppe]. Feel relief that we are at last doing something but at the same time horrified at the loss of life there will be.* Read out to Margaret that America thinks (or the press says) that one of their Generals should lead our European forces. Margaret said, well, of course, it's *their* war now. *We* might as well give up. And who was General Marshall – she'd never heard his name mentioned [he was US Army chief of staff and virtually a

---

* Allied Forces, mainly Canadians, suffered severe casualties during this raid, which many historians have come to see as pointless.

household name in America]. And why they were allowed
to blow their trumpet on the wireless every day she didn't
know. It was sickening. Bert said you couldn't tell him anything about the Americans. He'd lived there four years. They
were all braggers.

Friday, 21 August

Disheartening news from Russia [German troops were con-
tinuing to advance]. Margaret and Ma still maintain they
know what they are doing and all will be well. To me it
looks as if they are collapsing. Puzzled to know what kind
of people the Russians really are. If they are all Communists
they must be queer and if even some of them are as Chekhov
described them they must be queerer – governesses who
ventriloquise and men who burst into tears on the slightest
provocation.

Sunday, 23 August

Margaret and Ma saying, I told you so, now things will happen
when Churchill starts things moving. They take it for granted
the Russian visit means an offensive, but I wonder if we are in
such a sticky place that Churchill had to go [he had just travelled to Moscow for talks with Stalin]. Anyway if something
doesn't happen pretty quick it will be too late.

Wednesday, 26 August

A depressing three days what with the war and the weather
which has been constantly rainy or dark and lowering, ending
each evening with a thick drizzle mist – just like mid-winter

nights. And, then the crowning trouble of the Duke of Kent's death which has so shocked us all. Everyone who came in the shop this morning mentioned it as if it were of intense interest – something unusual with our phlegmatics. (Not one has mentioned Mr Churchill's tour!) One woman said 'It comes to them too, you see. None escapes.' And another, 'These blasted aeroplanes have brought nothing but trouble since they were invented'! [The younger brother of the King was killed in a plane crash.]

Bert comes back from Blackpool tomorrow. Expect something will have gone wrong while he is away. The kiddies have mostly spent their sweet coupons for the month and their ration cards are on their last legs. Why didn't the Government make them stouter? They should have realised that kiddies would be constantly handling them. And how badly they are printed. Most of our kiddies cannot wait to save for two ounces. They come in for a penny worth and cheerfully sacrifice the other half coupon value.

I asked 'Jacobs' what we should have to do with the broken biscuits which we have always sold to the kids before. He said, 'Well, there are so many rules and laws being broken every day, I should just carry on as usual'. So that's that.

Saturday, 29 August

We discussed the unfairness of the supplementary Old Age pensions. Auntie said she was paying her 10s per week back in tax to help keep others. She would be better off to leave work and apply for Supplementary but she didn't want her body and mind to become rusty. I said it was the same old story – the Government helped those who didn't trouble to help themselves but had no use for those with any backbone who strove to be independent. Listened to the moving description in the 9 o'clock news of the Duke of Kent's funeral. We were in tears.

Monday, 31 August

Went to an interesting lecture at the WVS by a National Fire Service man. Could not quite agree with him that *all* fires are caused by carelessness. We discussed probability of raids in this district. Bert said it would be a 'chance shot' if we had anything and Margaret and I said we had as important things here as many other towns which had 'copped it'. But Bert kept his pigheaded way and repeated 'There'll be nowt here'. We discussed the Duke of Kent business and Margaret at last voiced my own secret opinion that there was something fishy about the whole affair. I remarked that the broadcast news of his death seemed cold and callous and there seemed to be an air of constraint and secrecy more than was necessary, even in wartime. We agreed we should never know the truth of it.

Friday, 4 September

We seem to have no time now after work before blackout. Oh, the long dreary evenings cooped up altogether with the wireless going interminably! This winter will be worse than ever with the fuel rationing, for I suppose that is what we shall come to. We shall have no reading in bed and fires in the bedroom [on] cold nights. Think the Government has blundered badly over the fuel question – they should have tackled the mining question straight away at the beginning of the war. This propaganda only irritates me, newspaper notes, fuel flashes, etc., as I think it must do most people who have habitually to consider their pennies and can be trusted not to waste fuel for their own sakes – it is too hardly paid for.*

Thursday, 10 September

Margaret and I chortling because Bert has had notice he has to attend a fire and bomb lecture and demonstration or give good reason for absence. G.'s Biscuit traveller says he is fed up already with the biscuits points. He says everyone is wanting chocolate and sweet biscuits. He also said the Army had returned them (after the points started) two thousand, five hundred tins of 'Iron Rations' biscuits, with no notification of any sort, and there they were in stock with no prospect of getting rid of them. That was the Government for you. He advised us to do as other traders were doing with the cheaper qualities of sweets, which no one will have on points, and sell them free, because we could always plead, if reported, that they were deteriorating.

Saturday, 12 September

Usual crowd for Saturday night supper. O. M., who is an ardent Christian Scientist, spent a long time persuading Bella Hill to get her husband to read the 91st Psalm and meditate on it before going to bed. Bella Hill agreed at last and said she would have to hunt for a Bible, she hadn't seen one for ages. (Chapelgoers these!) I proffered my Laurence Binyon [poet

---

* While the rationing of household coal was contemplated, the idea was abandoned in 1942. Consumers were instead actively encouraged to be economical, mainly by means of publicity campaigns ('propaganda' to Kathleen), and sometimes supplies were restricted.

and art historian]. Henry Hill suffers dreadfully from asthma and this week has been particularly bad, and could not sleep. He came in later and agreed to try O. M.'s remedy. 'Owt, so long as I get relief'.

Monday, 14 September

Bella Hill says Henry Hill slept all through the night and felt pounds better. O. M. will be pleased. Christian Science has certainly benefited her.

Wednesday, 23 September

The views of the re-established [after its summer recess] *Brains Trust* that large stores are bound to supersede the small shops on account of better service and greater efficiency shows just how out of touch these sort of people are with the lives of poorer people. Their total ignorance of any life but professional and city life would be amusing if it were not so blooming irritating.

Saturday, 26 September

All the day long, whatever I do, my thoughts are of Stalingrad [and Soviet advances against German Forces]. Wonderful Russians! Shall we too stand the test, if we are put to it? Sometimes I quake and quake at the sheer horror of such fighting in our cities. Perhaps our greatest letdown is that we don't *like* fighting, even when we are mad, while the Germans love it anyhow, mad or sober. Meanwhile the Russians are getting madder and madder probably *with us* because we don't start something. What a prospect for after the war.

Tuesday, 29 September

Once down to the Food Office yesterday and twice today before I could get the Points Vouchers which are supposed to be handed over on demand. Their excuse was that they were busy. Apparently shopkeepers are never busy or only run their businesses as a sideline to their main preoccupation of keeping up with Food Office instructions. It grows worse every week – the forms to fill in and pamphlets to read. And every little mistake is the cause of a card which demands our presence at the Office immediately. How one-man businesses carry on is a mystery unless they have a permanent messenger to run back and forth to the Food Office. It would really be better and a great savings of stamps all round if instead of sending round these inspectors to 'snoop' they would send them to help the shopkeeper to fill his forms in, or over any difficulty he may have over the many rationing regulations, and point out any errors he may be making or small points of the law which he might be unwittingly breaking. This may sound ridiculous but I believe in the long run such a system would solve many problems for the shopkeeper and save time at the Food Office. What the powers-that-be don't realise is that a grocer cannot spend *all* his time getting the answers right – he must serve his customers in and between whiles.

Wednesday, 30 September

Noticed a great decrease in grumbling during the last month. It must be Stalingrad that is holding everyone's attention. Read out to Margaret that Lord Somebody was protesting that we were not cultivating parkland as we ought, and she immediately said, 'Well, how about making a start at Bretton

[Hall, near Wakefield] with Lord Allendale's little lot. Why wasn't his Park ploughed up? They filled all the public parks with vegetables. Hadn't he as much right to gaze on cabbages as we had?' I said 'Maybe it isn't arable. *Maybe!*'

Thursday, 1 October

Turning a street corner in Dewsbury we ran into a group of soldiers wearing gas-masks and [we] both gasped involuntarily. 'Good Lord,' said Margaret peevishly. 'We may as well be blown to pieces as "flaid [frightened] to t'death".' 'We ought to be used to it by now,' I said, 'what with practising at home and seeing these every time we come out.' We ought to be – but we never are. Just as we should be used to the blackout. Every time I put on my mask I think, 'It serves you right. This is a penance for not having lifted a finger to help prevent the war.' And every time I struggle with the blackout curtains I think, 'This is ridiculous – for grown-up, civilised people'. When there are bad raids and many killed, especially children – like the one last week at the school in the south [likely Petworth, Sussex] – my conscience troubles me that I am part of the world that allowed such things to come to pass. Perhaps other people are the same or perhaps I am just possessed of an Ultra Super Conscience – as the Americans would say.

Friday, 2 October

We are now wondering what to do with the poor quality chocolates and biscuits which the wholesalers have palmed off onto us during the last few weeks. Everyone wants the best on points – for which you cannot blame them. The Food Office certainly gave us permission to sell them free of points but at a reduced price which means at a loss in the long run. Bert is selling them on the Q.T. [quiet] to regular customers. But I am wondering how we shall go on – whether we shall have to take a quantity of inferior goods or get none at all. Apparently wholesalers can still make conditional sales though retailers are fined for it. The solution of the chocolate and biscuit problem is of course to make a few standard varieties so that all manufacturers are making the same. The wholesalers have the whip hand anyhow. Last week one tied up a thousand of Bert's points by promising this and that. When the goods were delivered there was only 80 points worth of goods in the delivery, thus immobilising 900 points for at least another fortnight. You cannot get anything without handing the points over *first*. Another wholesaler sent tinned steak and tinned salmon which at 24 and 32 points a tin still stays on our shelves. What with the wholesalers and the Food Office we are between the devil and the deep sea. Lucky we are that our *customers* are reasonable ones.

Saturday, 3 October

In the shop Mrs L. asserted loudly and defiantly that she wasn't going fire watching; they could do as they liked – send her to prison. It wasn't fit for women to go and stop at a mill all night. She said she would say her husband was deaf and not fit to be left. She will get off it all right. The Government is very kind to married women. We had the usual crowd for Saturday supper. We discussed the war. Bella Hill said she had heard several say they had sooner their lads went to the desert than stayed here to try to invade the continent for it would be slaughter – nothing else. I have heard several who have fighting men express the same view. We agreed that those who clamour for a Second Front don't know what they are inviting. We said that we owed Russia an unpayable debt and that it must be awful on the Eastern Front – especially at Stalingrad.

At supper we had buns. They were very leathery. Margaret blamed the dried eggs. Bert said they were like flannel and would make a good chest protector strung together. I said we could hang one on a string round our necks for a talisman against rheumatism as some carry a nutmeg. This led us on to superstition and thence to birthmarks. Auntie said the medical people said birthmarks could not be caused by anything that happened to the mother but when one knew of cases one could only say they didn't know what they were talking about. We then had instances from one or another, including a girl who had an orange on her neck which was white in blossom time and changed according to the season from palest green to orange colour, and another who had a fish on her arm, scales and all.

Thursday, 8 October

Bert plunged into gloom. He has got his income tax demand. He has got the idea that 'workers' are allowed more 'wage' before being taxed than business people. He keeps going into tempers and vows first that he will take good care he hasn't so much to pay next year, and then that he will sell the shop and have done with it. Margaret 'comforts' him by pointing out that he won't have so much pay next year anyway because we are gradually being deprived of turnover as one thing after another is rationed or goes on points. Another thing to upset Bert is the discovery that he should have been having discounts on butter, bacon, and cheese.

The wholesaler stopped these at the beginning of the war but now we find that a Government order has been in force all the time commanding that discounts on these commodities be paid.

Tuesday, 13 October

Agree with Australian Government that we should not have chained the German prisoners [thereby imitating Germany's treatment of British prisoners]. It puts us on a par with Hitler. And does no good for what do the Nazis care how we treat anyone, even their own countrymen? As for these Geneva Conventions and what not – what a farce! As if you can lay down rules for war as if it were a game of football. If it's war – it's war – and though one side may fight cleaner than another because they are made or trained that way, to talk of what they may or not do is daft. The Geneva Conventions will be stopping the war next and making us all start again.

Thursday, 15 October

This sweet rationing will send us all four completely nuts. One wholesaler is demanding transfer forms *at once*, another writes that on no account must we send them but wait and hand them over on delivery of sweets. It is obvious they know less than we do about this business.

Saturday, 24 October

Auntie came in tonight and we got off on the old subject of the Government and waste. Bert instanced our local Food Office sending out sometimes four stamped envelopes in one day, containing one small piece of paper with instructions. And at the month end we always receive points vouchers in a registered envelope. The postman says he delivers thousands each month. The postage bill for even a small place like Dewsbury must be enormous. Of course it is only taking from one Government department to put into another, but what a waste of time! I still think it would be cheaper and clear up a lot of muddles if the Food Office employed a man to deliver vouchers in exchange for points coupons *on the spot* and take note of any complaint or point out any error in filling [out] forms or in prices charged.

Auntie remarked that whenever she spoke with anyone who was not well they blamed lack of food or kind of food we were getting. She said she couldn't see their viewpoint as a good many of them were better fed now than they ever had been. At least they had to eat things that would nourish them now whereas before they ate 'trimmings' in place of solid meals. This led me onto the subject of biscuits. I said one family with about eight youngsters must have had nearly a stone of biscuits last week from our shop alone. I said I had seen the eldest girl buy a pound and distribute them to her young brothers and sisters outside the shop to go to school with. I noticed that our best biscuit buyers were the children of three families swarming with dirty, pale children, most of whom seemed to have chronic catarrh and in strange contrast to the little undersized kiddies the three mothers were huge strapping women who seldom went shopping themselves. They (the kiddies) always ask for chocolate biscuits first, then if not forthcoming, 'sweet' biscuits, then they will take arrowroot or tea biscuits after some hesitation but seldom will they have plain crackers.

Monday, 26 October

Went tonight with Bella Hill to a great meeting of the WVS in the Town Hall, admission by ticket only. Looked forward to this very much, thinking we should learn something of the work that is being done in the blitzed areas. The meeting started at 7 p.m. and at 8.40 we were on our way home somewhat disgusted. The lady (she was a real Lady someone or other [in fact, Lady Iris Capell, daughter of the Earl of Essex]), the Vice Chairman for England and Wales, after insipid speeches from the Mayoress and others, throwing bouquets at one another and occasionally a blossom to we [*sic*] 'groundlings', got up and spoke. She spoke from notes. She said how glad she was to see so many there to listen to her, and said that the WVS was doing such magnificent work and tackling such huge jobs, and nothing was too big for them, and we should be proud of all we were doing to help win the war, and how working for others brought a wider outlook (vista she called it), and many of us were realising for the first time that we had duties to others, and we were responding nobly. And that was all! There was a little more bouquet juggling and out we came, all a little bit flabbergasted I think. But on consideration I felt angry. To drag women, mostly middle aged, who have been working all day (and Monday is wash day with many of them), out in the blackout (large white invitation cards) to listen to such piffle is no joke. Members of the WVS expecting to hear of the grand work that *is* being done, in some detail, and non-members were equally bewildered. But I suppose we must be thankful we were not charged admittance to gaze on the elite of Dewsbury.

Tuesday, 27 October

I asked Mrs R. how she had enjoyed the meeting and she said not a bit. She says her husband said it served her right for going to hear a 'lady'. She might have known it would be a frost.

Bert is finding it difficult to get anything on 'points' except tinned beans and cut-up meat. Customers are clamouring for sweet tinned milk and syrup and dates and currants and raisins. Several are already planning to make 'spice' cake [for Christmas], though goodness knows where they will get ingredients. I asked one customer flat how she expected to be able to make cake and she said laughing, 'Oh, I shall go into the top cupboard'.

Wednesday, 28 October

Bella Hill and I went to the Wardens' Post for our Fire Guard lecture. We thought we were covered from fire watching by the WVS. Now we are told differently so are joining the SFP [Supplementary Fire Parties]. After, Bella Hill came in and we discussed the Jews. She said her auntie had written to the local paper defending Jews and had a letter from the Art Master at the Technical College – a Jew – and also one from a Jewish priest in Manchester. She said they had always got on well with Jews in business. Bert said the same – he had done well with them.

To the pictures this afternoon. Every time I go I say I will not go again. It always happens to be an American piffle. Today there were two – a John Barrymore [*World Premiere*] and another [*Flying Blind*]. Bored to tears and with cold feet I regretted my shilling (used to be ninepence). How boring these shouting Americans are – and how childish their

Flour, treacle and condensed milk are three of the items in this Ministry of Food photograph of suggested goods that people should keep in their 'emergency larder'. Also included were baked beans, coffee, cocoa, porridge oats, various pickled vegetables, lentils and rice.
Photograph © IWM DV110

humour. Their voices have no variety. Whenever they say certain words (and they always say them – 'But you Kant *do that*' twice this afternoon) they use the same intonation. I am afraid no amount of Anglo-American propaganda will ever make me irritant-proof against the *unlovely sounds* that Americans utter.

Sunday, 1 November

Fire watching. Went to Wardens' Post with B. and Bella Hill for our Fire Practice. They seemed at sixes and sevens there. Two who didn't seem to know much about it took us into a farm yard with several men who could only go on Sunday morning, and lighted a bomb behind a tin screen and we took turns at squirting and pumping. Then we were to be shown how to dodge smoke but the smoke bomb wouldn't act right but poured out a straight still column into the sky, and then rain fell and the Wardens said we would miss the First Aid bit and go back for our Yellow Cards. These Yellow Cards seem very important but to me as mysterious as the Labour Exchange Green Cards. B., who had complained of the cold all the time, dashed off to get her husband's dinner and I stayed for the Cards. But there was another class in progress and they hadn't had the time to fill them so we came away without. B. says they won't be any good anyway for keeping us from Civil Defence or other work, but as I am working full time I hope it will do for me. I dread being placed in a fire watching pool. The stories I have heard from fire watchers (women)! One gets cold every time she watches every week; there are four of them in a tiny room, unventilated and warmed by an electric radiator. Another watches with other girls at an Insurance Office in the town and they had to ring up one night and ask police protection against soldiers who were banging on the door to be let in and shouting disgusting stuff through the keyhole. The whole fire watching business is unsatisfactory.

Monday, 2 November

WVS. Went to our local WVS meeting where our new President asked for proposals for keeping the Party together. The old president being ill and having to resign, we are all pleased to have a new beginning. We have done nothing; no one even knew what equipment we had or where it was kept, and meetings have been irregular. It was proposed to have a monthly meeting and a monthly knitting circle. At the first meeting we are to overhaul all equipment and learn our jobs for an emergency. We discussed the Town Hall meeting and everyone said it was rotten. Those who go netting (working camouflage nets) were bitter about the 'platform people' parading in their uniforms but who never go near the 'nets'. It is hard, dirty, disagreeable work. The President said Dewsbury was a disgrace because of the large number of WVS there were and the small number of nets turned out. Then we got on the Civil Defence question, which is a sore point with the WVS whose ranks are being depleted by all this pell-mell conscription. There was some ribald talk when someone suggested that the best solution would be for all we younger ones to have babies. I pleaded it wasn't necessary in my case as I was already working full time. Everyone laughed as I was the only 'spinner' there. Then we got to the subject of illegitimate war babies. One said she'd heard there were hospitals full of them and the Government was going to bring them up. I wonder what sort of a race we shall have in future when everyone is sorted out back to their own country. A somewhat mixed one I should think. All these Poles and Americans and Dutch and Norwegians are bound to leave some traces. But this is the horrible part of war, worse than the slaughter – the loosening of restraint and decency, the stealing and the graft.

Tuesday, 3 November

Margaret says, why have they hung [merchant seaman] Scott-Ford [for selling secret information to an enemy agent in Lisbon] and only given the chap who left loose screws on the aeroplanes three years?

Thursday, 5 November

A beastly dark foggy day but everyone in a good humour over the African news [of the Allied victory at El Alamein]. Everyone coming into the shop this morning mentioned it voluntarily, a sure sign that they were pleased. No one seems to be *elated* – probably feeling as I did that there would be a catch later, in spite of the confident note in the announcements. But still everyone soberly pleased.

Friday, 6 November

Enemy still being pursued, but shall not allow myself to become excited. Cannot believe that the Germans will not yet make a stand and be too clever for us. Chief comment seems to be 'It's time we *did* do summat – by gow!' Our baker's lad pretended he thought *we* were running away and then apologised profusely. 'Of course, *we're* winning, aren't we?' in a mock surprised tone.

Saturday, 7 November

A few are saying 'Serve the b——s right' but a surprising number, men and women, are concerned about the awful carnage and waste of life [in Egypt]. Even Bert, who has always said 'Why don't they get stuck into them and let's get it over', remarked how dreadful it is. I think perhaps they feel as I do – a little shamed that we have to fight like this – sort of hitting a man with a stick who has only his hands to defend himself – but I take the view that the only way to treat the Germans is to give them their own medicine, only stronger. But I have been struck with the few people who have seemed *glad* that the Germans are suffering. Many remarked on the awful loss of life all over the world on both sides.

Sunday, 8 November

Listened to [Chekhov's] *The Seagull.* My nose bled. Margaret said, 'No wonder, listening to such stuff'.

In her response to MO's Directive this month, Kathleen made explicit some of her feelings about the ways in which she was living. 'The war, which has widened so many people's lives, seems to have confined mine within narrower limits even than formerly. The blackout and travel restrictions and getting tired serving in the shop all combine to keep me at home more than ever, so that I am with the same people day and night. Living and working with the same people is a strain normally. Under war conditions it becomes well nigh intolerable. This is why I am hoping and planning for a place of my own after the war, if only a bed sitting room.'

A little over a year later she enlarged on her hopes for the future. 'I feel I want a "broader" life after the war – to mix with different people and hear interesting ideas; in other words I want to expand. Have entirely lost "religion" but recognise the need for spiritual values.' (DR, January 1944.) She revisited this question in September 1944. 'My chief aim in life is to have a more interesting time after the war – by which I mean mix among a different lot of people who are interested in music and art and ideas generally. My life up to now has been spent mostly with "turnips". To do this I shall have to devise ways of earning more money, that great barrier to variety in life. I would like a small business I could run myself, perhaps sweets and tobacco. Failing this, at first I must have (fight for) a room of my own where I can expand mentally and not have to sit night after night with the family wireless' (DR, July–August 1944).

7

Looking Up?

November 1942–August 1943

To commemorate the Allied victories in North Africa, churches were permitted – indeed, encouraged – to ring their bells on the third Sunday of November. This was the first time bell-ringing had been permitted since early in the war. Previously it had been reserved as a signal of enemy invasion.

Friday, 13 November

Margaret says what is the good of ringing bells in the middle of a fight. Let's get it over before we start rejoicing. Look what happened when we were told to put flags out before – there was that Tobruk business – it was tempting Providence. But I think it will be very nice to hear the bells and I don't fear we shall think the war is over.

Saturday, 14 November

I am sure people are smiling more this week. There is a 'feeling in the air' though not much is said. 'We're to have t'bells, aren't we?' or 'He says t'bells are to ring', in a sort of half indulgent tone, as much as to say, 'They must have their little joke'.

Sunday, 15 November

Listened in vain for Mirfield peal. The bellringers must be at the war. We just had our own church's one bell and the wireless peals.* There were many people going up to church. What a long time since we first heard the good news. These last ten days seem – looking back – like a hundred. And even now one can scarcely believe that we really may let go and celebrate a victory – we have had so many false starts before.

Monday, 23 November

At our WVS meeting tonight we discussed how we should use the money we had in hand. Our President said she had been asked to subscribe something to the Christmas Treat for evacuees and proposed 10s. There were several dissentient voices, one saying that the evacuees were getting far too much now, that they had oranges anytime while we hardly saw one, and that if they broke crockery they had nothing to do but get more from the Town Hall while we couldn't buy it in the shops. Another said why couldn't we do something for the soldiers billeted in the town; Dewsbury did not seem to bother

---

* The bell-ringing this day was widely seen as remarkable and worthy of comment. The *Heckmondwike Herald*, 20 November 1942, p. 2, reported that 'An elderly farm worker, hearing the church bells on Sunday and feeling that some tribute should be paid, took off his hat, though he walked alone across the fields, writes a *Times* correspondent. Children playing outside a cottage ran indoors, shouting "The bells! The bells!"' Such stories, whether accurate or not, testified to the new mood of reassurance and relief.

about *their* entertainment. In the end the [money] was voted for the evacuees but grudgingly.

Sunday, 29 November

The American news commentator reviewing the month's events said today was the 30th November, so New York must be *24* hours in advance of us.* Perplexed about the French Navy. It was a brave thing no doubt but why *glorious*? They should never have stayed in French ports. Have no respect for the French no matter how America whitewashes their Quislings [i.e., Nazi collaborators].†

Thursday, 3 December

Soldiers' Wages. E. came to dinner. We discussed payment of wages for men in the Army, especially teachers. E. says the young girl with whom she works alternate weeks at the Co-op grumbles because she is made [to] work at all. She has about £5 a week coming in and sees no necessity to work. Her husband is a teacher and she draws his pay. E. says when Reg joins up she will have 27s apart from what she earns and will have to pay rent and rates and indirectly be helping pay for this lass to live in luxury. Margaret says all men in the forces should be treated alike and either all wages paid or none. Who

* Of course, New York is five hours behind GMT. Presumably this was a broadcasting error.

† On 27 November the Germans took over the major naval base at Toulon, and the Commander of the French fleet ordered the ships to be scuttled – and some seventy-five were. In early July 1940 Britain had offered the defeated French the opportunity to sail their navy to other ports, so that it would not fall into German hands, but the offer was declined, and thus Kathleen's opinion that these now scuttled ships should never have remained under (technical) French control.

the dickens in civil life could have 18s clear, when expenses were paid, for clothes and food?

Beveridge Report [laying the foundations for a welfare state, had just been published]. We had a rowdy dinner table. I happened to ask E. what she thought of the Report. That started Bert off at full tilt and we went at it hammer and tongs, I somewhat handicapped by a plate of scraped carrot. Bert said it was scandalous; where was the money coming from? Didn't he pay out enough? We [addressing his female listeners] didn't know – we hadn't taxes to pay. He wished he was a munition worker drawing his £7 a week and little to pay out. It was such as him that dropped in for it, and so on, and so on. E., when she could get in a word, thought it [the Beveridge Report] a delightful *fancy* but one that could never be realised. Margaret thought it sensible and said there was rows when the Old Age Pensions were started – the country was to be ruined – but we were still going strong and who would want to abolish OAP now. Bert said he was saying nowt about the OAP. It was this other. Where was the brass coming from? Out of such as him! By tea time he had calmed down to just grumbling. Margaret said the point about young widows was good. Why should they have a pension for life? I said I could [see] the scheme being dangerous for men – £10 if you marry a man, poison him off and you get another £15 for funeral expenses. It would put ideas into some women's heads. Margaret also said she agreed with not drawing the pension if working. Look at Mr and Mrs C. They must have had above £1,000 out of the Government and Mr C. kept on working until he was 70. And he had only paid into Insurance a short time before the scheme came out. And it looked as if they would both live to be 100. We [were] supposed to listen to Beveridge but were drawn into argument most of the time he was talking. Bert was reconciled and said it would be a good scheme when it got going.

Thursday, 10 December

Superstition. Mrs W. says her mother always wore *red* flannel underwear and a skein of grass green silk around her neck to ward off rheumatism.

Monday, 14 December

WVS. At the WVS tonight our Chairman asked for volunteers to wait on at the evacuees' party. There are no evacuees now on Dewsbury Moor and there was a little argument, but we finally all consented to put our names down, but with caustic comment because those districts sending many evacuees could only raise two waiters. We devoted most of the evening to discussing the proposed visit to the Panto [pantomime] after Xmas. Our Chairlady's husband has promised us £1 towards this treat.

Wednesday, 16 December

Went to pictures again today. About the fifth week in succession. Don't particularly like the films but feel an increasing need for change. The blackout seems more trying this year. Thank heaven that will be over after the war even if rationing does go on for years.

Thursday, 17 December

Bert has completed and returned the card from the Electric Department which had on it a diagram of the meter and a request that we copy the position of hands on our meter and return. I cannot see how this system of meter reading is either foolproof or craftproof.

Sunday, 3 January, 1943

At the WVS we discussed Conscientious Objectors. Young So-and-So was preaching at the Chapel yesterday. He was a conchie and apparently regular attenders had boycotted him. Strong views were expressed today, one going so far as to say all conchies should be hung – they were all out to make money out of the war. 'While our lads are fighting,' said one. 'By gow, if they offered me 3s a day dole when I came back I'd ...' 'There'll be work for everyone. Rebuilding and feeding Europe,' said another. 'There'll be no unemployment.' 'Why?' I said. 'Because so much will want doing. We ought to be better off than ever.' I said 'You mean a boom and then ...?' But the discussion hedged on to the many who were doing well out of the war and 'you needn't go short if you had money to pay with'. (One knew someone who bought a 35s turkey for *tea* because she could get nothing else.)

Thursday, 7 January

Bella Hill was telling me of the worry caused to her husband (a bus inspector) by conductresses absenting themselves from work. Yesterday 24 failed to appear for duty and Henry Hill had to rush round and find girls, whose rightful day off it was, to take their places. Even then six workmen's buses could not turn out first thing in the morning for even drivers had to be pressed to serve as conductors to get the most important buses on the road. Bella Hill said they were going to prosecute girls in future if they did not produce a doctor's certificate for even half a day off. And high time, I should think.

Thursday, 14 January

We discussed the punishment of War Criminals. Auntie said they would hide like rats in neutral countries. I said there were too many to flee, just as there would be too many to punish. It was a farce our Government talking of 'bringing to justice' thousands of beasts who are apparently revelling in persecution and cruelty for its own sake. To do so would take hundreds of years.

Saturday, 16 January

At the beginning of January we were promised eggs over the wireless, one each and twelve for priorities for the month. Our allocation arrived and on inquiry at the Food Office we learned that priorities were expectant and nursing mothers. Three applicants for 'priority' turned up during the week. (Seems as if the Government is bribing women with the offer of eggs to do their duty. No wonder the birthrate is soaring. Twelve eggs against other people's one!) We gave out the eggs and of course fell short for our ordinary customers. We are allowed 10 per cent overplus for such emergencies and then apparently have to use our wits to spread out the rest among our eager customers. We get no satisfaction from the Food Office. There they are always beautifully vague and manage to give you an answer which when you ponder it over leaves you more bewildered. It's the same with the circulars we get from time to time. One about these very eggs today, with a lot of 'It is hoped the retailer ...', 'It is suggested that ...', and so on. All nebulous and non-committal, not the sort of thing one can brandish in the face of outraged women who say warmly and truthfully (my sympathy is with the customer though I am a shopkeeper) 'I haven't had a shell egg since November. It said on the wireless ...', etc. etc. In short the shopkeeper gets the 'mucky end of the stick' every time. He is the buffer between the Government's wonderful paper schemes which don't come off and the housewives who want to know *'why?'* As for these 'priority' eggs, they should be given out at clinics or such places and not donned on the poor shopkeeper to distribute.

Tuesday, 27 January

Went to hear the Bournemouth Philharmonic Orchestra [playing at the Town Hall]. Two hours of bliss after a fortnight's foreboding that (a) No concert could be worth the extravagance of a 4s ticket, (b) I should be ill and the 4s *would* be wasted, (c) I should have to walk home in the blackout. Why was I so fearful? The ticket would have been cheap at 14s. I was not ill. And the bus home was easily caught for all was over by 8.30. The Town Hall was crowded. There were many young folk.

Monday, 1 February

To the Panto[mime] with the WVS, 21 of us, and afterwards to tea at the New Victoria, fish cakes and chips or Spam. (And we had discussed turkey and ham and tongue. But of course there is a war on.) The tea was 3s per head.

Wednesday, 10 February

Looking in M.'s [shop] window the other day, stocked with £5 and £7 and £10 handbags, and necklaces and fripperies outrageously priced, I mused on the easy time such people have compared with we poor grocers. There is no limit to the quantity of goods they may sell and no check on prices. I know M. went to London shortly after the blitzes and brought back large quantities of goods (unless the Government is lying about restriction of luxuries). I also know he bought a £500 business for his brother-in-law, and *paid for it in £1 notes*. No comment needed! But I wonder how many businesses today can squiggle even 500 pence without the Exchequer knowing. And how many can be so independent of the Banks?

Day Survey, 10 February.[*] Still seedy after my cold but rose at 7.30 as usual, arriving downstairs for the news. Had my breakfast, gave Bert his before Ma and Margaret got up. Kiddies swarming in with sweet coupons but we have little for them except liquorice. Bert keeping our boiled sweets for registered customers. Bert said 'Don't wash shop floor as it is such a nasty day'. Quiet interval. While Ma and Margaret had breakfast I knitted Army scarf and read *Celia* by [novelist] E. H. Young [1937]. At 10 Bert went into Dewsbury with Henry Hill to look at counter and fixtures Mr H. is disposing of. Few customers for potatoes, and Spam and cigs and sweets which we had not. Our best customer is to pay her bill. She was keeping me at it getting her groceries when

---

[*] This paragraph was in response to MO's request in its January 1943 Directive for Observers to write a detailed account of this day.

the baker came and then the railway van – the latter only bringing tinned beans. Having disposed of all these three, sat and read again (Ma and Margaret cleaning upstairs) until Bert came back very pleased with his bargain but completely forgetting linoleum Margaret had urged him to buy and send up with his purchases. Still he was too engrossed to worry about lack of customers. Got off the bread orders, and shared out the few buns for registered. Made morning tea and dodged from house to shop, serving mostly bread and potatoes. Busier after 12 with kiddies and last minute customers. Closed at 1 o'clock for half day. Had dinner leisurely. Decided not to go to the pictures. Helped wash up, then sat down and dozed over [George Bernard Shaw's *The Intelligent Woman's*] *Guide to Socialism* [*and Capitalism*, 1929] until 3.30. Weather meanwhile had cleared so prepared to go out. This took me a long time as I felt poorly but determined to master it. Finally got off at 4.15. Went to Library, paid 5d fine, decided Dewsbury had no attractions, turned back, called at sub-Post Office for Insurance Stamp and Post Office for Bert's Club money. Walked through Park and noted birds were singing as in April [this was a mild winter]. Had to dodge to avoid *flying* ducks. Home at 5.30. Felt tired and dismal, even boiled egg for tea did not console. Sat all evening in one chair without moving, reading and dozing. Bert grumbled rarely about the poor wireless programme. We all seemed out of spirits and went early to bed.

Saturday, 13 February

There was a play [by Adrian Alington] on the wireless tonight called *The Man in the Chair*, about a professor gloating over a helpless man, telling him that a previous victim had been buried alive while in a trance which enabled him to know what was happening though he could not move or speak. At this point Margaret switched off in disgust (although she likes thrillers in the ordinary way). I said I thought it in the worst possible taste when you consider all who have been and are being buried alive in this war. But the BBC often irritates me with this lack of tact and feeling. There was an instance on Sunday when after a beautiful religious ceremony and before the last words of the prayer had died away we were plunged violently, without pause or introduction, into a loud racing tune which went on fully a minute before we were told at the top of someone's voice that it was somebody's Players. I am not religious and I do not usually listen to religious broadcasts but this morning I did and I was not pleased to be jerked rudely from one mood to another, as if my mind and emotions were on strings like marionettes.

Monday, 15 February

To WVS where we were given two dozen towels each to hem and wash. These should have been done twelve months ago. Delay is due to former chairlady's negligence. We discussed the scarcity of fish and some were very heated over preference which they alleged was given to the Belgians in the fish market, some being seen to take 8s or 10s worth away and local women were refused any. One said she knew for a fact that the Market Men had orders from Town Hall to give the Belgians preference. Another said it was done so they would give us a good report when they went back to Belgium.

*There were around 240 Belgian refugees in Dewsbury, and a few more in Heckmondwike, according to a report from the summer of 1941 when they had a reunion on the day before Belgian Independence Day, around a year after their arrival in Dewsbury (*Dewsbury Reporter, *26 July 1941, p. 6). 'Most of them came from the Ostend area, and had many thrilling adventures before reaching Milford Haven, but it is gratifying to know that practically all of them now have homes of their own in this district. Most of them are in employment, and are very happy here, although a* Reporter *representative, who chatted with many of them, was impressed with their ardent desire to return to their own land, their relatives, and their friends, many of whom they have not heard of since they left them behind in their hurried rush to escape the furious German onslaught.' Their appearance was contrasted with that of the summer before. 'The youngsters romped, laughed and sang, thoroughly enjoying themselves, while the older ones were obviously quite at ease, conscious that they had regained their self-respect, and were able to lead an independent life. The Belgian Colours were everywhere to be seen, and although most of the refugees conversed together in their own language, most of them by now speak English – or rather Yorkshire – fluently.'*

Wednesday, 17 February

Pleased it is the *Americans* who are suffering reverses [in Tunisia] and depending on *us* to help them. What a blow to their self-esteem! All the same I wish our PM would not come back from his trips so buoyant that he makes us all float on air – for our balloon is so often pricked. *This* catastrophe was never foreseen and must make a hash of the Casablanca

Conference [between Churchill and Roosevelt the previous month]. No wonder Stalin is impatient.

Tuesday, 23 February

Stalin is not only impatient but sarcastic. That is evident from his reference in his Order of the Day to the absence of a Second Front [in Western Europe, for which the Soviets were actively lobbying].

Monday, 1 March

To the WVS. Poor attendance owing to the darkness and strong wind. Collected for wreath for Mrs H. Discussed proposed whist drive and whether it was to be held at Centre (the Baptist Chapel) or the Council School. One wanted dancing too. Exclamations from those who were Chapelgoers. They said it would never be allowed; we must be thankful even that whist was allowed on the Chapel premises – *that* was only a recent concession. This led to a long argument whether the Trustees had a right to say what should be done when they let the Sunday school. One lady said that at Socials where certain persons – mentioning no names but you all know who I mean – went home the young ones got up to dance and it [did] her heart good to see them. After this we drifted off WVS business on to stories of old Chapel-going days and the meeting broke up in laughter.

Thursday, 4 March

Mr N. the sub-Postmaster sent word to Bert to expect his fire-watching notice for he had inside information that himself and Bert and two others were being nabbed and also mentioned the place they would have to attend at. Bert sky-high of course. Saying they wouldn't get *him*; he'd his own business premises to watch and anyhow he was street fire-party.

Saturday, 6 March

Bert got his notice today and alternated between saying he was not fit to go and they couldn't make him go as old as he was. (On other occasions he always says how *young* he is. [He was fifty-four.]) And going without sleep knocked him up and what about the shop the next day, and so on and so forth. The worst week we have had for points for some time. Everyone spent up on fruit at the beginning of the period. We have most of our plums and rhubarbs left on the shelves with our points tied up. Marks & Spencer reaped the benefit of that little scheme. They had most varieties of fruit for sale.

Monday, 8 March

Bert gone down to interview Secretary of Chamber of Commerce. Has great faith he can influence Deputy Food Officer to get him off. Oranges today. Usual grumbling from mothers of over-fives and others. Much better to do as Margaret says and give one orange per ration book, old and young, or else send all to hospitals. Received form about shop assistants on Saturday and noted number of N.S.2 [National Service] to be given, if any. Henry Hill said I should have received N.S.2 when I registered. Ransacked house to find N.S.2 all day Sunday. No N.S.2. Down to Labour Exchange this morning fearfully, to confess loss of N.S.2. Young Labour Exchanger, after puzzling some time, said I never had one. I was too old for N.S.2.* Was going to bash Henry Hill when we met but anger was soothed when going to tidy up after ransacking I found a two-year-old birthday card with a ten-shilling note pinned to it, which I had completely forgotten, and which had been lying fallow all this time. I patriotically bought 10s Savings Stamps.

Tuesday, 9 March

Bert received his notice to fire watch about half a mile away. He says he doesn't think it right at his age and with all he has to do in the daytime. Margaret 'soothes' him with reminding him he *can* have a rest while most poor men have to work right through the next day. I make no comment. It will be my turn shortly I expect.

Wednesday, 10 March

There being nothing at the pictures worth seeing, I accompanied Bert and Margaret on their walk through the fields. On our return we called on Mr N. and found he'd had his notice too. He was very chuff. 'What did I tell you? Wasn't I right?' He said he couldn't get off to guard his Post Office but strangely enough the publican opposite, who was only 42, was excused on the grounds he was watching for the brewery who owns the pub.

* The National Service (No. 2) Act of December 1941 allowed for the conscription of women for wartime service, although it acknowledged many exclusions and modifications. Single women over thirty, like Kathleen, were not liable to compulsion.

Twelve half pounds of suet and 43 registered families. Bert had a brain wave. He rigged up an ingenious arrangement whereby every registered housewife pricked for the chance to buy a packet. This suits them down to the ground.

Monday, 15 March

To WVS. More discussion about where to hold whist drive. Argument among Chapelgoers as to whether relaxation of Methodist rule 'No Whist Drives' is to be interpreted 'Whist Drives only for benefit of Methodism', or 'Whist Drives for any cause'. The Church hall was suggested as most suitable since the Chapel schoolroom was deemed too small now the Wardens were joining in the scheme. Some wanted Town Hall but that was voted too ambitious and too far away in any case. We discussed possibility of raids on Dewsbury and said we were lucky to have escaped so far considering the targets in the district. Four elected on to Committee.

Tuesday, 16 March

L.L.'s traveller complaining that his firm (grocery and provision wholesalers) cannot get points goods. He had very little to offer. Bert complaining about Lord Woolton. Traveller said Woolton had done well in some respects but he never forgot his business interests. His boss was repeatedly going to London but could get no satisfaction. The big firms (such as M&S) were getting more and more and the small ones were getting less. There was no fairness of distribution and in turn as the wholesalers couldn't get goods, the small retailer was left without. Bert said he couldn't understand why these firms

were allowed to trade in lines they didn't touch before the
war. The traveller explained how it is. When an M&S store
(or any similar one) is bombed out in a seaside resort or place
where they sell these lines there is some juggling with the
Food Controller to have the licences transferred to branches
in industrial towns which formerly didn't sell these goods.
Whether it was legally allowed or not, the traveller didn't
know, but it is *done* and there you are. There is no fairness
about it.

It was sometime this month (DR, March 1943) that Kathleen wrote
about the food situation in Dewsbury and women's attitudes to
it, subjects on which she could speak with some authority. 'We
are able to maintain quite a large stock of one thing or another.
But we do not consider we are fairly dealt with as regards vari-
ety in Points goods. For instance, our allocation of tinned fruit
consisted entirely of plums and rhubarb, and consequently our
customers trekked to town half a mile away to buy where there
was a variety of choice – that is, Marks & Spencer's. Then they
came back minus Points for all of the last Period and grumbled
at us because they couldn't buy anything for three weeks. We
should have done the grumbling. There is the same trouble with
dried fruit. We get the same old thing time after time, prunes and
sultanas, while M&S get apricots, dates, dried apples and other
things. And again we seldom get apples and oranges from our
local greengrocer wholesaler who also supplies M&S. But apart
from these injustices (as we feel they are) we do not do badly. Our
customers usually seem satisfied and often praise us for our well
stocked shop.'

She then went on to write of her experiences with specific
aspects of provisioning. Eggs, she said, 'we get regularly and
give out fairly, which is more than many shops do if all we hear

is true. But we are never sure about Priority eggs, which keep
changing. We depend on the wireless for instructions and our
allocation is always at least one behind the current number. But

In spite of shortages, many shops managed to keep their shelves and
counters impressively stocked with goods – even if some were not quite
the goods their customers would have preferred.
Photograph © IWM D2374

our customers are equally mystified and I am sure we could cheat most of them and they would be none the wiser.' Points coupons 'are another puzzle to many customers. They say "I'll leave it to you. Give me some biscuits and make up the rest with anything – but no fish." (Tinned fish is a poor seller here.)' As for perceived luxuries, 'We have most bother over little extras such as apples or onions which take some stretching round and woe betide us if we sell any to non-rationed customers. We soon hear about it. Oranges are a very sore point. Mothers of older children are very bitter if they see green ration books produced for oranges. (This is a farce because most shopkeepers refuse to sell if they don't want to keep them for favourites of any age.)' Sugar and tea 'seem to be nearly everybody's bugbear. They cannot be made to spin out. Men folk and kiddies get the sugar. They will not give up having very sweet tea. The women go without much more frequently.'

Monday, 22 March

To the WVS. Mrs H. reported a not very good first meeting with the Wardens for whist drive. They seemed half-hearted and made difficulties. They wanted tickets to be 1s 6d with no supper included and said flatly they could not subscribe anything towards it. Regrets were expressed we had ever invited the Wardens to join us but now too late to back out. Talk then diverted to Wardens' clothes and the new issue of overalls; they had one only twelve months ago. One wife of a Warden said he was told he had only to go to the Depot if he wanted boots – there was plenty there – all sizes. Mrs K. said it was disgusting the way things were being carried on and money wasted. What the Government was thinking of she didn't know but they would get no brass out of *her* to fly up i' t'air and vanish, 'Wings for Victory' or not. Mrs P. said yes, it was as her husband said – the war would go on as long as money could be found for it and when all t'brass were done, t'war would stop. Them as could keep finding brass longest would win. It was a money war same as they all were. (Some murmurs of assent here.)

Monday, 12 April

To the WVS after words with Bella Hill who flatly refused to go, saying it was only a gossip shop and what good did they do. As she has never raised a finger or done a stitch of knitting I thought this was rich. We had a good meeting, though there was no response to the appeals for more to make camouflage nets. Mrs R. said why couldn't some of the 'organisers' take a turn – there seemed to be plenty of them ['Organiser' was the title used for most WVS leaders]. She supposed it was like the canteens – plenty of servers at the counters but no washers up. Well, if camouflaging was of such importance why didn't the Government pay for it – doing like any other war work – and there'd be no lack of workers then.

Tuesday, 20 April

Heard no grumbles about the tobacco increase, even from old age pensioners. But we are selling slightly less cigs. This will go back to normal in a little while. Women who formerly treated their husbands to 20 cigs when getting the rations now only buy 10 and say if they [their husbands] want any more they must buy them. Non-smokers, including myself, are very complacent and self-righteous. Heavy smokers say 'We shall have to have them whatever they cost. We're helping to win t'war aren't we?"*

Sunday, 25 April

M. came to tea. She says she has to report before a Board with a medical certificate to say her mother is not fit to be left every three months, although she is turned 35. She says she does not resent that; it is only part of the system, but she does resent that some of the women on the Board are of registering age – in fact have registered. This, she argues, is not fair.

Wednesday, 28 April

Went to the CEMA [Council for the Encouragement of Music and the Arts] Symphony Concert [by the Bournemouth Philharmonic Orchestra] in the Town Hall. Poor attendance – only half full. Dreading that there will be no more. Now heard three first-class concerts and have had my ears and heart opened to good music [Kathleen often evinced a yearning for 'higher' culture, to which in Dewsbury she had only limited access]. The wireless is no good for real listening – there are too many distractions in an ordinary household, not to mention violent opposition and sarcasm.

Saturday, 1 May

Cigarette sales definitely down this week. Hard from a business point of view but from a patriotic point of view good.

---

* 'The amount many working class husbands and wives spend on smoking alone is enormous when compared with their income,' Kathleen remarked a few months later (DR, September 1943).

Am always annoyed when told to eat less bread and save shipping that there is no mention of less smoking, which is after all less necessary than bread. I can't believe even the most weak-willed chain smoker would rather starve than not smoke.

Tuesday, 11 May

Where is Winnie? He seems to be lying low so is doubtless on one of his trips. North Africa I expect [he arrived that day in the United States]. The more we win the more people seem convinced of a long war, which is strange on the face of it, but really shows they are appreciating the difficulties before us. Several customers hopeful we shall get more fruit now, dried or fresh. I long for a glass of orange juice as Keats longed for his beaker of the warm South. Won't I turn vegetarian/fruitarian after this?

Thursday, 13 May

No buses this morning so there is a strike after all. What a beastly thing to do to the work people who depend on them. The trouble is over irregular hours, I think.

Saturday, 15 May

Men sympathise with the bus strikers. Women don't. So it seems from what I hear in the shop. The latter take the attitude that 'our lads in Africa can't strike'. It seems that many of the bus people have so many hours on and so many off during the day so that it takes them anything up to sixteen hours to earn eight hours wages, and as some live a considerable distance away it means they have to stay around the bus station waiting to be called on. Mothers of girls working on munitions are particularly angry when the girls have to walk home. However, now soldiers are helping with trucks – no fares but collections for the driver.

I have heard several people say they were against strikes of any kind – they were altogether wrong and did no one any good. And a good many said they were against strikes in wartime. And some seem obviously at a loss – torn between sympathy and irritation. The majority, apart from grumbling at the inconvenience, take no sides. It is supposed not to have union sanction but all the union people are out, leaving only inspectors, who I gather haven't to be in a union (one's wife said her husband had to go in with the bosses), and timekeepers, only a few of which can drive. A bus inspector I know was at it except for meal intervals from 4 o'clock a.m. to 11 p.m. and says it will be like that until it is over. Many of the men joined the union after the girls' strike some time ago.

Tuesday, 18 May

People are more and more fed up at having to walk out of Dewsbury, especially as it is so warm. It is a very unpopular strike among the general public. Henry Hill (our friend the bus inspector) says they have had yet another meeting and only decided on staying out by four votes. He says that if there had been a secret ballot the strike would have been over; as it was, the silly lasses were looking around to see how their friends and sweethearts were voting and doing the same. (Three cheers for democracy!) Henry Hill looks played out. Up at 3 a.m. and on the go until 10 p.m. for days is too much

of a good thing. But there is a lighter side. Yesterday he said as
he was hoisting a stout lady up the step ladder into the waggon
she fell back on him and squashed his 30 cigs! He says he has
never done so much pulling and shoving in his life. It is an 'ill
wind', however. The soldiers are delighted. One has already
made over £12 in tips. He was very put out when his waggon
broke down and he had to miss 'two b—— trips'. Henry Hill
says it is sheer pleasure to work with these sergeants. Only a
wish or suggestion has to be expressed and it is carried out –
with no argument or fuss. They wear crash helmets all the
time.

*The discontents of these wartime bus conductresses and drivers
were over both wages and the hours of work, which often involved
very early starts (4.30 to 5 a.m.), late endings (near midnight),
much waiting-around without pay during the day, and erratic
work schedules. Absenteeism sometimes lengthened the hours and
heightened the strain for those workers who did show up. A few
months later Kathleen wrote that 'I think the bus strike here in the
summer was justified although it did inconvenience the war effort.
The conditions were bad and public attention was drawn to that.'
(November 1943 DR).*

   *The six-day withdrawàl of service produced a few temporary
changes (Dewsbury District News, 22 May, p. 1). On Sunday
'quite a number of ponies and traps were seen on the roads';
another effect 'was to reduce considerably the numbers of young
people who stroll around the centre of Dewsbury on a Sunday
evening – a habit which has long been deplored'. These Sunday
customs of youth had been remarked on by Kathleen a year
before (April 1942 DR). 'The Market Place at Heckmondwike
is crammed every Sunday evening with "paraders", lads and
lasses of fourteen to twenty, who saunter in large, giggling,*

shrieking groups up and down the pavement, indulging in horseplay and using foul language. Young folks have to let off steam somehow when they have been cooped up all week, but no one will convince me that this is enjoyment, not the real sort of fun they should be having at their age. They are just plain bored stiff, though they don't know it. And no wonder. Many of them live in such small houses that their parents are glad for them to get out and make more room. There is nowhere for them to go but the streets, except the pubs and Clubs. And what streets! Heckmondwike on a busy day is drab and ugly enough but on a Sunday evening, unenlivened by the bustle and stir of business – Crikey!'

Heckmondwike, with the approach to Market Place shown here, was a near neighbour to Dewsbury, and very similar in character. The industrial towns in this part of West Yorkshire came close to merging into each other.
Photograph © Kirklees Image Archive

Wednesday, 19 May

The bus strike is over [it ended the previous night]. The people have returned to work under the same conditions as before; they have lost nearly a week's wages to no purpose. WVS meeting. We discussed the Dam disaster. One said she lay awake all night listening to the bombers going over and worrying about our lads up there, and thinking about the floods in Germany, and feeling sorry for those decent Germans who were suffering from the catastrophe [hundreds of German civilians died as a result of these dam-busting raids on 16–17 May]. But she was soon told off. One said there were *no* decent Germans, they were all alike; one that that was not the way to look at it, we had to concentrate on winning; and several said that the Germans had no pity for us when they were 'tops'. Everybody seemed hazy about the quantity of water – one said four million gallons, one four hundred, but neither really conveys any meaning to us, or to me at any rate, any more than the talk of so many hundred thousand prisoners.

Several people in the shop today have remarked on being wakened by aeroplanes flying over, which comment is unusual.

Thursday, 20 May

Overheard in the hairdresser's: 'Isn't the Dam affair wonderful? All those floods! It *must* interfere with their munitions. And they can't do anything about it. There must have been thousands drowned. It's a pity in a way. I mean, mothers there having feelings for their children the same as we have. One doesn't like to think of the poor people being drowned.' Hairdresser: 'We mustn't look at it that way. They don't worry about us in the least. We've got to go on and win the war.'

Saturday, 22 May

Several letters in the local paper about the bus strike, all con-
demning it. One from a soldier, one from a soldier's wife, one
from a woman munition worker.

*These three letters (Dewsbury Reporter, 22 May 1943, p. 3) all
contrasted the strikers' conduct with the absence of individual
freedoms in the Forces, whose members were fighting on behalf
of everyone. 'A soldier's wife', writing on 13 May from Mirfield,
thought the strikers 'should stop to consider all the advantages they
have over the soldier who is fighting to defend his land. Compare
the amount of wages earned, too [British soldiers were notori-
ously ill-paid], and yet how many of the bus men love to drink their
nightly beer and criticise as to which country we ought to invade
next. At the moment perhaps it is lucky for them that soldiers'
wives are not government officials or else the order would be: "If
you are not satisfied with the job you are doing for your country,
here is a suit of khaki, or air force blue, and a serviceman's pay."
If their wives and children have then to go out to earn money to
keep the homes, maybe the bus drivers left will take them to work
cheerfully and willing[ly]. So, whilst we can wait patiently for our
men's return, after we have worked a wearisome day in the factory
or on munitions, please don't let us have to trudge home, where
household duties await us.'*

Wednesday, 2 June

Auntie was here. We talked of Giraud and de Gaulle. She said
de Gaulle had not been treated right. He had been cold shoul-
dered after carrying the burden all the time, while Giraud had
only come over when he saw how the wind was blowing. I

suggested North Africa was so anti-British they *daren't* put de Gaulle in for fear of an uprising.* Auntie said, well, none of the French were to be trusted. They had borne a grudge against us since Napoleon's day, for these last hundred years. Bert said any soldier in the last war would tell you that Germans were to be trusted before Frenchmen any time. Auntie said you wouldn't get her cousins, who lived in Germany before the last war, to say a word against the German people, although there was a lot of militarisation even then. They were splendid to live among. Whenever her cousins holidayed in England, they were greeted by all their neighbours on their return with garlands and branches. They always rued they were here when the war broke out and so couldn't get back.

Friday, 4 June

Had yet another visit from insurance men to invite Bert to take up six Endowments for Wings for Victory Week [5–12 June]. Don't know how the scheme is worked but doubtless the Companies will get a nice bit out of the things. There seems to be no lack of petrol for them to run around with. Bert was discouraging. We had a shop full of customers or possibly they would have been more persistent. I shall go along in the old sweet way taking no heed of Wings for Victory or anything else. I put my small savings in regularly each week and if

* Generals Henri-Honoré Giraud (1879–1949) and Charles de Gaulle (1890–1970) were rivals, each seeking to lead the defeated French against the Nazis. The Americans supported Giraud and the British de Gaulle – in the summer of 1940 Britain had recognised him as leader of the Free French (while the United States continued to recognise the Vichy regime). The American President was decidedly hostile to de Gaulle. At the Casablanca conference in January 1943, Churchill and Roosevelt demanded that the two work together. In the end Giraud was no match politically for de Gaulle and resigned.

everyone did the same there would be no need to waste 1s for every 1s 6d taken in a special week.

Saturday, 5 June

Olive and Auntie to supper. We discussed sleeping and dreaming. Bert said he never waked to consider whether he slept soundly or not. Auntie has slept on her sofa partly dressed ever since the first air raids. Olive described a frequent dream she has where she is flying high in the air and cannot get down, but is wandering all night over church steeples and mill chimneys. Margaret and I have similar experiences: when dropping off to sleep faces appear before us in rapid succession; mine are grotesque, hers are terrifying.

Monday, 7 June

No ration books to be given out this week on account of Wings for Victory. Only A and B given out so far [referring, apparently, to names listed alphabetically; see 8 June]. Hear various reports. Some say they had no bother and were not in twenty minutes; others were angry at having to wait an hour and a half, and complain that standing twice in a queue is beyond a joke. People who went at lunch time and evening after work seem to have fared best.

Tuesday, 8 June

The *News Chronicle* correspondent [8 June 1943, p. 3] rather irritated me with his continual harping on what Russia had done and what she had suffered and what she was doing; as if no other country had done or suffered anything, as if we had been sitting with folded hands for two years and were only now getting down to it. I can see we will have to shout and blazen 'our year alone' up and down the world after the war. Neither America nor Russia will like us to refer to that. As for Russia's sufferings, her own hands are not clean from atrocities to other people. I hope the correspondent stays long enough to get a few facts to take back to Russia with him.

Could get no points vouchers at Food Office today. They protested they were so behind with their work through being upstairs in the Victoria Hall all last week giving out [the new] ration cards. When asked what we were to tell our wholesalers when they ask for vouchers before we can have goods, there was no reply. This is a ridiculous idea, taking out of the Food Office all the clerks into another department to do different work. And we have yet another 24 letters of the alphabet to go through, besides exceptional cases. At this rate we shall not see another points voucher before the new rationing year. Of all the daft ——!

Wednesday, 9 June

One of our wholesale travellers came today and read the Riot Act over this voucher business. Every shop he visited in Dewsbury had no points for him. The wholesalers are not supposed (in fact they have recently been instructed or ordered on this point by Lord Woolton himself) to allow any goods out without *first* receiving the points. He says he has never in all his travels come across such a place as Dewsbury Food Office and if there isn't a row kicked up by the Chamber of Trade there certainly will be by infuriated wholesalers whose business is being hindered.

Sunday, 20 June

Mr D. is convinced Hitler will have a pot at us with all he's got, including gas, before he goes down. He says Hitler doesn't plan these things, there are others behind him. A man who only got to a corporal in the last war hasn't enough about him to lead nations – he is just a puppet or figurehead.

Friday, 9 July

Much talk among customers of the new food concessions for expectant mothers, and many ribald remarks. One said she was born twenty years too early. She had no help in bringing up her bairns. One said it was ridiculous depriving babies of up to six months of their sweet ration – all babies liked chocolate even if they couldn't eat sweets! Another grumbled at cut in fats and bacon, saying there were no oranges to be got anyway; and another, who has just had a fourth baby, said they could have extra eggs and oranges who wanted to qualify for them. She wanted no more children – but it isn't what you want, it's what you get. Two or three seemed scandalised or skittish because unmarried mothers were included in the scheme, and all seemed unanimous that the interest in kids would not last after the end of the war. 'They'll be calling us for having them when unemployment starts again. Anyway, let them have kids that can afford them. Oranges and eggs!'

Sunday, 25 July

Margaret came upstairs to waken us at 11 p.m. to say that Mussolini had resigned. Not surprised. We all thought a revolution in Italy the next step.

Thursday, 29 July

Alice arrived from Northants. She had a decent journey except for bungling at N—— where she had to wait three hours. We took her in the Park to see the ventriloquist and on to the bowling green.

Friday, 30 July

Terrifically hot. Set Alice on to pull peas to forestall pilferers who are robbing gardens just now. After shop closed we went to see bowling tournament in Park [held in Crow Nest Park during Dewsbury's three-week 'Holidays at Home'].

Saturday, 31 July

Ma and Alice to Mirfield. Ma overcome by heat on return. All into Park in evening. Hotter than ever. Storm during night. Alice insisted on pulling curtains. Nearly smothered.

Monday, 2 August

Fire-watching with M. Awakened by a loud knock at 4 a.m. It was the police sergeant and constable to see if we had heard strange noises as the picture house next door was fully lighted and a door open. M. conducted herself with dignity although sitting up in bed. I never undress, as I trust neither the beds nor the lock of the cottage which opens straight into the street, but my stockings rolled down over my shoe tops and (I afterwards found) my hair net dangled from one ear. When they had gone I pondered for some time on the strange scenes that must be going on all over the country through fire-watching, and the more I pondered the less I liked it. Say what they like it's no work for women.

Bank Holiday. Arose about 9 a.m. A typical showery Bank Holiday. Breakfasted altogether off bread and dripping. Proposed to Cousin Alice who was staying with us that we should walk into Dewsbury to book seats for [J. B.] Priestley's *When We Are Married*, given by the Repertory Company [the Court Players at the Empire Theatre]. Walked through the Park – a damp, warm and sticky morning – Alice talking all the time. A long queue at the Empire necessitated a long stand before we could get seats for Tuesday evening. Walked slowly home to dinner at 1 o'clock. (Dewsbury a strange place with shops all shut but all mills and transport working.) After dinner I was so sleepy with the weather and with not resting properly at night owing to having hefty Alice as a partner when I am used to sleeping solo, that I went and lay on the bed for an hour. Then up again, still languid, and a walk in the Park was suggested. By the time we were all ready rain was pouring again. I sat and knitted with my outdoor things on. Alice produced her jumper. I said if that was intended for her it would not be half big enough. Ma and Margaret backed me up in this. Long argument whether she should pull back and begin again. Still not convinced it would not fit, Alice decided to leave it until she got home to measure with another jumper. Now fine so we walked through the Park. There was sounds of fun from the Marquee. Before we got home rain was peltering down again.

Tea, with tinned apricots and tinned milk, to celebrate. I read at intervals when the din and chatter would allow. About 7 we decided to go to see a Concert Party in the Park and found a decent seat. For a local effort it was unusually good and lasted three hours. The sides of the Marquee were lowered so more people could have a view but they had to stand in the rain. Home at 10.30 to supper of bread and dripping and after listening to Haw-Haw* and European news – to bed.

This is the third successive August Bank Holiday that has been wet and muggy and the third I have spent in similar trivialities.

---

* William Joyce (1906–1946), an Irish-American fascist known in Britain as Lord Haw-Haw, broadcast propaganda for Germany, mainly in an effort to undermine morale. By this time in the war he was probably regarded by most listeners as a comic figure.

8

The Weariness of War

August 1943–May 1944

Thursday, 5 August

Alice went home today to our great relief. Visitors at a shop in wartime are a great strain. Since Mussolini went a lot of people seem to think the war as good as over but if they considered Sicily they would know different. If it is taking all this time, men and munitions, to capture one small island, how long is it going to take to conquer Europe?*

Tuesday, 10 August

Had a strange affair today. Mrs M. registered a daughter with us several weeks ago. Today we have discovered that when

---

* The British (including Canadians) sustained 12,572 casualties in the 38 days of battle, the Americans 9,811; 5,159 were killed. These were heavy losses for what had been expected to be a quick victory. (Carlo D'Este, *Bitter Victory: The Battle for Sicily 1943* [London: Collins, 1988], pp. 551–52 and 597.) Enthusiasm for the Second Front was being tempered in many circles by a growing recognition of the probable casualties.

the new rationing year started she turned in a book belonging to another daughter and we never noticed the different name and had been supplying rations to the wrong daughter. On enquiring of Mrs M. where the original daughter was obtaining rations, she seemed all at sea, having apparently many daughters, all rationed at different shops (many women have the mistaken idea they are 'better done to' when having one ration instead of many). We advised her, after much vain argument on her part, that one book was as good as another, to take all down to the Food Office and get them all re-registered at one shop.

Sunday, 15 August

Depressed over many things, chief among them winter shortly to be upon us, and the blackout to hand this very night. A good many people seem to think the restrictions will be relaxed somewhat and better street lighting given, although nearly everyone thinks that we shall be for it sometime during the winter, either with gas or without. But certainly, opinion seems to be that Hitler will have a 'good crack' at us before going under.

Tuesday, 17 August

WVS resumed after long interval for holidays. Discussions on forthcoming Merchant Navy Week and door-to-door collecting. All agreed it was hard work selling flags and often unpleasant. The public is sick of flag days. Relief that Merchant Navy is to be envelopes instead of flags. Discussion then turned to the unpreparedness of Dewsbury in case of blitz – uncooperativeness of the post wardens with our branch of WVS. Then we talked of Russia and how she had saved us. Some said that there were a lot of Hitlers in this country and it was a wonder that Russia would fight for us after the way she had been consistently snubbed. (Quite disregarding the fact that Russia is fighting for no one but herself.) There seemed to be general agreement that Russia would want a big say in what happened after the war. America was in poor esteem. 'They don't *want* us, don't Americans,' said one vigorously. 'They'll have won this war like they won the last. We never heard t'last o' that.' One said her cousin had been training for an officer twelve months in America and was glad to get home. He said the Americans thought little of us.

Friday, 27 August

Heard many remarks in the shop today about Mr Churchill's fishing trip, some amused, some scathing, but all were sarcastic about Mary's presence with her father. 'It's just a holiday trip,' said one, 'and then they tell us to stop at home.' 'I thought she reckoned to be in the ATS,' said another. 'By gum, if one of our lasses had wanted time off to go abroad!' 'Who's she, anyway,' said another, 'that she's to be treated different to other folk?' [Mary Churchill, the PM's youngest daughter, then in the ATS, sometimes accompanied her father abroad – this time to Quebec City.]

But these impending big events leave me cold. One can't live at top pitch all the time and even an invasion of Europe would be only *one* event among the many that crowd upon us. I am war-sick and appalled at the prospect of another blackout. It isn't as if there will be anything but trouble and rationing and general upset for years after the war. But a surprising number of people are convinced that Christmas will see the end of the fighting.

Saturday, 28 August

Had the usual party to supper. Talk turned on today's article in the *Daily Mail* on State Medical Service and all voted it a fine one ['Cure by Charity has Failed', p. 2]. O. M. said it was disgusting that hospitals had to be continually in debt in order to appeal to the public. Auntie said poor people would never get a square deal while the present hospital system prevailed. She had had some experience of outpatients' experience. It was heartrending to see sick people sit for hours on cold hard benches waiting their turn to see the specialist and if they were not agile enough being pushed to the back, for lack of system. Of course, Dewsbury Infirmary was a by-word in the district – many doctors would not send patients there. Batley was much better as regards the kindly treatment of patients, but that didn't alter her argument that with proper State supervision all hospitals would have to toe the line and treat patients more humanely.

Monday, 30 August

To a small whist drive at Mrs H.'s in aid of Merchant Navy Week. Mrs R., full of the concert her husband is sponsoring in the Town Hall for the same cause, was indignant because some refused or would not promise to buy tickets at 2s 6d and 3s 6d each, and turned very nasty, saying it was everyone's duty to support such a cause. Mrs B. spoke up and said that each must decide for herself whether or not she could afford to go. There was then some unpleasantness and the evening finished badly.

Tuesday, 31 August

To the Empire to see the 'Court Players' in *The Chinese Bungalow* and home in time to hear part of Churchill's speech, in which he seems to be explaining and justifying us to Russia. Am more and more amazed at the number of people who expect Christmas to see the end of the war.

Wednesday, 1 September

Mrs B. has taken St Dunstan's collecting boxes to Bella Hill for her to find collectors for the weekend. When Bella Hill protested she had no time, Mrs B. mildly threatened her with the displeasure of Mrs L., the WVS Organiser in Dewsbury, who may think Bella Hill is not doing sufficient voluntary work and pass her name for an 'interview'. I do not believe Mrs L. has this power but Bella Hill, who is only 34 and has no children, was intimidated and took the boxes. This is either an invention on the part of Mrs B. or a subtle form of blackmail in order to get unpleasant jobs done on the part of Mrs L.

These flag days are a perfect pest. This week St Dunstan's and the Merchant Navy Week clash. Last week a child all the way from Heckmondwike was selling for Mrs Churchill's fund, all round the district, thereby breaking the law regarding her age and upsetting our selling prospects when our turn comes. People are fed up – the nice ones are resigned and pay, but many now grumble or refuse to pay altogether.

Thursday, 2 September

J. H. was in a cinema in Worksop with another soldier when a film of a bad raid on England was shown. A woman behind kept up a running commentary to the effect that such things were impossible; of course it was all faked, folk couldn't carry on when bombs were falling like that. At last, J.'s pal could stand it no longer. He turned round and told the woman to shut up; he'd been bombed out of two homes, his child had been born dead through a raid, he hadn't a stick nor stone of a home left, and when he got out of the army he hadn't so much as a pair of boots to go to. The attendant spoke to him but he was worked up and wouldn't be quiet, so Jack took him out, but not before he'd wished bombs on Worksop, just to waken the b——s up.

It seems to me that Britain is divided into two definite camps – the ones who have suffered through the war and those who have been only inconvenienced. How anyone can sail through four years of this and yet be complacent is astonishing and yet there are thousands and thousands with still pre-war minds and outlooks.

Friday, 3 September

Only heard one comment all day on the 'National Day of Prayer' and that was a woman who, noticing a bill hung up in the shop announcing Prayers at Church today and Harvest Festival next week, said 'So that's why t'old lad were ringing his bell so early this morning. I thought there must be something special. He's a lad for services is t'Vicar.' When I turned on the wireless and heard some parson's voice droning I turned it off. These Days of Prayer seem to me utterly ridiculous. Our enemies are praying too and how can the Lord satisfy us both? Besides it seems to me disgusting to ask God to bless such bloody fighting and I am not *so* convinced we are in the right. The time for prayer is when we were on the slippery slopes of 'Peace'. Why were our church leaders so silent then?

Monday, 6 September

To Harrogate with Margaret to visit O. M. who dotes on this snobbish place. The shops have lost their glamour. Utility does not suit them. We fed well while we were there although we were rather self-conscious about queuing for meals. I had my fortune told at a little shop sandwiched between two grand emporiums. Five shillings worth – hands, cards, crystal and all. Madame told me my lucky colour was blue, water was 'prosperous' for me, I should be called for an 'interview' and change my job before three months and change my residence to somewhere beside water before three years, where I should prosper in the handling of liquids (sounds as if I'm to be a seaside barmaid). I must guard my health, keep my feet and back warm, take olive oil, cod liver oil, iron pills and four glasses of water every day. Otherwise I had nothing to fear for I should live to be 83. She condoled with me because my 'fate' (meaning a lover I suppose) was not yet to hand and said I must go out more, particularly at night (sez you!), and that I must stir myself because if I was not married before 45 I should never marry. And that was my five bob's worth.

During the 10 minutes I was with her, three women tried the door; each time Madame made an appointment in twenty, forty minutes time, and so on. I calculate that even at 3s 6d a time – her cheaper rate, 'just the palm' – she can earn 14s to 21s per hour and all cash. No income tax on that unless she banks. O. M., who believes every word, is talking of having a trip over in the spring to have another 'reading'. While there are all these silly women about, who shall blame Madame for accepting such eagerly given money.

Wednesday, 8 September

Heard the news of Italy [it had surrendered] at six o'clock but what with colliding with Margaret on the stairs, she tearing down, I tearing up, and both of us bawling for Bert, we rather missed the details. But it sent us off to the Merchant Navy Concert in good fettle. At the bus stop there was a small crowd but no one said anything until Margaret asked if anyone had heard. Then everyone spoke but no one excitedly. A woman said she was pleased; a man said when one country of a combine gave way the other [Germany] must collapse sooner or later; another said Italy was a grand place – he's soldiered there last time.

After the Concert in the Town Hall (a poor turn-up) we all stood and sang 'Land of Hope and Glory' and '[God Save] The King', except one young man in front who was furious when we were coming away and said he didn't mind standing for t' 'King' but hang standing for 'Land of Hope and Glory'.

Thursday, 9 September

Went to see the 'Pictures to Live With' Exhibition [of contemporary paintings] at Templefield School but were more impressed with the school, finished two years ago [and built on modern lines]. I thought of the high, severe rooms of my school days and then wondered why, even now, children are reluctant to go, when you'd think it would be a joy to work in such a beautiful pleasant place. I do not understand art so was reluctant to ask anything of the lady guide. The landscapes bored me; the back alleys and sordid streets had not the charm for me they apparently had for the artists, perhaps because I live 'agin' 'em and they don't. One I liked, all shapes and shadows, coloured richly in brown and pale blue. Another mystified me. A sailor embracing a girl on a seat while a corpse new risen out of a graveyard beckons him with six arms and a man aims at it with a peashooter from a window. Strange? Yes. Art? I don't know. But a picture to live with! Decidedly not! [Modern art was not to the taste of numerous MO diarists.]

Wednesday, 15 September

Had a loud and prolonged row with Bert over this Sydney Page business [this 18-year-old had refused to work underground in a colliery, and then been imprisoned]. Bert stuck out that the miners did right to strike [in support of Page]; they should go out for all they could get; they deserved it and no lad ought to go down the pit who didn't want. Margaret said *all* strikes were wrong in wartime and I said afraid or not, young soldiers had to stick it; besides there was something fishy about the business. Bert said 15,000 men couldn't be wrong; they thought it was well worth sticking up for. Margaret said then if it was a good case, why wasn't the Union supporting the strike? Bert would not answer this but kept repeating 15,000 men can't be wrong. Would we like anyone belonging to us to go down a pit? No, we shouldn't! Let them in t'Government send their lads down instead of telling miner's sons to go. We hadn't seen men being brought dead out t'pit and he had. And lasses here coming out of factories with six and seven pound a week. No wonder the miners were fed up. They ought to be t'best paid workers in t'country. I said all miners weren't badly paid and in any case when they'd earned a wage they gave up for the rest of the week. I quite agreed they should be better treated but that [it] was up to us to demand nationalisation and in the meantime there was a war on. Surely some of those miners had lads in the fighting line. It was disgusting to strike in wartime. Bert only kept saying 'They do Right'!

Strangely enough Mr D. earlier in the day surprised me by sticking up for the miners. He is a rabid Conservative but seems lately to be changing to an equally rabid Socialist. He said the miners were treated shamefully – the Government took care none of their relations went down the pit. There was too much of this – you must do this and you must do that.

Friday, 17 September

Margaret roused to indignation once again by the Moscow Celebrations [for recent Russian victories]. Wasting all that ammunition, she says, very likely some we have had to give them. They want to keep their celebrating until the war's over.

Sunday, 19 September

To the Pioneer Cinema to see Civil Defence Films. There was a good turn up of WVS and Civil Defence people. The Regional Commissioner spoke on road accidents [many a result of blackout conditions], asking us to do our best to prevent these and not to be indifferent to the enormous casualties, which would shock us if they happened in mine or railway. The films were *The WVS*, *Tunnelling for Rescue Work* and *Malta, G.C.*

Saturday, 25 September

We had a practice at the Rest Centre this afternoon which went off very well, I think.* We got there at 3 and immediately blacked out the Sunday School, lighted paraffin lamps and got out the things [that is, supplies of emergency goods]. Small children of the neighbourhood come in to act as casualties and received a ticket at the door to say what attention they required. I was put in the ambulance group, goodness knows why, because I cannot bandage a finger successfully; maybe to make the team of two look more imposing. Luckily, we had no serious cases, only 'cuts and bruises', and several small boys submitted to being practised on after being bribed with tea and biscuits. Meanwhile, the ladies in the 'Catering Department' struggled outside with the soup boiler and got soup ready in record time. (Secretly bring it to the boil on the geyser – the gas was supposed to be cut off – before taking it outside.) A large bottle of 'VEROX' and two tins of casserole steak went to that soup's making for, as one WVS lady said, we were not all wasting our Saturday afternoon just to cook and eat vegetables. It was certainly good soup when finished and the kiddies polished it off in good style; I only feared real patients before the 'incident' was over. But everything seemed to pass off much better than we expected, which was a good thing as all Dewsbury Centres were being tested that day and we didn't want to be disgraced.

* Rest Centres, which were staffed in Dewsbury and most other places by the WVS, were intended to give temporary refuge to people bombed out of their houses. In 1941 there were 33 Rest Centres in Dewsbury (*Dewsbury Citizens Handbook: Official Handbook of Useful War-time Information and Advice* [c. 1941], p. 22); 24 of them were tested during this exercise. This was a time during the war when exercises to cope with the consequences of possible air raids were being conducted all over the country.

Sunday, 26 September

While listening to Albert Sandler [and the Palm Court Orchestra] we thought we heard the siren. Sure enough, on switching off the wireless we heard it dying away. So out we went and paced up and down and our neighbours joined us. We finally got tired as nothing seemed to be happening and went to supper. At 10.30 Bert came in and said it was the All Clear we had heard; the Alarm was half an hour previously. Not liking to think we had been made fools of, we hotly disputed this and were only convinced when Bella Hill came in and said the same.

Monday, 27 September

It seems something went wrong with one of the sirens, which sounded the Alarm and then all the town sounded All Clear to reassure us. Haven't we been chaffed today over our fire-watching effort.

Most people seem to be in sympathy with the men in the Barrow strike. I could forgive anything of anyone who has to live in such a God forsaken hole. I spent half a day there in 1940, when things were booming, and thought I had never seen such a dreary, depressing place with thousands of prams full of pale sickly babies (two or three in each), and horrible grubby shops. The only decent looking place was the cinema outside the station – where we got a jolly good meal. It struck me as a place without lightness or hope, and the people with no energy to get out of it. What was it like in the years of depression? No wonder the workmen are sore when they remember how they were neglected.

Barrow-in-Furness, a shipyard town in north-west Lancashire (now Cumbria), had been in a bad way during the Depression. Ironically, unknown to Kathleen, Mass Observation's star diarist (it is now generally agreed), Nella Last, lived in Barrow and wrote relentlessly, producing one of the longest diaries in the English language. Her writings are now available in four books, all published by Profile Books: Nella Last's War *(second edition, 2006), edited by Richard Broad and Suzie Fleming, and three volumes edited by Patricia and Robert Malcolmson –* Nella Last's Peace *(2008),* Nella Last in the 1950s *(2010), and* The Diaries of Nella Last: Writing in War and Peace *(2012). This unofficial work stoppage at the important Vickers-Armstrongs shipyard saw around 9,000 workers on strike by 24 September; the dispute was to last a total of eighteen days. Nella Last undoubtedly wrote about these disputes but her diary is missing for these weeks.*

Friday, 1 October

A woman in the shop today said she hoped the war would go on a good long time yet. Her husband had left her with nine children and gone off with an ATS lass. He was a soldier and therefore her pay for all the family was much more than he had ever earned. Extra money for every child. In civil life one unfaltering wage or unemployment pay to do for the lot. This war is a godsend to thousands.

Monday, 4 October

Glad the Barrow people have gone back. Still sympathetic with them though they have now put themselves in the wrong [the strike was widely seen as illegal and disruptive to the war effort].

We had another WVS meeting tonight and were given another badge. Our Centre practice report was good. We were congratulated on the speed with which we prepared tea and soup for the 'homeless'. One Centre baked potatoes which were not ready until 8 o'clock. Another group took an hour and a half to prepare tea and biscuits for thirty people.

Our window cleaner says the Government is only getting what it asked for in these coal strikes. They should have taken more interest in the miners before the war. A miner deserved a wage for going underground before he did a stroke. For his part he'd rather go to fifty feet up than five feet down. No lad of his would go in the pit. Let some of them that were doing all the talking go down and send their lads down.

This seems a sore spot with many people – this sending or threatening to send the young into the pits [to compensate for the declining number of miners]. I have never heard anyone not in sympathy with the miners, though many deprecate strikes in wartime and say they are wrong. But they say you can't wonder if they do come out – the way they are treated in peacetime, put on short time and so on. It's a case of chickens coming home to roost in most people's eyes [many felt that the miners had been badly treated in the past].

Sunday, 17 October

To the public baptism of M. G.'s nephew. E. B. sat with me and we both previously told M. G. we should not 'process' round the church. However, the party was placed near the font so all went off smoothly and well; the baby did not cry and the Vicar afterwards preached a sermon extolling the whole family and welcoming the new member of the church. Personally, I thought the whole thing a farce. I can never understand anyone of M. G.'s intelligence being so church ridden. I found the service boring and the singing unspeakably dreary.

Friday, 29 October

To the meeting of the newly formed Esperanto Society to discuss the possibility of forming an Esperanto class. Only five men and myself present. Decided to advertise in local paper. No one but myself completely ignorant of the language.*

Friday, 5 November

Margaret thinks the way boy Craddock is being made a hero is disgusting – ruination for him and an encouragement to other lads to do as they like.† This case will make magistrates so nervous they will shirk sentencing youngsters at all. They err now on the side of leniency. I think that whenever a child is proved guilty of bad behaviour his *parents* should be punished as well.

Sunday, 7 November

To the Parish Church to hear the Archbishop of York [Cyril Forster Garbett, 1875–1955]. Disappointed to find him

* Esperanto was an artificially constructed language designed to be spoken by people from many backgrounds and to help foster international understanding and harmony among diverse cultures. It was created in the later nineteenth century and was usually conceived of as an auxiliary language to existing 'natural' (albeit parochial) languages.

† A juvenile court in Hereford had ordered Dennis Craddock, aged eleven, to be birched for theft, a punishment that seems to have been carried out immediately and with no opportunity for his parents to appeal. The conduct of the authorities was called into question and the case attracted much publicity.

uninspiring and (seemingly) very old. The church was crowded but, as usual, everyone afraid to hear his own voice. Fire-watching with M. G. She kept me up until midnight discoursing on the satisfactions of religion and joy of believing. But I remained unconvinced. She dismissed all critical books as trash. But she admitted that the great failing of still too many parsons is arrogance. She says that they preach a humility they are incapable of practising.

Tuesday, 9 November

Bought a poppy and was given the cheapest kind although I paid sixpence. The collector grumbled that people were jibbing at paying 3d where before they could pay a penny. Heard many protests at having different priced poppies. I suppose this is to get more money out of the snobbish ones who will only pay well if they can display that they have done so. Mrs R. says she has never bought one since the British Legion refused to help her brother – a non-member – to buy a wheelchair.

Wednesday, 10 November

To Esperanto class. Only four students – one doubtful – besides the Society members. But we decided to carry on and one of the members gave us a lesson. We are to be taught gratis if the Technical College does not charge for the room.

Sunday, 21 November

Fire-watched with M. again. We reviewed all the girls and women we knew who were getting out of war work. A. (40), ex-teacher, now married, who, when asked to do something, gave out ration books for a few weeks in the summer and has since rested calmly on her laurels. She has a char, no children and her husband is out all day. B. (34 and childless) has never had an interview [for national service]. C., in her early twenties, does nothing at all, simply stays at home to help mother – mother being very well known and influential. (Why are tribunals made up of local people? There's bound to be wire pulling.) D. (44) twice found jobs by the Labour Exchange and twice explained she has been working for two years. E., her sister (28), no children, doing nothing whatever, never been asked to do anything. F., G. and H. in their late forties never troubled to register.

We talked of people we knew to whom the war was a tiresome nuisance, and those to whom it was a heaven sent blessing because it gave them a regular income. This led to M. telling of her Vicar saying someone had told him that forty years ago men had to bring up families on 28s per week, but he could not credit it. When M. pointed out that 28s forty years ago was a wage not attained by many, 20s would have been more frequent and 15s very common, he was dumb-founded. He then said he couldn't imagine how men were raising families on £4 per week; they must be paying 20s to 25s for rent and rates alone. M. said she was so disgusted at this ignorance of facts (who of *his* parishioners live in houses with combined rent and rates [of] 25s?) that she did not reply. I said soothingly (?) that he must be excused, having come to religious work by way of Osborne [Royal Naval College on the Isle of Wight] and a naval officer's way of life; and anyway it was the Bishop's fault for planting a man with such a back-ground in a working class district. M. (surprisingly for one so devout and 'church-minded') stuck to it that a parson ought to know or make it in his way to find out how his flock really did live.

M. said (apropos of naval officers) that the real ones were riddled with snobbery; that the temporary ones (like her brother), although supposedly equal, were jolly well made to know they were jolly well not.

Saturday, 27 November

Not a single customer has mentioned the Berlin raids [four had been made on the German capital within a week]. But they have been very voluble over the very fat bacon and the dark raisins (they seem to think light ones are better for some reason) and concerned over oranges for Christmas.

Monday, 29 November

To the WVS to a pie supper which was to be brought from the Municipal Canteen but which never came owing to the thick fog. We sat round the fire waiting until 9 o'clock, discussing spiritualism and table-lifting and fortune telling. Most of them, being chapelgoers, professed not to believe in anything of the sort, but each either said they had seen a table lifted (one said she had seen it go up to the mantel shelf and fetch a glass of beer!) or had had a dream which came true or had their fortune truly forecast. One described the similar dreams her son and she frequently had though miles apart.

Then the chairlady read out that we had donated 10 guineas to the prisoners of war, and everyone sat back and smirked and looked self-satisfied, although the whole of that sum was raised by the sale of toys which my sister made and gave.

They think, evidently, that threepence each every time we meet, about once a month, enables us to work wonders.

The unfairness of this war strikes me more and more; that some have to give up all and others are untouched – even their imagination is unstirred.

Tuesday, 7 December

To the Esperanto Class. Only six attended. The Headmaster came in and remarked on the smallness of the class. We pleaded that influenza was keeping some away. He then said we might try it until after Xmas. Our President was very bitter about Churchill's boosting Basic English.*

Monday, 13 December

Heard various scathing remarks about the will of old Mr W., the local millowner. Auntie said he had minded to leave his brass well in the family and none to the people who had earned it for him. She recalled that once in the 'depression' she went into the office with 10s 3d which represented a week's hard work (she had very poor work in her loom) and asked one of the young Mr Ws if he considered that a fair week's wage for a fair week's work. He said he would look into the matter and shortly after went to her loom gate with 4s 3d which she said they must have been collecting for such an occasion for it was composed entirely of sixpences and three-pences, all worn quite smooth. Mrs D. says the gardener who worked for Miss D. W. (now famous as a Whitby fisherman)

* This was a simplified 850-word version of English devised by linguist Charles K. Ogden in the 1930s, and seen as a competitor to Esperanto as a prospective universal language.

refused to wash floors as part of his duties, and was shortly afterwards mysteriously called up.

The local mill-owner under discussion was John Ely Walker, of Knowle House in Mirfield, who had died on 24 October at the age of ninety-six. His prominence was such that the Dewsbury Reporter *devoted all of page 3 (excepting advertisements) of its issue for 30 October 1943 to highly respectful and celebratory accounts of both his long life and the funeral service held three days earlier in Ravensthorpe Congregational Church. He was a 'captain of industry', with mills in Mirfield, Dewsbury Moor, and Whitney, Oxfordshire, 'which constitute one of the largest, if not the largest, group of rug and blanket mills in the country' (James Walker & Son). His Low Mills in Dewsbury Moor were less than a quarter mile from where Kathleen lived and worked. He was 'one of the influential personalities of this district'. In the newspaper's brief reference to his relations with labour, it was said that he had found 'work for many hundreds of work people. Moreover, he was a considerate employer who earned the respect and esteem of those who worked for the company.' (This language was less effusive and more pro forma than in other parts of the obituary.) Mr Walker's will, proved 3 December and thus just recently known about, left an estate with a net value of £130,000, to be executed by his two eldest sons, both blanket manufacturers. This substantial sum was roughly 650 times the annual income of the average West Yorkshire working-class family. All the beneficiaries of his will were members of his family; he left nothing to charities or the local community.*

The 'Miss D. W.' referred to by Mrs D. – 'famous as a Whitby fisherman' – was Dora M. Walker, a daughter of the deceased and the author of several works dealing with Whitby's seamen and fishermen, with whom she had a strong affinity. They Labour Mightily: A Tale of Inshore Fishing in War and Peace *(London and Hull: A. Brown, 1947) included two sketches first published in the* Dewsbury Observer *in 1932–33 and a broadcast from June 1940. A 1933 photograph of her and her father in a Whitby-built boat faces page 16 and one of her with five crew of a fishing boat faces page 31. Her other post-war publications included* Freemen of the Sea *(1951), an account of the lives and stories of mariners and fishermen,* The Panorama of Whitby Shipping *(1960), and* Whitby Shipping *(1971). She was actively involved with men whose labouring lives were dependent on sailing the North Sea. These close connections between a woman from a wealthy mill-owning family and the seafarers of Whitby were undoubtedly exceptional. In later years she was Curator of Shipping Records and Models at the Whitby Museum.*

Tuesday, 14 December

Strange how the most conservative and prim and proper people are now uttering Socialistic phrases and airing quite revolutionary views. Whether it's the influence of Beveridge or of Russia or just that we have now 'evolved' to this stage, I often wonder. Anyhow, it all 'gives more spice' to life.

Sunday, 19 December

Waiting for the bus I listened to the conversation of a group of women, one of whom had just been to purchase a Noah's ark, second hand. She said her sister had bought a doll's pram secondhand last year for £2 10s. This year they were asking £8 and £10 and she thought that too much. Yes, agreed another, I would pay £4 10s but no more. I think people are profiteering. Yes, said a third, four pounds is enough for a secondhand toy.

All this without batting an eyelid. They were better class working women, and I am jolly well sure even if they were getting plenty of money just now they could not afford such sums. But they would pay it to be equal or better than their neighbours. There is no snobbery so bitter as the snobbery of the 'respectable' working class.

Thursday, 23 December

Very irritable this evening through (1) being overtired with shop work, (2) wondering if the baker *will* deliver all the bread he promised tomorrow and how I shall placate customers if he does not, (3) reading the whole of *The Brothers Karamazov* [by Fyodor Dostoyevsky, 1880] this week when I am too tired to take it in, (4) eating too many mince pies, (5) having to listen to R. Frankan's show which is the BBC's prizest flop up to now. Customers have been enquiring for mincemeat for weeks and we have replied they must not hope for it. All three wholesalers warned us there would be none for us and the wireless said there would not be enough for all. Then the D. B. Company delivered a huge jar (6½ lbs) and Bert said what the devil was he to do with that among fifty housewives. Margaret said 'give it to me' and took it. Bert said alright but if anymore came in to make up a respectable quantity he must have it back. Luckily none has come. We have had many awkward moments because Broughs [provisioners, at 27 Westgate], the Co-op [which had numerous branches], and other multiple shops have been *teeming* with mincemeat, no restriction so far as their customers' jam ration would allow. *Our* customers have even swapped their customers' jam for mincemeat. We can only reply that as usual the big shops get it and the small ones go

without. We are so indignant that we usually arouse our customers' sympathy and then all is well. But it is very wearing,
this constant explaining, explaining. And besides it *is* unfair!
This time we were able to offer soothing syrup in the shape
of apples to come. Meanwhile we enjoy the mincemeat without one prick of conscience. As Margaret remarked when
Bert gave her a piece of ham to boil for Xmas morning, 'It's
our ham, isn't it? What's the use of keeping a shop if you
don't have what's going?'

Friday, 24 December

Safely through the day at last and able to shut up at usual
time, half past six. The rush we expected in the evening came
earlier in the day. All bread safely disposed of (8 dozen large
loaves, 34 dozen teacakes ordered and no mishaps except that
I forgot Mrs S. and had to rob our own bread ration for her, but
Margaret says she will bake a couple of loaves on Monday).
The apples were not eaters but Bramleys and so big we had to
give one per family but everyone was so pleased to have even
one apple they never murmured. They one and all seemed to
intend to eat them raw, and did not consider cooking them to
make them go round better. We are now at 7.30 (washed and
dressed for holiday!) listening to a Dorothy Sayers' Nativity
Play [*He That Should Come*]. Bert is fretting for carols. He is not
in the least religious and usually has no patience with hymn
singing (he prefers Lovejoy) but he clings fanatically to the
things of his boyhood [in the 1890s] and carols are 'the thing'
for Xmas Eve, just as, because his mother always had some
new adornment for Xmas, we must not put down the rug we
made two months ago until tonight.

Xmas Day

Had a decent day though quiet. Breakfast at 10.30 off boiled ham. Visited Cousin Edie to cheer her loneliness. She was still indignant over the parcel of groceries which her workmates had made up and sent to her. She considers it 'charity', as she considers the supplementary pension her aged mother is receiving. I think she must be the last 'independent' soul in England. Everyone else has got into the way of taking everything that's going. The Atlantic Charter [August 1941, which stressed individual rights] will make scroungers of us all.

Duck for tea. And spice cake (without cheese) because we gave customers extra for Xmas and ran short. Then listened to the wireless, the only thing which pleased being [Lewis Carroll's] *Alice in Wonderland*. Discussed the question of 'white lies', which was put to the *Brains Trust* the other week. Agreed that truthfulness is impossible in a shop these days and that those Spartans who would not lie to save their lives should spend a winter behind a grocer's counter.

Monday, 3 January, 1944

Bert says he will take the wireless extension upstairs and then he can listen when he goes early to bed. 'Yes,' I said, 'and then we can lie in on Sundays and hear the news instead of having to get up for fear of missing something.' Bert sneered. 'One of these mornings you will come down and find the Invasion has taken place, and you've *missed* it.' This waiting [for the Second Front] is nearly like a woman waiting for her baby – tension and weariness and thought of coming misery and pain and hoping for glorious relief from fear afterwards. Though goodness knows we have no need to fear – we have no part to play in the war and no one to worry for. Our role seems to be that of onlooker. I cannot when I think forward, which I find myself constantly doing, imagine our lives, which have not been 'upheaved' by the war, being greatly disturbed by the peace. There will be no 'rationing' to worry over and no black-out but otherwise things will remain as they are. This is not a satisfying thought in a world war but that is our circumstance.

Many people seem to think something may happen any minute. But the more sober ones think a movement is likely in the spring, when the bad weather may be over. As one housewife (40) remarked, 'They'll have to be sure and be quite ready *this* time. They'll not be able to retreat as before.'

Friday, 7 January

Just turned on the news to hear about the new invention [jet propulsion] as Bert opened the shop. He told a man who came for cigs and he must have heard it at 7 for he said without any emotion 'Ay, we've been working on it for ten year.' Not another person mentioned it all day. I began to wonder if it is so wonderful after all, for the *Daily Mail* pushes the news into a minor column on the front page, continued to back, after the BBC sounded the trumpets so loudly. So glad it's a *British* invention and not American – we should never hear the last of it.

Saturday, 8 January

Auntie came in excitedly this afternoon to ask if we had been out to see the new aeroplane which had just left a trail of vapour in the sky. Then old Mrs M. came in and said that a machine had been doing that sign – writing in the sky. These are all the remarks I have heard about the new aeroplane being over here. Every time I hear a plane I run to the door but there is nothing but 'old fashioned stuff' in view.

People keep coming to see if the oranges have come yet and going away with pained expressions. 'Another wireless promise,' they say. When I point out that they have up to April to expect them, they laugh sarcastically and say 'Ay, if we *do*.' Strange how the bread trade has declined since Xmas. The baker reports slack trade all round and the yeast man says he is selling no yeast to the bake houses. What do people eat during these slumps? You'd think they *must* have bread.

Sunday, 9 January

A man in the shop yesterday, when we had the 8 o'clock news on, 'It's t'Russians 'ats winning this war, as per usual. They're real 'uns, aren't they? It'll be all over before we begin.' Which set me wondering what *would* happen if Germany did crack up before we got on to the Continent. The Russians would regard *themselves* as the liberators of Europe and what then? There's one thing – we shall have a shock when we *do* get inside Europe and see what a state the people are in. *They* won't have much interest [in] or energy for a brave new world.

Monday, 10 January

To the WVS to hear a lady from Leeds appealing for more Street Group Leaders [i.e., members of the Housewives' Service]. When she finished there was a stony silence and then Mrs C. said she was afraid there was no hope of business on Dewsbury Moor; the folk here wanted something giving, not having to pay out. The lady said we should not be asking for anything; we were doing people a kindness really and they would bless us after the war. The only Savings Collector laughed derisively and said 'They never get to the Certificate

Making bread and rationed goods stretch was a constant concern.
As part of a study carried out by the Wartime Social Survey,
housewives were given a poster of sample portion sizes, seen here
on the kitchen wall. As the mother cuts bread for her child,
she will check the size of the slice against the chart.
Photograph © IWM D18844

stage. When they have a few stamps they want to cash them.'
The lady said we mustn't mind that; we must be prepared for
disappointment and rebuffs. Mrs C. said she had had enough
collecting for the Red Cross. At one house the woman asked if
the envelope had to be sealed, and on Mrs C. saying she could
please herself she said, 'Well you *look* honest. You don't *look*
as if you would take anything.' Mrs B. said yes, people were
sickening; some of her penny-a-weekers which she collected
monthly always looked at the calendar to see whether there
were four or five Fridays in the month and paid accordingly.
Finally it was decided that we should think it over and the
local Organiser should come and see us in three weeks. When
the party had gone there were general murmurs of disapproval.
The meeting had no faith in Dewsbury Moor's generosity. We
said we should just have to form a group among ourselves,
and get stamps when we had a meeting. I did not volunteer
as Collector because I don't finish until 7 and I am nervous of
the blackout. A young married woman near here was molested
when crossing the road from her neighbour's to her own home.

Tuesday, 11 January

Went to the Sadler's Wells Opera *La Bohème*. The Empire
was packed. I know one bus conductress who was going three
times and another girl who is going every night. One of our
customers, definitely not a highbrow, went to see *The Barber of
Seville* on Monday and she was so charmed she is going again
to see *Madame Butterfly*. She said she wished she had taken
her eldest lad, who loves music. She said the gallery was full of
young girls and children but you could have heard a pin drop.
Much more popular than two years ago.

Wednesday, 12 January

Went to see [*The Life and Death of*] *Colonel Blimp*. Fairly enjoyable; the costume and colouring was delightful although the length might have been cut a bit.*

Saturday, 15 January

More excitement and indignation over the blowing up of the oranges than I have heard for many a day [time bombs had been placed in ships carrying oranges from Spain]. I laughed at first – it seemed so daft – but quickly found I must not be so frivolous. Oranges are serious business. Said one woman, 'Suppose a child got a bomb in one or those oranges. Aren't they devils?' I said 'Suppose a poor shopkeeper got one in a case, you mean!' 'Well, anyway, that Franco [fascist leader of Spain] is as bad as Hitler. They say he is in German pay. Whatever will they think of next? Even oranges!' Even oranges! This is a twisting the lion's tale indeed.

Tuesday, 18 January

No one has remarked on the strange behaviour of Russia but Mr C., a traveller, when I asked him what he thought of the *Pravda* affair, said, well, he had expected we *should* have trouble with Russia, and we should probably have a great deal more. Meanwhile I am wondering if the Poland affair has anything

---

* *The Life and Death of Colonel Blimp* was impressively produced and photographed and, unusually for a feature film, over two and a half hours in length. Its perspective on the British army was less than respectful, which did not endear it to the Government (Churchill tried to suppress it), and an 'enemy alien' who featured in the story was portrayed sympathetically.

to do with it; perhaps they are offended at our offering to help settle the dispute or perhaps our diplomats in Cairo are too la-di-di-da and they are offended. It all makes one uneasy.* Not even the return of Mr Churchill can quite compensate. Meanwhile the Second Front can get going now he is home [from Marrakesh, where he had been recuperating from a viral infection]! I suppose we have been waiting for that!

Sunday, 23 January

Whatever is coming over us? New Year's Honours for char-women and now George Formby [popular comic actor and singer-songwriter] broadcasting a *Postscript* [radio talk] and doing it jolly well. He was sincere, which is a rare and delight-ful broadcasting virtue.

Monday, 24 January

Daylight lengthening in the evening but hardly moves in the morning. How anxiously we watch it and pore over each day's timetable. What is our interest in a Second Front compared with our impatience for returning summer.

Wednesday, 26 January

Queued fifteen minutes for oranges, the first time in my life. Do not enjoy rubbing up close to my fellows. An old lady in

---

* *Pravda*, the official Soviet newspaper, had printed allegations, attributed to sources in Cairo, that two prominent Britons were having secret peace talks with Ribbentrop, the Nazi Foreign Minister. This was a time when Moscow was disput-ing its border with Poland, which it wanted to push further west, against (of course) the wishes of the Poles.

front said she was getting oranges for her daughter but could not afford them herself on old age pension. I take these tales, which I hear frequently, with a pinch of salt. Many old people spend on 'luxuries' and then grumble because they haven't got enough for necessities. Admitted they don't have an overplus but they are certainly in better case than men I know who are trying to bring up a family of five or six on £3 15s a week.

Thursday, 27 January

Oranges came today. Three cases. We got out two bucketfuls of bad ones. One woman said 'Are these what have been lying at the bottom of the sea?' No mention yet of the new landing in Italy [at Anzio, south of Rome]. Wardens tonight to test our gas masks. Agreeably surprised that ours were in such good condition after five years. Said that many were in a dreadful state; they had seen one today full of oil, one full of whitewash and one full of potato peelings. They said how disagreeable and awkward many people were. One woman said she would never put one of them things on, gas or no gas.

Monday, 31 January

To WVS. The War Savings 'Campaign' resulted in one woman promising to sell stamps when we had a meeting and among her immediate neighbours. We talked of the Japanese prisoners. Several said indignantly that the Government should never have made the disclosures. All said they were rather their boys were dead outright than in Jap hands. One woman, whose son was a prisoner in Italy, said he had never received a parcel in two years she had been sending [them] but now he was in Germany he hoped to do. He said the Germans treated them much better than the Italians; they were warmer and cleaner, had had more exercise. He was helping a local bricklayer, though some were in the copper mines. They were near Berlin and had air raid shelters. Two or three said they understood the Germans treated prisoners better than the Italians did. 'It's time it were over,' said one passionately. 'Look at money 'ats being spent every day. Look at planes, lost. They said Hitler had no-an [none]. And skies swarming with 'em. It's time we got over there and finished it.' There was a chorus of approval.

Someone said something about the boys in the mines. Opinions seemed divided. Some said that it was hard on some boys who weren't used to a rough life.* When someone protested about the money paid there was a general exclamation they shouldn't allow t'women to charge so much for board and lodgings. One said they say they won't work when they get down but this was indignantly shouted down. 'We shouldn't say that. Give t'lads a chance. They're new t'job. It's not fair to say they won't work because they want more spending brass.' One said, 'Well, anyway, miners deserve all they get. They were thought nowt on before. When they were coming out wi' 2s a day, nobody worried about them. *My* husband wor in t'pit and he says his sympathies are with the miners always. They deserve all they can get. Let some o' t'kid-gloved uns go down and we shall soon have changes in t'mining industry.' This woman also said that some union official said he was

* Because of the severe shortage of mine-workers, a new policy, agreed to in November 1943, allowed for compulsory recruitment into the mines. A proportion of men aged 18–25, on being called up for national service, were mandated for pit work, and at least 10 per cent and as many as 20 per cent of these conscripts were randomly assigned to the mines. Those compelled to work in the pits became known as 'Bevin Boys', thanks to the surname of the Minister of Labour and National Service.

sick of the name of [Ernest] Bevin. This also led to choruses of approval.

There was general agreement that we should have gas attacks.

Then talk turned to being cold in bed. One said she wore to sleep trousers from a pyjama set, a thick nightdress, a wool coat, a wool bonnet and had two hot water bottles; another had pyjamas, tied round the ankles, long wool stockings above the knee, a wool coat, a flannel to lay her face on (*and* a husband!); another wore a bonnet, two wool coats, a nightdress, a vest, bed socks and a bag for her legs made from a wool skirt, and two hot water bottles; another wore a cap, a cardigan, two vests, nightdress and bed socks and one hot water bottle. The interesting point was that all these were comparatively young women. The older ones derided them and said they made themselves soft and said hot water bottles were 'weakening'. Mass Observation should conduct an enquiry into bed-time habits. I know of a young man who has a soother to go to bed with – he has never broken the childish habit. That is true because he bought the soothers off my cousin, a dozen at once, and (being a single young man) apparently thought he should explain what he did with them. I also was told of a man who slept always with a rag doll after his wife died.

Sunday, 6 February

Young N. F. to tea. She is stationed at Tadcaster now. She had scathing things to say of the NAAFI – that they did not do their job as they should, and should not make all that profit, and that the YWCA and YMCA are doing the job they should do. She likes Army life and is undecided about her life afterwards, although she has a good shop job to go to. She thinks she won't like the standing, for now she has a cushy office and seems to make tea all day long.

Wednesday, 9 February

Down to breakfast at 8 o'clock. Bread and marmalade. Gave Bert his breakfast. Then swept and dusted before Margaret and Ma came down at 9.15. Was going to help Ma complete the *People* crossword but were unusually busy in the shop for Wednesday so she did it herself. J. H. came with sweets at 11 a.m. for which we were thankful as we were quite without on starting the new [points] Period – always a calamity because the kiddies take their sweet coupons elsewhere. We closed at 1 o'clock for half day. I had already washed and dressed for going out. Swallowed some dinner (minced meat and greens and potatoes, and milk pudding) and went off at 1.30. Called at Library and got *Three Guineas* – V. Woolf, *The Playboy of the Western World* [by John Millington Synge, 1907], a book about old Wakefield, and a Baroness Orczy [best known for her 'Scarlet Pimpernel' novels] for Ma. Then to the hairdresser to have a trim and set. Wish Joyce would come back from Land Army. This girl [her new hairdresser] messes about and chips and chops – why don't these folk learn their job? Then glanced in at the Make and Mend Exhibition, and got two bars chocolate at Woolworths, walked all round Smith's Bookshop, nothing doing, very cold so into pictures to see [J. B. Priestley's] *When We Are Married*. The supporting picture [*Colt Comrades*] was tripe. The news feature was at least two years old (talked of the French Vichy being in possession of Tunis and the siege of Malta) and the star not up to the stage version. Syd Howard [born in Leeds] billed but not a very big part. Home to tea, fried frozen fish and a mince pie at 7 o'clock. Then Ma and I had a quiet evening (no wireless thank heaven). I read V. Woolf, did a little writing. Off to bed at 9.30 when Margaret and Bert returned.

Thursday, 10 February

Just listening to the broadcast news of the Germans occupying the Cistercian monastery in Italy [Monte Cassino] and that the English did not know whether to destroy it and the Germans or preserve an ancient building [see below, 17 February]. Margaret and and Ma violently support the destruction of the monastery, saying that no building, however ancient, is worth the life of one soldier. Margaret adds that after this war there will be a different spirit; we shall think less of ancient buildings and more of modern human beings. Old things are alright and perhaps very interesting, but that didn't mean we need worship them. I agree that the monastery must be destroyed but feel doubtful about this new spirit abroad.

Friday, 11 February

Our tobacco traveller remarked on the great rise in the sales of snuff. We ourselves sell a fair amount, practically all to women, and not all old women. One or two send the children for it; one always asks for a 'little brose'; one always pretends she wants it for her mother-in-law and the mother-in-law always pretends she wants it for the daughter-in-law, so presumably they are both 'addicts'; one motions mysteriously; and one and all put it away hastily and furtively. So I conclude they are all ashamed of the habit.

Thursday, 17 February

What a to-do in the House of Lords. It's time old Lang retired from public life if he is so out of touch. I agree with Lord Latham that a building is not worth one of our soldiers' lives. There seems to be a lot of tender consciences over this Italy which most of us have never seen and are never likely to.* As Margaret says, why should our lads be sacrificed to preserve the playgrounds and 'cultural' shrines of such as the Archbishop? It leaves me cold this concern for beauty (which I admit is valuable and worth seeing and which I shall probably regret all my life that I cannot see) when human beings are in question. I never remember the long years of unemployment and misery raising such a storm in the House of Lords. There has been all this commotion about the Benedictine Monastery and now the Pope is protesting about something or other. Not all his followers are of his opinion, for an old lady, a Catholic all her life, said to me today she couldn't understand what we were hesitating about, costing our lads' lives every day. I suppose her country and patriotism comes before her religious scruples as is the case with the Pope. He never raised his voice in protest throughout this war until now, or throughout the Abyssinian oppression.

* Seventy-nine-year-old Cosmo Gordon Lang was former Archbishop of Canterbury (1930–1942); on his retirement he was elevated to the peerage and sat as Baron Lang until his death in 1945. The debate concerned the preservation of works of historical and artistic value, mainly in Italy, as the Allied forces advanced, notably the legitimacy of the bombing of the abbey of Monte Cassino, thought by some to be a sanctuary for German troops, which resulted in the wholesale destruction of the monastery's historic buildings. The action was even controversial within the Allied military command.

Monday, 21 February

The WVS tea party at L.'s Cafe went off very well. Eighteen of us sat down to fish and bread and *butter* and scones, and cake and pineapple and cherries. Then we went to the pictures. G. H. says he was in a Wardens' Post the other day when a midwife rushed in and asked for a doctor to be phoned for but they had no directory or list of nearest doctors and a policeman seemed as helpless. G. H. happened to be able to give the woman the number she wanted. He says he would raise Cain if he was in charge there.

Saturday, 26 February

We are looking with alarm at our diminishing coals. All the summer's surplus has vanished in a month. By the end of March we shall be like so many more around here, quite without, which will be a new experience for me; I suppose I am lucky to reach 38 [her next birthday] and never have been hungry or cold indoors. There seems to be a slight hardening of the former sympathetic attitude towards the miners, but most of the grumbling is against the mythical 'they' (in other words the Government) who are responsible for so much discomfort. My sister Margaret has no sympathy with the miners; she says no strikes are justified in wartime, much less at a critical time like this; that the miners, when they get more wage, simply play half the week to avoid more income tax. The yeast man, who comes from Pontefract, agrees with her and cited instances of having rows himself in the pub with miners over the subject. He says the money that is being swindled out of the Government is scandalous. He gave an instance of a friend who went down a pit (pit named) and saw new machinery buried out of sight until after the war, so the pit owners could claim help. He said there was no remedy while so many owners and shareholders were MPs.

It is a vast and irritating subject. Whatever the rights and wrongs of the miners, it's no consolation to me to sit shivering and think that they have good fires and abundance of coal whatever happens.

Tuesday, 29 February

Mrs H. came in very upset because she had read in the *Daily Herald* that some expert had said that national flour will not keep very long – it starts getting maggotty. She said she couldn't finish her breakfast. Have heard no other comment on this. Many women say that home baked bread is much better than the baker's – they seem to think it is doctored at the baker's.

Thursday, 9 March

Rumours and hints and whispers of the invasion increase. One customer said that the 18th was definitely fixed for the great move and another just afterwards told me that there would be no invasion; the Germans had had enough with the bombing and would soon be calling for a halt. But one and all say fervently 'I wish it were over.'

Saturday, 11 March

What are we to make of the miners? Are they just irresponsible? They remember past years of neglect and indifference and all is mixed and muddled with present grievances. Very old chickens are now coming home to roost. Z. B. [her sister-in-law] not very satisfied with her new job. As one of Bevin's part-time workers, she is supposed to work only thirty hours but, she says, the firm is expecting her to take full charge of all the books, which is a full-time job, and are only offering her half-time pay. As she says, she is only filling time; her husband can quite well support her, and although she is willing to do her part-time bit (which is more than most married women she knows are), she objects to being exploited. A factory worker wouldn't stand for it for an instant!

Sunday, 12 March

And now, just when I am fairly launched on my Esperanto course, comes this news of the Basic English Boost [see above, 7 December 1943]. This is some of Winnie's doings, I am sure. If this isn't Imperialism ... !

Tuesday, 4 April

People around here seem to be strangely reserved about the strike [of miners, which had started in mid-March]. They seem to carefully avoid expressing an opinion. Of course, in a district like this, where everyone has someone who is or was a miner, or knows someone who is, it is easy to tread on someone's corns. I would take the general attitude to be sympathy with the miners mixed with some mild reproach. From what people do *not* say, I guess they feel the Government must be asking too much or the men would not have come out. At any rate have heard no one (save my sister who thinks any strike in wartime is treason) blame the miners for not obeying their union leaders. When I complain in the shop that we have no fire the only response is, 'Ay, it's a do, isn't it?' The only pit worker's wife I have talked to made no comment beyond being very pleased that she had money to tide them over a good few weeks, not like some who have nothing. She knew one chap who said the first day 10d was all he and his wife had between them. But I have an idea this woman did not approve of this unofficial strike. She said they would not go in before Easter.

Have waked every morning this week thinking of the strike and this morning awakened myself by exclaiming 'The trains, what about coal for the trains?'

Disputes and discontent were rife in the Yorkshire coalfields. This unofficial strike by 1,500 Dewsbury miners was in fact about to end, partly because of the stern intervention of the Minister of Labour, and Shaw Cross and Thornhill Collieries resumed work by the middle of the week. Several other local pits had also been 'out', along with 90,000 other miners throughout the county. The mood of resentment among the miners was palpable. 'The miners feel that their work is vital and valuable only when it is scarce, and that at other times his is a job no one wants. At a recent miners' meeting of Dewsbury district the bad feelings prevailing in the coalfields was evidenced. The men said, in no uncertain tones, that whatever they get they have to begin by begging for it, then negotiating, then threatening, and then striking, and yet the public refuses to take a sympathetic view of their case. Workers in almost every other industry receive increases or adjustments without these endeavours, but the miner finds himself given a £5-a-week minimum – and not many are getting the bare minimum – and within a short time a deduction is made from his earnings on the home coal question.' (Dewsbury District News, 15 April 1944, p. 7.)

The miners felt put upon, exploited, and their work devalued. They remembered well the working conditions of the 1920s and 1930s, and they feared a return to those conditions, and that they might be forced in the future to accept whatever they were offered. For while coal was seen as essential, no other Britons wanted to work in the mines, and young miners who had been called up in the Forces showed little enthusiasm for returning to work underground. Given these realities, it was reasonable to foresee an industrial culture in which the supposed free market would be actively overridden by state coercion, with miners on the losing side. The Government's key goal at this time was to maintain levels of coal production (they were in danger of falling) that would not undermine the war effort.

Kathleen's final words in her diary this day were:

Feel neither noble nor braced to face the trials promised us shortly. Only experience one vast and mounting mood of exasperation; what with waiting for the Second Front, and the prospect of yet another year without holiday and another blackout looming before us after all; and then all this wrangling in and out of Parliament; and the prospect of more and more rows when the war *is* over.

Monday, 10 April

Thought we were to spend Easter with an empty grate but our man brought us two bags of coal and so with two bags of wood we got and a few cinders we shall have a tolerable fire for a few days. But we used to think nothing of burning a ton in a month in winter. Mother feels the lack of fire dreadfully. It's hard on the old folk who have nothing to do but sit, when they have not the consolation of a fire.

Easter Monday has passed pleasantly with walks in the Park and reading and dozing. After dinner Bert complained he could not get a seat for people sunning themselves in the warm sunshine. They picnicked on the grass and altogether made a holiday at home of it.

Crow Nest Park, a short walk from Kathleen's shop and home, was the main site in Dewsbury for outdoor leisure and recreations, including wartime 'Holidays at Home'.
Photograph © The Francis Frith Collection

Tuesday, 11 April

Hiked nearly to Huddersfield with the 'Women's Bright Hour' from the Chapel. Nearly prostrated three of the older ladies (all over 70 with bad hearts) so that we had to put them on a bus.

Friday, 21, April

Siren last night, first since October. We all got up. Bert knocked next door but could not rouse them. We three and two wardens were only people in view during the half hour's alert. All over by 12.50. Bert grumbling because none of his party turned up – he does not yet know who is in his party. This morning it was amusing to question people – most had never heard it. Those who did had not got up with the exception of a woman alone with four little ones, and an old man who lives alone. Margaret and I recollected when we were going back to bed that we had both left a considerable sum of cash upstairs and our gas masks, and our decent clothes.

Tuesday, 25 April

Rumours increase. Most people think anything may happen anytime now. From a traveller we get word that a policeman told him of a convoy which took 4½ hours to pass him. Our window cleaner, who is also on NFS [National Fire Service], reports that only seven are left out of his company, the rest are off to Dover. Bert, wanting to return a wooden case to London, found that no goods whatever are being despatched south.

Bert also found at his Fire Service lectures that the whole section did not know half they were supposed to know and what they had been taught was all wrong. A new lecturer has discovered this. The old one has got a new *paid* post in Civil Defence. More is expected to come of this.

Everyone taken aback because there are no new taxes – especially on tobacco, although many pretend they are not [the Chancellor of the Exchequer had just announced his

Budget for the coming year]. One lady customer was very perturbed; she did not see how we were going to pay for the war this year if there were no new taxes. It took much explanation to convince her that all the old ones stood as before. Apparently she thought all taxes were cancelled every year and the Chancellor thought up new ones.

Sunday, 30 April

There was a pretty general belief around here that this weekend would be Invasion weekend. Several times customers have told me that 'the moon and tide will be just right on Saturday'.

Monday, 1 May

To the WVS. Very poor turn-up so we could not arrange the rota for duty if we had a blitz or if we had a batch of refugees from the South Coast. Our leader warned us they would be poor class. Groans. Margaret and I told of when we were at Wakefield in 1940 and had the Channel Island folk plumped on us [they were refugees]. How dirty and lazy they were and how the men got drunk and fought and rowed to get into the women, who were separated from them. This led to talk of sexual matters in our own district. There are seventeen unwanted babies at the present time in the Maternity Home, most of them of women whose soldier husbands had forgiven them but would not take the child. One member after another cites cases of unfaithfulness of married women, personally known to them, supposedly respectable people, and several spoke of disgusting conduct in public places or on private property. One said it was sickening the way very young boys and girls carried on in a field opposite her house in broad daylight. Someone said sarcastically 'They'd need talk about raising school age to eighteen,' and there were exclamations of derision. Also there was some sarcastic talk about raising soldiers' dependants' pay, and cries of 'They'll never want t'war to end. What about t'mothers? They're treated shamefully, far worse than t'last war.' One woman said the case which most riled her was when the soldier husband had forgiven and accepted the baby and the wife would be drawing 12s 6d allowance for it. 'And that comes out of respectable folk.'

Just a few days before, in her Directive Response for April 1944, Kathleen wrote of 'the large number of married women who are going off the rails. I am brought up against cases of "loose living" and unfaithfulness every day in the course of my shop duties. In almost every story married people – mostly married women with growing up families – are concerned. Not all can plead that their husbands are abroad. They are quite brazen about it; though not all as open as the one who told a friend of mine that when a woman had once known a man she couldn't keep off men and if her husband was not available someone else would do. The wonder is that some of them bother to get married at all. But I suppose there are monetary advantages – war and widows' pensions.' She returned to this theme in mid-April 1945. 'Morally things have deteriorated. There seems to be a general carelessness and indifference to public opinion. Great laxity among both married women and young girls. There are no soldiers billeted here now but American officers in Leeds seem to draw them to that city' (DR, February–March 1945).

Monday, 15 May

To the WVS. Our leader told us we were to have chevrons to wear when on parade, according to our length of service. Everyone mystified, and most were indignant at this waste of time and money. The leader said she had been told to tell us that a deputation had waited on the King about these chevrons and he had been graciously pleased to grant permission for us to wear them and we should think it an honour; but someone said she didn't think much of honours that had to be asked for. I thought it would be that Lady Iris Capell, who once lectured us [26 October 1942], who would be spending her time running round asking favours of Royalty. Everyone made fun and we called ourselves Corporals and Sergeants. Then the leader wanted to know how long we had been enrolled and everyone fell to arguing with each other, for the war has now been going on so long, I think they were all taken aback to consider when they began.

Thursday, 18 May

The siren went at 4.40 p.m. yesterday and all clear an hour later. There has been much discussion in the shop today whether it was an accident or a practice, but everyone seems convinced that it was not 'real', 'not in an afternoon!'

9

Bursts of Activity

June–September 1944

D-DAY [Tuesday, 6 June]

The German retirement from Rome without a fight greatly puzzled us. Margaret expected the city to go off with a bang when our troops were well in – she seemed to picture a vast mined booby-trap. But nothing happened, only we seem to be left with a large baby to hold – in the shape of providing food for the millions.

Then during the 8 o'clock news this morning [BBC announcer] Frank Phillips (was it?) threw in a brief remark that the Germans said their naval forces were engaged with our landing craft. 'It sounds as though they have begun,' I said to Bert, but doubtfully. Perhaps it was just a fake or a practice. I told a man who came into the shop just after but he said 'Oh', uninterestedly. Other things occupied my mind. I had to go down to the bank by the 9.40 bus. Waiting for the bus several women joined me. One said 'Well, it's begun! Eisenhower [has] just been speaking. And they are speaking foreign to occupied countries.' A young woman said, 'Well, now for the killing. Our —— was there when they tried to get on Crete. He saw them being brought off again. He knows what it's like. He said that was nowt to this.' I hesitated whether to slip back home to put on the wireless, but the bus came. Inside I sat next a friend. She said 'Well, they've begun at last. There'll be some lads slaughtered by now. I'm just going to the station to see if my lodger can get back to London.'

At the bank the entire staff were at their desks but listening to a wireless or talking together in undertones. (I remember I had time to wonder resentfully if it was there always or just brought for the occasion.) The girl at the counter apologised for keeping me waiting, and asked if I had anyone 'there'. 'No,' I said, 'we are among the fortunate ones. It must be dreadful for those who have.' 'Neither have we,' she said, 'but we shall all be in it now.'

I went to Smith's for little pin flags but could get none. Back on the bus spoke to no one, but alighting, someone coming up B—— Lane shrieked my name urgently. It was a woman to whom I only say 'Good morning'. 'They've invaded,' she panted as she came up with me, very excited. 'Six o'clock this morning. It's all been on the wireless.' I appeared to be surprised, not wishing to disappoint her by saying I knew already. I went in home and found Bert standing in the living room doorway keeping one eye reluctantly on the shop and all his attention on the wireless. Bella Hill had run in after I left to tell them to put it on. By this time there was nothing to listen to. They were all three excited: Margaret and Bert keeping up running remarks, but Ma went very quiet and though I kept drawing her attention to Ann

Driver [presenter of the BBC's *Music and Movement* radio programme for schools] drilling the infants, she obviously heard nothing.

I tore off the edge of the *Daily Mail* and, with paste and pins and coloured pencils with which we cancel ration books, made little flags for our wall map which has been hung in readiness a fortnight. Bert complained they hurt his finger as he pushed them in. I tried with drawing pins and then a few large-headed fancy pins. I gave up trying to make 'Union Jacks' and 'Stars and Stripes' and just put British Empire and U.S.A. We squabbled where they should go. We didn't know where exactly to put Russian flags so left them in a heap in White Russia for the time being. Two women came into the shop before dinner who 'had not heard the great news'. Everyone else who came in was greatly excited and could talk of nothing else. I heard more talk of the war today and more interest taken in it than at any time since we came here in 1941. Most mentioned that we should have a lot of casualties and should have to expect 'him' to give us something back now. Mrs M. said she had just visited her sister, who had a boy who was probably in it, but found her not as upset as she expected. Mrs L. said the news made her poorly – it made her feel awful – but she cheered up a little when we showed her the map.

Later. Bert keeps bringing customers in to look at the map as if it was his idea to have one. He was irritated because he could not find Normandy on the map – obviously thinking it was a town. We listened at 5 to the Forces Programme and at 6 to the other.

At 7.30 Margaret and I went to a lecture at the WVS. A warden was talking to us. He said he would not keep us long as of course we should want to hear the King at 9 as he did himself. He asked us to co-operate with the wardens by keeping open house for air raid casualties and so get them off the streets until they could be attended to. He told us of some grim experiences in danger towns and warned us that Hitler would not 'sit down' under this pummelling, and then finished the lecture by demonstrating phosgene and mustard gas.

We got home at 9 o'clock and heard the King, and the news and exciting commentaries by the Correspondents. The Archbishop we found too tedious and shut him off. 'He's too dreary,' said Margaret. 'Yes,' said Ma, 'but not so bad as that awful chanting, intoning on this afternoon.' I agreed and said, 'If our lads went in dirging like that, we should lose the war this week.'

To bed at 10 o'clock. And so ends this eventful, historical day. We feel excited and happy, and yet grave and sad – all at once. But above all relieved as if something had been taken off our chests so that we could breathe better.

Wednesday, 7 June

Everyone surprised that we have got onto the Continent so quickly, but convinced that Hitler has something up his sleeve. Heard many *wish* that the war would be won before blackout time but say they were prepared for another winter, and only one said September would see us through with the war. Not quite so many war references and more sober toned but still a good many compared with past months. People seem elated because we have 'taken them by surprise' but not puzzled (as I am) that this could be when all those ships were crowded in so small a space on Hitler's doorstep.

Thursday, 8 June

To the first of the meetings for Fireguard training, to which I have been 'conscripted'. A packed room – 96 women altogether. There were three instructors to introduce the unpleasant subject and reassure us that we had nothing to be alarmed about – we should not be called away from home. They were so soothing I felt that we were frantic sheep being soothed before the slaughter. I came away convinced there was a catch in the affair – a snag that will come to light in due course.* In the meantime B. H. is 'having eggs' because someone has told her that she will have to crawl on her hands and knees in a lot of smoke while men look on and laugh. She is regretting having given away her slacks, and is already planning to miss that night. Margaret says she never heard anyone so daft and wouldn't a couple of bombs on Dewsbury Moor brighten the ideas of quite a lot of folk, and teach them the war is still on. The best part of the day for me is going to be the war Correspondents' reports after the 9 o'clock news. These are thrilling and incredible. I am still amazed that we were ever able to get a foothold at all.

Oh, if the weather would only clear. Last week we were messily irritated with its unsummerlike behaviour. Now we anxiously watch every variation – distrust every cloudy sky and rising breeze.

* With the successful opening of a Second Front in France, there were fears (with reason) of German retaliation. In a few days this occurred, and from 12 June V1 missiles (aka pilotless planes or doodlebugs or flying bombs or buzz bombs) were launched against the South-East and caused widespread terror through the summer. They prompted the final major evacuation of the war: see below, 12 August 1944 and following remarks.

Monday, 12 June

To Esperanto class where we were engaged with adverbial participles. From discussion of the many forms and tenses of the verb we passed on to wondering how Basic English dealt with some of them and if all forms of even the commoner verbs were included in the 850 basic words. If so, there will be more than 850 of them alone; if not, how do they get the language over to foreigners? Mr C. said they avoided many words altogether – for instance, no one could love or die in Basic English, which raised a laugh but sounds incredible. Our Czech member says they take this international language business much more seriously on the Continent.

Wednesday, 14 June

To Bradford for the day where we found their 'Salute the Soldier' week in progress. In the Park we found selling booths and guns and soldiers but only a small crowd owing to the intense cold and frequent rain. We joined a crowd round the Cartwright Hall and found the Princess Royal [Mary, daughter of King George V] was expected. We waited to see her and were struck by her graceful bearing and the fact that she wore no makeup. She made the wives of the officials clustered round her look insignificant and yet she was only in Khaki and they bedecked with furs and pearls. Finished up the day at the 'Prince's' to see [the popular French actress] Alice Delysia in a French comedy [a play, *French for Love*]. The first time I have had a day off since September.

Friday, 16 June

Many comments about Hitler's new weapon [the V1 flying bomb]. 'He's always thinking of something fresh.' 'They must be clever.' 'He's always one ahead of us.' 'We shall soon find a way of stopping them.' 'It's not a new thing. We discovered it in 1930.' (Various dates given for this 'discovery' by various people – from 1917 to 1939.) 'Saving pilots, you see.' 'They discovered they could do it at the Schneider Cup Races [international aerial speed contests held between the wars] and said bombs could be dropped by wireless. And then we let Jerry pinch the idea. Always too late.'

Monday, 26 June

To the WVS. A lady telling us of the Prisoners of War Society. Very interesting. Hope this is the last year for these poor men.

Cherbourg still not captured in spite of everyone talking these last two days as if it were all done and settled. According to many people, when it falls the war is half won. 'We shall soon be in Berlin when we get that port for our big ships.' 'If the weather hadn't been so bad we should have got Cherbourg before and now be in Germany.' 'Only 200 miles to Berlin from Cherbourg.' [A serious underestimate.]

Monday, 3 July

Everyone now expecting the war to finish this year.* A traveller today said we should be in Paris at the end of July and

---

* 'I am war-sick', Kathleen wrote in her June 1944 DR, and this must have been a very common sentiment. Imaginatively counting the days until war would end was almost universal from mid-1944, with probably most predictions overly optimistic.

Berlin in the autumn. The general opinion seems to be that the Russians will beat us to Berlin – and many say that will be because we want them to – that this is arranged. The Germans have made a bluster with the flying bomb – they'll only find us less lenient over peace terms.

At this point there is an exceptionally long (one-month) gap in Kathleen's diary.

Wednesday, 2 August

Went to the Fireguard lecture. This time on fire-spread. Cannot help thinking these lectures are unnecessarily prolonged though the man shortened this as much as he dared, giving us one hour instead of 1½ hours. But all he told us could have been told over and over in half an hour if taken out of official jargon and put into simple language. One stout lady was indignant because we are having more lectures than at another place, and she also wanted to know why young girls should not come to them and also why men were not compelled to attend. This last is a particularly sore point with all. They do not see the difference between Fire watching and Fireguarding – at least the only difference they see is that the former is *mostly* done by men and paid, and the latter is pushed off to women and therefore unpaid. Some take it more sensibly. As a young lady said to me, 'If this is all the war we are going to have to put up with, just coming to half a dozen lectures, I'll come and be thankful I'm not being bombed.'*

* Fire Guard, as one authority has said, involved 'a huge force of civilians upon whose ordinary life a tedious and often dangerous task had been superimposed' (Terence H. O'Brien, *Civil Defence* [London: HMSO, 1955], p. 608). While this work in Dewsbury was undoubtedly tedious, it was rarely dangerous.

Tuesday, 8 August

The Fireguard course is ended. Cheers! We finished with a practice at the old empty cottage on the moor – those of us who did not desert after enrolment. There was grumbling as usual, this time on the lines of 'The war is as good as over. Paid fireguards are being dismissed. And if we do get anything it will not be fire but flying bombs.' Our instructors led us into a field behind the cottage, soothing us with kind words and jokes for fear we should stampede and bolt. First we had a stirrup pump drill to a derisive running commentary by a crowd of Cockney kids. The cows whose field we had usurped formed a grave circle about us while their leader licked the pumps all over and drank out of each bucket by way of testing our kit. Then we learned the effect of water on magnesium. While these fires were being tackled one pump burst and two others had to be discarded. Finally we had our ordeal by smoke. For this we had to wait in the cottage bedroom until smoke filtered through the floorboards, then creep down the pitch black stairs into the room where the fire and smoke were. Here we had to crawl round the room on hands and knees after a hefty fireman, much more fearful of possible bugs than of the smoke, and stand while our lecturer made his final remarks, and stagger out into the blessed fresh air where a crowd of apprehensive ones waited to be kippered.

Saturday, 12 August

Been waiting with dread a call to the [Women's Voluntary Services] Centre but no more evacuees have come yet. Where on earth we shall park mothers and children in this district I don't know. B. says flatly she will go to no Fireguard drill on

Sunday mornings. She has her husband's dinner to cook and it's all a farce anyway. She says talking of prosecuting non-attenders is bosh – the police are refusing to take the cases up.

While this was the first explicit mention in the diary this summer of evacuees, they had in fact been a major story in Dewsbury for the previous five weeks. Around 800 children from London arrived in early July and were distributed throughout the Heavy Woollen District, 325 of them staying in Dewsbury itself. Seven hundred more were expected a few days later. In the course of the month, as a consequence of the flying-bomb attacks on south-east England, around a million people were evacuated to safer parts of the country; over 4,000 of them were delivered to Dewsbury. (Another 800 were expected in August, but, to the relief of local officials, they did not arrive.) One can imagine the scenes of confusion, congestion and fright and the many instances of individual hardship that must have been evident when these evacuees alighted at the train station – where, it was said, 'Large crowds gathered ... as if expecting a royal visitor, cheering and waving to the evacuees as they filed into the waiting buses'.* And then they had to be found places of refuge. As the press, which was supportive, remarked, 'Tired of their long journey and by their ordeal in London, some youngsters were inclined to be fretful, but sympathetic handling by the WVS and other helpers soon made them feel at home .... Adult and child had the same story to tell – of how they had been without sleep for weeks, and had tried to do their daily duties in between dashes into shelters, and how they welcomed the chance of a good sleep.' As usual, mothers and children were harder to billet than children on their own, but past experience had proven useful. 'In cases of mothers with large families ... the billeting officers arranged for

---

* *Dewsbury Reporter*, 15 July 1944, p. 5.

their accommodation in houses which have been kept vacant for such an emergency.' By the end of July there were probably over 2,000 new evacuees in Dewsbury, about half of the total number that were then newly billeted in the Heavy Woollen towns.*

According to a newspaper report the day that Kathleen mentioned evacuees, 'Until this week the billeting office at Dewsbury Town Hall was inundated with evacuee inquiries, but there was a big decline in the number of dissatisfied evacuees and disgruntled householders .... Since the evacuation began, 45,000 women and children have been received in the East and West Ridings from London and the Southern Counties, and another 25,000 have arrived by private arrangement with relatives and friends.† *Some people were said to be making excuses for not billeting children; and later in July a letter to this paper from a resident of Back Brook Street complained that people with larger houses were not pulling their weight. 'This billeting should not be left to working-class people just because they are working-class people who are being evacuated.'*‡ *By contrast, other reports suggested a general willingness to render aid to these hard-pressed southerners. 'The response to the appeal made to householders to take in the refugees from Hitler's flying bombs has, on the whole, been good. Many people undertook to take in evacuees before being requested to do so and hundreds signified their willingness to assist when a canvass*

---

* *Dewsbury District News*, 15 July 1944, p. 1 (for the quotations); and the issues of 8 July 1944, p. 8, 22 July, p. 1, and 29 July, p. 1. The town's other paper concluded one report by noting that 'Countless stories, humorous and tragic, have been current in the district concerning the evacuees. Some of the children who have come into the district have lost one or both parents through the war.' (*Dewsbury Reporter*, 22 July 1944, p. 8.) Throughout the reception areas of England, the responses to evacuees in the summer of 1944 were better organised and less hostile than they had been during the first two years of the war.

† *Dewsbury District News*, 12 August 1944, p. 5.

‡ *Dewsbury District News*, 8 July 1944, p. 8 and 29 July 1944, p. 5.

was made.* *It was almost always the case that some householders in any reception area balked at the prospect of housing evacuees; and while they could be compelled to do so, billeting officers were usually reluctant to employ their full powers of coercion since they knew the results were likely to be dismal and further intervention necessary, usually by removing the evacuees to other premises.*

Kathleen wrote again about her experiences with these evacuees – this time in response to the first question in MO's Directive July–August for 1944. 'If you live in an area to which evacuees have come, please give as full an account as possible of their reception, the views of the local people on the evacuees and vice versa, and any personal stories and anecdotes which you know to be authentic.' Kathleen wrote about these matters in September, and she had a lot to say.

'Our first batch of evacuees,' she said, '25 children, were received with the usual protestations that there was no room for them. Room was speedily found. All our WVS ladies turned up on duty and most of them who probably could took children. Their evening meal at the Centre was unsuitable. Meat pie and potatoes and rice pudding. Too stodgy for a boiling hot day. Many of the children too tired and excited to eat. Many would not undress, being used to shelter life. All were placed out the middle of next morning. Families together or near. One boy expressed a desire to go on a farm as he had been on one when previously evacuated. Mrs B. the Dairy woman was sent for. She agreed to take him and in the end two more boys and a girl. The reception of these children at the station was made into an occasion. People streamed down to "watch them arrive", as if it were a circus. The next lot were rumoured to be mothers and babies. For days before the arrival we WVS were besieged by anxious householders

---

* *Dewsbury Reporter*, 15 July 1944, p. 5.

(especially childless couples) with requests that their name be put down for a child if there were any – they could just push an odd child in. But there were no odd ones, only women with one to four little ones. Dismay and refusal to take them on. The billeting officer had to use compulsion at last. Most of them placed by dinnertime the next day. One woman was kept hanging about until 7 o'clock when her "landlady" finished work.' All these incidents had probably occurred in July, and some probably involved Kathleen, a member of the WVS, directly.

Kathleen went on to report that 'The attitude to these women was mixed. We kept telling one another that we should be thankful we were not moved from home and make it as easy as possible for them. But the women themselves soon began to demand things and expect things doing. They would not help with the housework in many cases and nearly all of their children were quite out of hand. Difficulties were caused in the shops by such things as eggs and tomatoes, of which there is apparently abundance in London. And taking the all round, the impression is here after eight weeks that they take too much for granted.' She did not think that 'closer acquaintance between Cockneys and Yorkshire folk makes for better feeling. The difference of outlook and way of living is too great.'

Some particulars were mentioned. 'Our next door neighbour took a woman and baby into her home and things go as well as may be. She preferred to be boarded so Mrs Hobbs charges her 15s per week for everything, including soap for the baby and milk. The evacuee washes up and gets the vegetables ready. Otherwise her time is spent tending her child and reading women's magazines. When holiday time [presumably in August] there seemed nothing for it but to take [them] with them to Mrs Hobbs's mother in the country. Mrs Hobbs paid her mother for the keep of her lodgers. The evacuee herself paid not a cent – not even her own railway fare.

Mrs Hobbs is wondering just what "board and lodging" covers. No wonder that everywhere Mr and Mrs Hobbs go the evacuee goes too, putting baby out to nurse to her mother, who now lives near. Mrs S., an elderly and deaf lady, took twin boys of six, and cannot control them. They are very ragged and have no decent boots, but when she wrote for boots or money and coupons their mother wrote back to say she was very poor but had sent some sweets – off the children's own ration pages! But Mrs S. knows that there are several grown up workers in this family.

'Boots seem to be the big problem. Apart from the buying there is the mending. Unless there is a handy "foster-father" to patch up, mending is a big item. And to apply to the authorities means months of waiting before boots are forthcoming. There is a general idea that the children were sent up with the oldest clothes possible so that new ones would be provided.'

This was not the end of the complaints that had reached Kathleen. 'Eating seems to be another sore point. They (the children) – the women board themselves usually – do not "care" for our plain Yorkshire food. As one woman said, "I cooked a good dinner with Yorkshire pudding and meat and veg and V. messed about with a potato and gravy and then left the table saying, 'I know what I like, in the pantry'. But I fetched her back and made her sit down, telling her that what was good enough for Mr L. and me was good enough for her. All she wants is biscuits, biscuits, and dipping them in her tea and messing about. And pictures! They'd go two or three times a week. But I make them wait till Saturday and then we all go together. Eight years old isn't old enough to roam the streets." Two or three customers grumble about getting meals ready for their evacuees, saying they don't eat "right" meals.' (We should keep in mind that in such disruptive situations as evacuation, billeting, and strangers being thrown together against their wills, problems were much more likely to

be spoken about and reported than arrangements that had gone
smoothly and were largely trouble-free. Good news had, as usual,
little visibility.)

Monday, 14 August

People now expecting the war ending very soon. Margaret met
M. W., who excused herself in a moment because she wanted
to run home and put the wireless on to see if the war was over.
(This quite seriously.) T. B. came into the shop and said that
his mates at work were saying 'cease fire' would sound this
weekend. The most cautious estimate is the year end and the
most popular about the middle of October.

A traveller has explained to us how Woolworths and other
big stores have salmon and other things in the window when it
is not being allocated to this district. They simply buy largely
in the zone in which it is being released and send it out to
their branches. But it will take some explaining it to make our
customers understand this.

Holidays at home now over. The last week being good
weather, we were able to enjoy the events in the park outside.
The twice-weekly dancing round the bandstand to gramophone records for threepence has been a huge success.

Tuesday, 29 August

The favourite time for the war's end still seems to be the
end of October, or as our customers say, 'There'll be no more
blackout,' regardless of the fact that the blackout is even now
descending upon us at 9.30 without the slightest relaxation of
these horrible regulations. But people are very patient. The
only grumbling I have heard this week is about the buses

finishing so early in the evening. Pro-Russians are silenced. No more do we hear of the wonders they do on the Eastern front and the blunders we make.

I must say I am not so prepared for the war's end as I was for the war's beginning. *Then* I cried war for twelve months to the disgust of my family. *Now*, having settled that the war must last until next summer, that is twelve months from D-Day, against a *solid* enemy, who only finally gives up because his homeland is bombed to bits, I am nonplussed to see that the enemy is only an extremely hard crust and within all is hollowness. Of all the amazing and unbelievable things that have happened in this war, the sight of Jerry taking to his heels is the most unbelievable.

Thursday, 31 August

Have noticed no remarkable elation at our success in France [Paris had just been taken]. Just quiet, sober conviction that this is the end.

Thursday, 14 September

Wretchedly ill and low spirited for a fortnight. Had dreadful pain and thought I was booked for the hospital but the doctor, when summoned, said it was only rheumatism and I could get up in three days. I returned to duty in the shop, feeling that if I had been 'private' instead of 'panel' I should not have been treated so callously. I hate this semi-charity business. Put everyone on the same footing – either give everyone state medical service or make everyone pay privately.

Incessant rain and steamy, dark days. Struggling with a lassitude which makes the simplest action or thought demand a tremendous effort. Everything takes an amazing long time to perform. I seem to be swimming slowly and ponderously at the bottom of a deep, dark tank, and what goes on at the other side of the glass does not affect me at all. People and things grow more and more remote. My job seems to matter less and less, and as far from the war . . . ! It may end tomorrow or go on for years. Either way it is all one to me.

10

Winding Down, Looking Ahead

September 1944–August 1945

In contrast to all the preceding chapters, this chapter offers an abbreviated version of Kathleen's diary during (roughly) the last year of the war. The passages selected represent what we see as the highlights of her writing during these months. When an entry has not been reproduced, a line of asterisks appears, or some of the omitted content is presented in a summary, or an ellipsis indicates a deletion.

Sunday, 17 September

Relations, some from Northants, descended on us for tea. They thought our bread very white compared with theirs and ate enormously. In their casual way they had brought with them an American soldier. I thought him a Pole until he was introduced as 'Frenchy' on account of his grandparents' nationality. His name really seemed to be Randolph and he apparently had no surname. It seems at breakfast he had aroused the wrath of all his hosts *and* the billeted soldier by saying 'When Roosevelt whistles, Churchill runs'. They were struck with the brightness of our street lights for this, the first night of the relaxation [the blackout was partly lifted this month], but I explained the Moor lamps had been brighter for a fortnight because they were gas-lamps and did not need much manipulating.

When they had all gone Margaret said it was alright but she didn't like Americans on principle. Ma couldn't get over the soldier and young M. cuddling at the back of the group when waiting for the bus – 'and only just acquaintances'. I thought we must add [to] our thankfulness to be free of the flying bombs our freedom from regiments of soldiers cluttering up the place and disturbing 'the even tenor of our way'. In a way there is as much difference between the North and South of England (when I say North I mean here locally, I suppose) as between America and Europe. We are America – only knowing of the war by hearsay; the South is Europe – up to the neck in it. We are critical and intolerant. They are busy on the job – theirs will be the task of clearing the mess up. And I don't just mean that the flying bombs have left.

Tuesday, 26 September

We all read the paper at once this morning to learn about the Social Security Plan [inspired by the Beveridge Report]. Bert said it would never get past the big Insurance Companies. Ma said why had Children's Allowances to come first. The old folk should be considered first – they had the least time to live and enjoy it. I couldn't understand why the pensions for childless young widows isn't dropped – they are as well able to work as spinsters.

The baker said they would have to give more wage or he

wouldn't get enough to cover income tax and other deductions; there wouldn't be enough to live on. I asked the first
customer what she thought of the Plan. She said 'What's that?
Oh, what they've been saying on the wireless. Well, we shall
have to pay for it ourselves – they'll give us nothing.' Another
came in. 'What's this about pensions? Someone told me we
are all to have pensions.' The first said disgustedly, 'Well, you
can see what it is really. Money for kids. Then they have 'em
shot when they grow up. It's all a gag. We shan't get anything
without we pay it ourselves.'

People now seem resigned to a longer war – Xmas at the
earliest for peace.

Wednesday, 27 September

Poor Mrs F. disappointed. She thought that she would start
drawing widow's pension immediately, and was very crest-
fallen when I said it had yet to be approved by Parliament, was
only a suggestion, and in any case would not operate for ages
yet. 'It was in the paper,' she said. 'It looks as though I must go
on working another two years till I'm 65. It's too much for me
walking a mile and a half and standing and lifting and tugging
all day. What do they want to put it in the paper for, like that,
if we are not to have it.'

Friday, 29 September

Young Mrs J. said she wished the war would be over so that her
husband would be home. 'But that will not be yet. We shall
have a hard time first. Look at the way they have had to fight
at Arnhem [in the Netherlands, where British troops suffered
significant setbacks]. Wasn't it awful when they told us on the

wireless. Everyone at the mill was roaring that morning.' 'Yes,' (weeping) said Mrs M., 'but they are making more of it than D-Day. It couldn't have been worse than D-Day. That were proper slaughter. They didn't give those lads medals. Why give these medals?'

Saturday, 30 September

Bert has arranged to have his car done up although he is not expecting to get petrol until the spring. The garage man says orders are pouring in. He thinks it was planned to release petrol in about a month because we thought the war would be well over, but Arnhem has altered that plan, and set us back three months in everything. Mr W., traveller, says October will see the finish; but his is the most optimistic opinion I have heard. Most people say Xmas. Personally I think early spring.

Wednesday, 4 October

Have decided not to continue with the Esperanto class, for obviously English (American version) will be the international language. And Esperanto is anyway too heavy and cumbersome for modern needs. Instead have joined a WEA [Workers' Educational Association] lecture course on 'America' which promises to be interesting [her classes started later this month].

Some wool from the WVS to knit garments for the 'occupied' children [in Europe]. My hairdresser was rather sarcastic when I told her of this and said, were there no British children who needed to be knitted for? I said, well, didn't she think it was partly propaganda, a sort of bribery of the continental countries? She said, yes. America and Britain would now be sort of rivals for the admiration of these foreigners. I said evidently France and Belgium had not suffered from food shortage as much as we thought. In fact they were better off in that respect than we were. She said, yes; she knew an airman who had been hidden in Belgium two months and he had gained four pounds. And we are given (as great treat) a pound of oranges in three months. But I said didn't she think Poland and Greece would need much help, and she agreed they must be in a dreadful plight.

Wednesday, 11 October

Am more than ever convinced that we shall not see a settlement of the war this side Xmas. Customers are bringing in a strange story that 'points' will be finished by Xmas. If this is so, pity the poor shopkeeper.

Sunday, 15 October

No mention made now in the shop of the end of the war. Customers have returned to their usual glumness or indifference or whatever seals their lips. They seem more concerned about the goods which may go off 'points' – tinned meat, tinned fish, dried fruit and biscuits, one said. When I asked her who had told her that fancy tale, she said it was in the Sunday papers. I pointed out that if these things went off points there would be little left *on* 'points', and the scheme would be a farce. We get these wonderful tales from time to time and in the next breath people grumble at scarcity and ask why we must send food to France, which has abundance.

* * *

Monday, 30 October

B.H. had a letter from her evacuee regretting she had returned to London with her baby last Sunday. B.H. says [she] will not have her back. Is tired of being out of pocket for entire strangers. Her list of grievances include having to pay for evacuee's holiday, fare and board; having to pay fares wherever they went; having to provide milk, oranges and chocolate for baby out of the 15s she charged for board; having big electric bills owing to evacuee burning light all night ('in case baby wakes!'); extravagance of evacuee in food matters (requiring bread and butter with bacon, etc.); having to entertain evacuee's soldier brother and friend every Sunday (camping three miles away); having no board at all for last four days; and (crowning impudence) being asked to make a cake for evacuee to take back to London. 'I got on alright with her,' says B.H., 'as far as temper goes. She is good-tempered and agreeable and all that. But I think Cockneys are both damned cheeky and lazy. If things get worse I suppose I shall have to have her back, but I shan't if I can help it. They wouldn't do it for us – they say flat out they wouldn't.'

Thursday, 2 November

Mother received the bill for re-pointing her house – £27 12s, of which less than 30s is for materials. Other is wages. Absolutely no hope of getting the tenants out of it although it was only let while they 'looked round'. Lawyer says all advantage with the tenant these days and if anything happened to Mrs P. the tenancy would automatically descend to her daughter. So no prospect of selling house. Mother has no ready cash. Margaret and I must foot bill between us. Calculate that more than two years rent is lost in this one item. See a future of pottering out sums of money on this house for Mrs P. to live in comfort while we live in this daft building. Who would own property?

Thursday, 9 November

At WEA class. Dr S. last night asked if anyone would entertain some of a party of Canadian soldiers for the evening who were to be conducted round Templefield School. I spoke for three and we waited expectantly all this evening but none turned up. Possibly it was because only eight were spoken for out of a company of thirty.

Friday, 10 November

Heard no comments today on the PM's Mansion House speech [the previous day] nor the fact he was completely sozzled. Margaret and I argued while listening that he was or wasn't but before the end we had to agree he was and trembled lest he not get through it. Not that there was anything important – only a suggestion of heavy losses in Holland. Hearing no remarks I ventured to ask a traveller if he heard 'Winnie'. He said no, and when I said he had had one over he laughed as if it was a huge joke and said, well, at the Lord Mayor's banquet everyone got fresh, but it was a pity the speech was broadcast. I said yes, it would be pie for the Germans.

* * *

Monday, 13 November

Mrs H. the WVS leader called to rest on her rounds gathering in
the Poppy boxes and delivering chocolate to evacuees. She says
she is about tired and thinking of resigning. The WVS seem to
be the mugs for every group in the town which has an unpleasant
job to pass on. The British Legion had palmed Poppy selling
on to them now. She said did we hear the PM's speech? She
thought it disgusting when other countries were listening. She
says he ought to have remembered himself and his duty and at
least waited until after the speech. She says her husband thought
it a joke and stoutly defended the 'culprit' when she protested.
'He'll not have a word against that man,' she said indignantly. 'I
thought it disgusting!' Mrs H. also thought that there would be a
swing over to Labour when the soldiers came home, but it would
not be a good thing for the country. She said that after boasting
and shouting the war would be over by Xmas, our leaders were
now saying another six months. She preferred the Russian way
of getting on with the job and not so much talk. (This is the only
comment I have heard about *the speech*, but she says at every
house she called at there were scandalised comments.) Mrs L.
said aggrievedly she thought the war was as good as over or what
was the use of allowing us more light.

Tuesday, 14 November

Mrs M. met Margaret and asked her what she thought of the
PM's speech – said she had thought it 'queer' but had hitherto
mentioned her suspicions to no one. B.H. had a letter from her
evacuee saying they were having good nights and she was set-
tling down in London. B.H. relieved. I pointed out that there
is no point in coming back here as we may have [V2] rockets

anytime. There were buried at the church here yesterday two victims of a flying rocket that fell on Luton last week.

Acute shortage of paper bags. One paper dealer informs us we must not use our ration of sugar bags for other purposes than weighing up bulk sugar but does not say what we are to use for wrapping sweets, peas, rice, soap flakes or dried fruit. Our cake traveller says he must have all cartons back – one for every one delivered every month – and adds 'God knows where I am going to get the petrol for this collecting business'. He formerly called every three months. He said the Government was now putting plastered cardboard partitions into the huts they are erecting in London. Hence shortage of boxes. I told a man this who said angrily, 'Why can't they build proper brick houses? Putting folk to live in huts!', and when I pointed out it was no use building houses to have them knocked down again, he was only half convinced and clearly had no comprehension of what it must be like in London. He was a type of man who should have known better.

Margaret said it was a pity we couldn't be conducted in parties round London (compulsorily) so as to brighten a few blockheads their ideas. She also says she does not wish the Americans any harm but she hopes a few rockets will fall in New York before this is over.

During the following two months Kathleen wrote a lot about the efforts of independent retailers to protect their interests against what they saw as the unfair competition of chain stores. There were numerous well-attended meetings in Dewsbury and Batley, and three organisations were vying for the support of shopkeepers. This was a major issue in commercial circles at this time.

* * *

Sunday, 10 December

Women in the shop were talking about the deaths of two local infants, one twelve days old (abnormal), the other five months old (suddenly by pneumonia). 'Ah,' said one. 'No good can come to babbies this year. It's a lion year.' 'Yes', said the other. 'My twins were born in a lion year; the one died at a fortnight and look at the lass – deaf and dumb.' 'What's a lion year?' I asked anxiously. 'Lions only whelp every seven years,' I was told, 'and when they do – look out for t'babbies. It's ill luck having children in t'lion year.' First time I have heard this superstition. Don't know whether it is just a local one or not.

Monday, 11 December

Joined the Dewsbury Musical Appreciation Group, and went to first meeting, a Service of Carols. Very enjoyable – particularly the Hallelujah Chorus. The performance of the *Messiah* in January promises to be packed in the Town Hall, but how strange that orchestral concerts are so poorly attended [other evidence suggests that they were mostly well-attended].

* * *

Saturday, 23 December

Bread came at half past 9 last night so got up early to get off orders (400 teacakes). Then we cleared a space for [them] if oranges *did* come. Unusually slack until nearly 12. Everyone off into Dewsbury seeking oranges. There were ugly scenes.

Not enough to go round. Only getting two per customer and then had to buy a basketful of vegetables. A pound of nuts if you spent 10s 6d at one place. At one shop there was a free-for-all fight and the police had to be fetched. Our own customers drifted in after dinner, chastened and orangeless, resigned to waiting until after Xmas when there will be plenty. Rest of day busy but we shut at usual time. We had visitors but they went early and we came to bed by 9 o'clock.

Sunday, 24 December

After finishing writing in bed last night, slept for a time but was overtired and kept serving people in the shop, worrying about oranges and the war – the war – which seems to grow more and more gigantic and overpowering every week. At last sick of tossing, I determined to put on the light and read, but before I could do so I heard an unbelievable sound – the sirens! Mother woke me as soon as I spoke. I shouted to the others and then wondered if I had dreamed it. But Bert and Margaret were already dressing and Ma out of bed. I got up like a slow motion picture – irritated at being roused, at the things going at Christmas (something which has never happened before for us in five years) and the senselessness of things in general. Then we heard planes – and a bang at a distance which shook the house. Bert, who had been out, came in and reported something dropped over Barnsley way. The night seemed to be filled with noise. We went out – it was very dark but fine – about 5.30. Only one full-dressed warden was about. Our neighbours stirred; otherwise not a voice. The sky-noises died away, the warden went away, others went in for tea. Margaret went out again. A plane was heard. 'One of ours,' we said comfortably. 'A fighter.' On it came, straight for the house it seemed, just scraped over with a strange rattling sound, making the doors and windows rattle. Margaret came in with a white face. 'Wait for the bang!' We stared aghast. One of *them*. But it passed and the weird noise died away. 'I saw it coming over the church,' said Margaret. 'Straight for me, it seemed. A funny flickering and a rattling noise. I couldn't move. First time I've really had the wind up in this war.'

There was a strange silence and then we gave little exclamations to relieve our feelings and began to joke. Mother, on her knees lighting the fire, said calmly 'If there's one for us it's no use getting panicky. It will come just the same.' There were more distant noises and we went out once again. Another thing rattled over filling the sky with echoes. 'It's a fighter *this* time,' said Bert. 'I never heard a plane sound like *that*,' I said. 'I tell you it's a *fighter*,' said Bert. 'It might be a new sort. Can't *we* have new things?' 'If that's one of ours, it's falling to bits,' I said. 'Do you think these things would be over and ours not up?' Bert stumped in angrily.

I was alone in a world so silent I could have heard a pin drop a mile away. Not a glimmer from a window, not a door on the move, not a voice. After a minute I went in, trying to digest this new experience. There was no reason why we shouldn't have it – have had it long ago – but we had stuck to the idea that we never should. Well, we should have to adjust our viewpoint apparently. The all clear went at 6.30 and the others went to bed. I had a wash before the fire and then composed myself for an hour or two in an armchair. So begins Christmas.

9 o'clock evening. Did not go out in the morning so heard no comments. Ben and Zillah sent a taxi for us at 2 o'clock. We were surprised to see the fog in Heckmondwike. Ben and Zillah did not get up, they said, until their doors and windows rattled violently. Then they were soon out. Ben said definitely that no planes had been in the sky – only flying bombs. He thought they had been sent from a stationary point in Holland because they all followed a line, but the radio said later [they were] from planes over the North Sea. We had a pleasant family party, just the six, talking of long ago. Barely had we finished supper when the taxi came – three-quarters of an hour early. The fog was thick now, with one man driving and another guiding us off the kerb with his torch, we crawled home, glad of no mishap. Now we are considering bed – to catch up on lost sleep.

Monday, 25 December

Slept fairly well but kept rousing and listening. 'The first six months will be the worst,' I kept telling myself, and 'Use is second nature'. A thick fog prevented any walks this morning so I fled from the wireless and snuggled into two eiderdowns on the bed to catch up with writing.

* * *

Saturday, 27 January, 1945

Ma up today, her 79th birthday, the first time since Tuesday. We prevailed upon her to stay in bed because of the bitter cold and lack of firing. The bedroom was so cold she had to cover her head most of the time, and take her meals with great difficulty. The windows were frosted to the top for six days and we had constantly to replenish hot water bottles to keep her warm. Working has been great misery and though we have had the gas fire it gave out no heat. I have constantly worn wool underwear, a wool jumper, two wool cardigans and an overcoat. We have no water upstairs – all frozen.

The weather has distracted our attention from the Russians, who seem to be resuming their old place as gods in many people's estimation. A constant cry seems to be 'What are *we* doing? Can't *we* make a move?' and generally and fervently 'I hope they get there first. The Russians will stand no nonsense. They are not as soft as we are.' For myself I am expecting them to come to a full stop any time and then think we shall start. But it's strange that minefields and weather seem no barrier to the Russians as they do to us.

Tuesday, 30 January

Relieved that blessed snow had fallen in the night and now is thawing fast. Our pipes thawed at 3.30 and we have a burst so with the water cut off we have to carry bucketsful from next door, up two flights for the lavatory. Astonished at the progress the Russians are making. Surely Germany will collapse after all.

Coal came today when we had swept up the last bucketful of small and Margaret was deciding to bring forth the large cobblings she hid away during the summer. Several feet tracks in the snow to our side door, which is evidently thought to be our coal place. We only keep cinders there when any and anyway it is always locked. But have heard of several coal thefts. Most people seem to get it weekly and burn it up and then be without fire several days. We have kept going with wood and coke.

Wednesday, 31 January

Snow all gone marvellously. A pleasure not to be frozen to the marrow. Shall not soon forget this winter. The Russians still progressing. Now the Germans are suffering a little of what they inflicted on other people. Heard no word of regret that the Russians are pounding on or pity for the populace. Some hopes now of the war being over this summer.

* * *

Thursday, 8 February

Going downstairs again after going up to bed found Margaret switching off a wireless talk. 'I am not religious,' she said, 'or I should perhaps look at things differently, but where's God's justice in all this?' 'We have brought it on ourselves,' I said, 'with selfishness and carelessness, and lack of foresight. It's no use blaming Germany, any more than any other country. She was only out for her own ends the same. You didn't blame America for the state of the world when her gangsters were riding high simply because they didn't go into other countries or turn political."* 'That doesn't prove why the Jews should suffer and the Poles for other people's sins.' 'You shouldn't look for justice and appeal to God to get you out of messes of your own making. God is helpless to do anything if we refuse his aid – isn't that the correct Christian outlook?' 'I don't know anything about it or understand God,' said Margaret irritably, 'but I still don't think there's justice in it.' 'You don't *understand* God,' I said. 'You *experience* Him. At least that is the way I have always thought it was. Like being in love – something that happens to

---

* A few months before Kathleen had pointed to some of the roots of her pessimism. 'The most bitter thing I have learned since 1939 is the depth of unreasonableness and degradation the human mind is capable of, and the dangerous and unlimited possibilities of mass emotion (not thinking solely of the German question), and the ease with which it can be aroused and directed. Another thing is I do not expect so much of people. I regard them tolerantly as one would children, realising that not one in ten has mentally and emotionally grown up.' (DR, September 1944)

some and not to others. I have never known either so couldn't say.' 'Well, I don't think there *is* a God,' said Margaret. 'Probably not, as we think of Him. We are not yet grown up. Personally I cannot think what there is so lovely in this life on earth whatever awaits us in another existence. Our generation has never known comfort and happiness and never will.'

Having exchanged religious views and though not coming to any agreement, getting some satisfaction through this unusually frank talk, for deeper things are not usually discussed in our household (not being time perhaps), I went off to bed. But Margaret still cherishes a grudge against God!

Sunday, 4 March

Last night we had the sirens at 1 o'clock and had to get up to please Bert who went out and patrolled. Bitterly cold. Very annoyed because we could hear no planes. An hour before the All Clear, which went on and on until we were sure something had gone wrong with the works. Felt very irritable. Two people mentioned the alarm today, both sounding more interested than dismayed. Apparently most people had not even heard it. One person gives the war four more weeks; several I asked said Whitsuntide. Personally I think there will be no definite sudden finish to the war like last time but it will gradually peter out into gangsterism. But can raise no great enthusiasm about it. If anyone had told me two years ago I should not be elated at the prospect of peace I should not have believed it.

Wednesday, 7 March

Great indignation in the family over the reprieve of Elizabeth Marina Jones. Ma says it will cause trouble with America.

Margaret says, why let her off? She will be out by [the time] she is thirty to do some more damage. I think the system is daft altogether. Why have laws and trials if one man can set all aside? If the law is such a bad one that everyone shrinks from carrying it out, then the law should be changed. Why bring sex into the matter? To let off both might ease the conscience of some but to punish one and not the other – or to punish them differently ... We shall continue to have these crises until we all bestir ourselves to improve social conditions. And that is the whole root of this reprieve business. Those of us with tender consciences feel that we share in the guilt of that murder.

The family was discussing the so-called 'cleft chin murder' of 7 October 1944. Private Karl Hulten, a 22-year-old US Army deserter, and Elizabeth Jones, an 18-year-old Welsh waitress and (self-described) striptease dancer, had been convicted of the murder of George Heath, a London taxi driver (with a cleft chin), and both were sentenced to death. Hulten was about to be executed; Jones had just been reprieved by the Home Secretary and her sentence commuted to life imprisonment. (Kathleen's sister was correct in her prediction, for Jones was released from prison in 1954, before her thirtieth birthday.) The case was discussed by George Orwell in his 1946 essay, 'Decline of the English Murder'.

* * *

Saturday, 24 March

Cannot honestly say I have perceived much excitement about the Rhine crossing. Do not think the bombing by twelve-tonners and suchlike has raised any remarkable enthusiasm. Rather I think people are sick and weary of the whole dirty business and do not bear the strain now so well. 'Let's get it over' is the general outlook. 'It's high time. It's gone on long enough.' One woman typifies, I think, the opinion of many women (though often unspoken). She said 'I don't think it's right, all this bombing. We know they are enemies – but I don't think this is war, do you? It's murder.' (This question of what is right and wrong in war – the rules of warfare – always puzzles and saddens me. As if war was a game, instead of the murder it is, and we set out on it with a book of printed regulations. Surely after this lot [i.e., amount of destruction] the glory and sporting view will be finally de-bunked.)

Tuesday, 27 March

Strange not to feel elation over prospects of the war being over soon. Rather I feel irritated, especially by the newspapers, and would like to say 'Oh shut up, and get it over, do'. Comment seems cautious. One man said it would be all over by July, another said Whit [Whitsunday in 1945 fell on 20 May]. But most people don't remark at all on it. They will believe it when it's happened, I suppose, but they have been led to rejoice prematurely before so are cautious. And very tired.

What if there is no end to the war? If it just peters out? What about flag-waving then? I can see it's going to be different from last time when everyone went mad. I do believe we've learned a bit of sense since then. Anyway, there are no flags to buy.

Wednesday, 28 March

Bert very 'chuff' this morning. 'I told you this, I told you that. We shall hear any time now.' We keep putting the wireless on and then turn it off in the middle of the news – 'Nothing fresh'. 'It doesn't alter so much in two hours,' says Ma. 'No,' says Margaret. 'But suppose Hitler commits suicide and we don't know straight away.'

Easter Sunday, 1 April

The people who have told me during the last three days that Peace would be declared this weekend! Well, here we are at the end of Easter Sunday and 'resistance is stiffening'. Shall expect Peace when the last German soldier has been captured.

The bus strike (West Yorkshire) planned for the holiday did not take place after all. A last minute meeting decided otherwise. As one driver said to Henry Hill, 'It's all very well for these young married women who are getting Army pay in any case, but I've three kids to keep and I need my wage.' Most of the drivers intended to turn up anyway. One woman whose husband is a railway signalman swore about it. 'Bloody well coming out on strike again and my man putting in all the hours he does at a stretch. It's time something was done for the railway men.' But there was a good deal of sympathy with the bus people – many families around here having a girl 'on the buses'. The awkward hours are a real grievance with their mothers. The reason for the unrest is overtime rates.

Events in Europe were now moving quickly. By the middle of April there was no doubt that (as Kathleen wrote) 'the war will soon be over – but how soon is soon? We are cautious of prophecy beyond "It won't be long now".' This, of course, was true, and the prospect of war ending gave rise to other thoughts. 'Whether there is a great and earnest wish for the war to be over is a question I often ponder. For such a highly industrialised district we have been singularly free from air attack. We have once had flying bombs pass over and were more curious than afraid. We have felt little of direct war. But financially almost everyone is better off and everyone has a feeling of being wanted. I think they expect both these things to stop after the war ... One might almost say that life has got geared up and smoothly running under war conditions (in spite of the absence of so many young men and women) and there is yet no thought of another way of life.'

*   *   *

Tuesday, 1 May

The *Daily Mail* splashing headlines that war may end today. Don't believe it. The gangsters will fight in every hole and corner.

Bella Hill came in this morning in a bad temper because her husband, Henry Hill (bus inspector), supposedly enjoying his weekly 'day off', was sitting glued to the wireless waiting for peace to be declared. He had, upon hearing that, to rush down to the bus station to make arrangements for taking the work people home (drivers and conductors to be bribed with extra pay to do this), then the buses to cease – anyone not a worker who happens to be from home will be stranded. Never heard anything so daft. It's going to be as bad as the general strike [in 1926]. Bella Hill wanted to start spring cleaning as

---

* DR for February–March 1945 (answered around mid-April 1945). A couple of months before, in early February, she had mentioned another aspect of local well-being – that the Dewsbury district faced 'no serious housing problems' (DR, December 1944–January 1945). She discounted people's grumbling. 'I should say on the whole they are rather better for six years of austerity.'

Henry Hill would not go out but he said No – she would look silly cleaning on V-Day. However, tired of waiting for nothing and exasperated beyond measure, she shut herself in the parlour with brooms and a whitewash bucket to commence operations.

Mr and Mrs D. came to tea [from Mirfield]. I warned them they might not get home. Mr D. said Pooh! V-Day would not be celebrated till the weekend. Everything was settled up but the news to be held back until Sunday. He was very indignant over the feeding of German prisoners on so much meat while he could have so little. I said we had to stick to the law but he said 'No, tit for tat. The way we civilians have been tret is abominable.'

We all think [Heinrich] Himmler is bargaining for his life at the expense of others.

Wednesday, 2 May

Quite bewildered by events in Italy where we have been bogged so long. This sudden collapse of the Germans is startling when we have had to struggle so hard against them. The Italian surrender has at last made an impression on our customers. They have more to say and seem inclined to think the war may end soon.

Thursday, 3 May

Margaret woke us at 11 p.m. to tell us Berlin has fallen. Customers (about three or four) are cynical about Hitler's death and think he has been smuggled away. 'But they are all liars. How can you believe any of them? He may crop up somewhere else yet. This "Donitz" seems to be a better sort of man, not a Nazi.' (I'm at a loss to see how they make this out but it seems a general opinion that he must be a better man if he doesn't like the Nazis.) Mr B. says the war is over now but they won't tell us until the weekend. The baker told us about their holiday two days *after* V-Day but when I mentioned ours [in Scarborough] all customers have a dicky fit – apparently poor grocers are to be still at war. One lady in the shop was lamenting shortage of Spam when old Mr C. rounded on her indignantly. '*Spam*! Don't you know t'war's over?' As if to say we don't need that wartime diet now.

We told everyone that they would have to 'clour' (starve) for a day or two by way of celebrating V-Day and one lady quite believed it and scuttled off home to prepare her family for short commons.

Friday, 4 May

No one believes Hitler dead. 'T'Russians can keep on looking. They'll not find your devil' – seems to be the general opinion as expressed by one emphatic lady. Though of course the pro-Russians say he will be found very soon. 'And they want to hang him up by his heels *living* – never heed waiting till he's dead. Shooting's too good for him.' Another expression of prevailing opinion in our shop. A dire, bloody end is still hoped for Hitler.

We began the day about fifty-fifty in favour of Saturday being declared V-Day. There were some doubters who pointed out there was still a lot of land held by the Germans and one Thomas of a woman [a sceptic] who said we should have to wait twelve months. Also a disgruntled few who said it would be Saturday because then they could be done out of their 'pay for nowt'.

We put up a notice as requested by the Food Office about shop closing and bread supplies but few really bothered to understand it and only one woman was concerned about bread supplies. There seems to be a background of bewilderment and amazement behind the fatuous remarks and cynicism. But towards the end of the day opinion had hardened pretty solid that Monday would be 'The Day'. 'Mr Churchill's disappeared. He's gone to Berlin to help receive the surrender, and then he'll be back to talk on Sunday.' [He was, of course, still in London.]

Mrs H. said her husband (a signal man at a busy junction) said they had instructions to stop work immediately for two days. She had asked him if they would stop the trains there and then wherever they were in the middle of the tracks and he said, No, go into nearest station. Nothing would pass on the railways for two days. The whole business gets madder and madder to me. The only people who will be working in the British Isles will be grocers and milkmen.

Monday, 7 May

The strain of wondering when 'It' will be is getting on people's nerves. 'Why can't they tell us without all this mystery? They know well enough when it will be. Having folk wondering what to do ...' is the note. The baker told us he was coming at V-Day but not for two days after. He is bringing no extra so that we are in a queer position. Went into Dewsbury to bank this morning. Everything as usual – no trimmings as yet.

At 1 o'clock we were warned 'It' was very near. We were by now getting the feeling that we were watching by someone's death bed – these kinds of warnings are most ominous. What is this idea of letting us down gently? And *is* the war over or are the Russians still fighting? After dinner we went to Cleckheaton for shoes (I had searched Dewsbury and Scarborough in vain for size 3s and been told there was none made). Back at 3.30 we were told it had said on the wireless that the war was over and Churchill was speaking at 6. What were the actual words I don't know, but apparently something ambiguous, for one customer after another came in and said 6 o'clock would see Churchill making his announcement. We kept the wireless on continually from *then* (3.30) for fear of missing something. There was a sudden panicky rush for bread for half an hour. I have not broken news of *two* days without baker. I shall just save for regular daily customers and blow it. They must bake their own. After bread failed everyone seeking yeast. None until tomorrow. Nothing at 6. Very flat. Shut [shop] at 6.30. Listened again to wireless till 7. Nothing doing. At 7.45 happened to try again and heard flat announcement that war *was* over and our V-Day was to be celebrated tomorrow. Went out to post feeling quite exasperated. Why all this blah? Why couldn't they have said earlier instead of all this caution. If anyone *was* feeling gay and 'celebratory' this business would knock all the joy out of them. Not that anyone is. Most that I have talked to feel this is no time for rejoicing with the war only half won, with so many bereaved homes, with trouble with Russia looming. On way back from post saw that flags were appearing and streamers being put up. We have not an inch of anything.

Tuesday, 8 May

As I feared people rushed in from 8 a.m. seeking bread. When Bob came with only half an ordinary day's ration I was in despair but cheered up on learning he was only missing tomorrow. Everyone clamouring but I insisted on regular orders being fulfilled first. Bob said at Ravensthorpe he had to lock his van between every trayful he carried into a shop because women were raiding it. By 11.30 everything was gone – bread, potatoes, etc. – we closed at 12. After dinner I went to bed for an hour but up in time to hear PM's speech. Then walked into Dewsbury in the pouring rain. Met five drunks on the way at that time (3.30). Nothing doing in Dewsbury. The bus station was not too busy. In front of the Town Hall the Salvation Army was just playing 'God Save the King'. Only two soldiers stood for this. Everyone else walked and talked as usual. Town Hall decorated and one bank; several shops had flags from upper windows but weather was dreadful and made them hang limply. There were about 100 people scattered about the middle of the town in groups talking, or sheltering in doorways and the Arcade. Walked straight through it and up Heckmondwike Road. Met a few people but in the Park was not a soul. Heard bells from St John's, the Parish [church], and across the fields through the mist, Mirfield. Had tinned plums for tea by way of celebration.

After we went on bus to Ben's [in Heckmondwike]. They had not seen a soul all day except the milkman. Listened to the King and everything. Struck by stress on ourselves and America and lack of praise of Russia. Margaret said again and Zillah agreed that we were celebrating too soon. Walked home at 10 watching the bonfires – it was now dry – and amazed to see so many beautiful fireworks. (Someone has been storing up.) Stayed to watch Mrs H.'s. She said – hadn't it been a daft business altogether? Hadn't it been a farce? And Russia was still fighting. Russia hadn't announced anything. She supposed the BBC had made all these plans and they had to be carried out on the dot, but things were very funny. She didn't like their look at all.

Home with mixed feelings. Relief, yes, but also foreboding in my heart. Margaret said she wouldn't be surprised if the fighting flared up again.

Midnight. Expected a rowdy time tonight when pubs closed but up to now a strange quietness has prevailed. No traffic has passed for some time and no people about.

Wednesday, 9 May

Better weather today. Opened shop from 9 to 12 but nothing to sell. People seemed puzzled why we rushed to celebrate without waiting for Russia. A day would not have mattered after 5½ years. To Mirfield after dinner. Into the churchyard with Auntie and then to the Ds. They remarked on the strain of Monday. They were left without bread. Their shop had unkindly sold to all-comers without considering regulars. Home at 9.30 to listen to 'Story of Churchill' and watch from the window the distant bonfires as the sky darkened. They gave an explanation about Russia which was no explanation about our conduct. Why could *we* not have waited until everything was signed and sealed in Berlin? Instead of being so discourteous as to bring off on our own with the celebrations.

Thursday, 10 May

Another day of Peace Celebrations and I shall be in a mental home. Today, after waiting until 4.30 for the baker, he came at last with such a small quantity of bread that I was in despair about orders. Am just about tired of apologising and prevaricating for someone else's shortcomings. He said the night-men had yet another night off making [bread] – making three – and consequently there were no loaves made. This is all due in the first place to Winnie. He gave it out in the beginning that everyone had to have two days holiday, and two days holiday the conscienceless ones have *had*, irrespective of rhyme or reason. There was no need to slap it into the middle of the week, in any case. We could just as well have celebrated on Saturday and had Sunday for a day of meditation, which, though I am far from religious, I believe would have suited most people far better. There were then hints of supplications but no real guidance about these 'essential services', and everyone has just pleased himself – and hasn't there been a glorious muddle! The postmaster at Heckmondwike was aroused early on V-Day by an army of postmen who demanded instructions about letter delivery. He referred to Dewsbury and they couldn't tell him anything but finally decided they would all call it a holiday. At Heckmondwike station, the clerk tells me, the unnecessary part of the staff duly turned up but two signal men, ticket collector and porters were minus. Some mill-workers turned up, hoping to get extra pay, only to find themselves locked out. And Bert made out his lists for his travellers in spite of my efforts to induce him to realise they would not come. As Margaret said tonight, 'Thank the Lord it's over. If they'd made as big a mullock of the war as they've made of the bit of peace we've already had, heaven help us.'

I suppose they have postponed Winnie's speech so he can let off steam for a few days and get *his* 'razzling' over. If and when I am a very aged grandmother and my descendants ask me to describe my experiences and thoughts on the Great Victory days, I shall have to confess that for most of that eventful week I was exasperated beyond words and that my thoughts were very 'bready' during the whole time.

* * *

Thursday, 23 May

Most of our customers have taken the news of the food cuts calmly and in a tolerant spirit. 'Of course starving people have to be fed. And we've never *starved*. But what about Jerry's rations over here? Aren't they to be cut?' Every other person expressed concern for those living alone and said the lard ration would not be worth the paper it was wrapped in. About two appreciated the fact that here was another blow to the poor grocer, and to his takings. They were so concerned with the fat reduction they had not grasped they would have less points, and when I announced this to a shopful of ladies there was consternation.

The ration cuts have taken away the jolt of the General Election. No one has mentioned this to me *first* but *everyone* to whom I have broached it is either dubious or very indignant, (1) because they say it should have not been held until the war is over – there is a lot of fighting yet, and all our men are abroad; (2) out of sympathy with Mr Churchill. These (and there are many) say it is a dirty trick to do the minute he has won the war for them. [The Labour Party had just withdrawn from Churchill's coalition government.]

I have only heard one person who does not agree with my own view that there will be a big swing over to Labour. Most people whether 'red hot' or no seem to think that. But personally I think this 'forcing the issue' will do them harm among the 'floating votes' and possibly among their own followers. I feel as I did over the celebrations that someone is standing over me and urging me to do something that I want time to think out.

Why has this 'German Government' been allowed to carry on for a fortnight? Why wasn't it shot-up? Why are we not allowed to have a look at Berlin? What sort of a farce will an international trial be for war criminals? Russia will scoff and refuse to take part.

Friday, 31 May

To first general meeting of WEA, where we only got through half the agenda, forming a branch and election of officers, and must have another meeting next week to finish. Several trade union representatives present as 'watchers'.

The potato shortage is the last straw and is causing more dissatisfaction than the cuts in rations. There has been much grumbling. We were quite without for ten days and our customers complain that no one else will serve them. 'What I want to know is, have we won this b—— war, or not?' 'We're to feed Jerry first and have what's left.'

The potato failure has just come in nice time to influence the Election. For my part I feel as if I am between the Devil and the Deep Sea, for I have faith in neither the Tories nor Labour. Neither of their pre-war pasts will bear scrutiny. But it is high time we had a change after ten years, and I do believe that the resources of land (and the land) should be common property. So I shall vote Labour. There will probably be a stalemate with no party having a working majority. It's a case of choosing the party you *dislike least*. They say the Forces are already largely for Labour. They undoubtedly will be when they find, on demobilisation, what rations they will get for the next twelve months.

Kathleen wrote intermittently in June, mainly about the election campaign, political speeches on the radio, and remarks she heard about Churchill – whose speeches did not go over well – and his prospects. On 5 June she remarked on 'An old lady grumbling about

the terrible weather we are having. I said "Yes, I don't know what
we can blame for it now the war is over – the election perhaps."
"Well," she said, taking me seriously, "I shouldn't wonder. As soon
as we get the war over and the fighting and banging stops, we have
another upset. We shan't have decent weather all summer."' (In
the end Labour won handily in Dewsbury, as in many parts of the
country.) Then there is a very long gap in Kathleen's diary, lasting
for six weeks from the first of July and related to a serious illness.
When she resumes writing she is living in a truly new world.

Saturday, 11 August

Home from hospital yesterday but feeling weak yet. They
have managed very well in my absence. The newspapers still
full of the new atomic bomb. And me congratulating myself
I should be able to live out my life – even to ninety – before
the nations could summon energy for another war! Now war
is abolished. We shall just be destroyed without warning by
some country which doesn't like us. But why do all writers
stress as one of the benefits of the atomic age the abolition of
hard work? Surely work is just what is needed to keep us from
getting into further mischief. Wars, in the long run, are caused
by words, and busy people haven't time for words. Besides,
what is physical strength for if not to use in toil.

* * *

Wednesday, 15 August

The announcement [of Japan's surrender] was not made at
9 o'clock and disgustedly we went to bed early, all of us, even

Margaret, for we were tired. We said it would be days yet even if the Japs played fair and tried no tricks. Even Margaret, usually sitting until midnight, was abed by 10. We were all awakened by a great hullaballoo in the street. For some time we lay and grumbled about mothers who let boys and girls and even young children be out at such an hour. We drank the coffee Margaret had provided for me and this brightened our wits considerably, for Alice and I exclaimed together, 'Do you think Peace has been announced?' And so it has as we learned this morning. We got up then, of course, and ran from front windows to back. We could see the glow of a bonfire in the next street and on the church tower a white cross glowed. The bonfire crowd seemed to be confined to the rowdy element of the neighbourhood. At intervals a strange and solemn procession passed down the road. First came a group of toddlers, hand in hand, then older children, and lastly two buxom women in aprons, one carrying a furled flag. They marched along without speaking, round the entire block, presumably with perhaps a pause at the bonfire, and then round they came again. This rite was kept up until 4 o'clock and then the fire burned out and the revellers went home. Bert brought us up a cup of tea, while I explained to Alice that these were all Glasgowites who had been celebrating so promptly. Then to our well-earned rest for a few hours.

Bert opened shop at the usual time in spite of our protests, but there were few customers until mid-morning. Most people took the news very calmly. All had some reference to our prisoners. This time we had plenty of bread for everyone. Closed at 1 o'clock for our usual half day. For dinner Margaret opened the tin of turkey saved two years for this occasion, which also is her birthday. We also had the chicken presented to me by Mrs D., salad, fried potatoes, and apple pie and coffee. Five years ago today Margaret promised the Red Cross a penny for each plane brought down, little dreaming how much she would have to tip up before the end of the day – 185. We laughed as we recalled this but all agreed it seemed more like twenty years ago. We were all so tired we rested all afternoon and were pleased we had no callers. For tea we again had a 'spread' – bottled plums, custard and special birthday cake.

Henry Hill came in during the evening, very tired, having just finished at 7 – starting at 4 in the morning. He is a bus inspector but had to act as conductor all day because although drivers turned up for normal duty the girls didn't. He said they had the cheek to go into the station during the afternoon in Sunday attire, expecting to ride home, but the men refused and told them to walk.

As darkness fell we watched the bonfires start up on the hills all around and saw *some* fireworks. There was no noise in the street tonight. Not even later when the pubs closed. (Probably no beer!)

Epilogue

Kathleen's postwar diary-writing is very scant, and concludes in July 1946. Her glum outlook in 1945 persisted into the following year. There was, she felt, little to be optimistic about. 'No confidence either in my own or the country's future,' she wrote around early March 1946 in a Directive Response (for December 1945–January 1946). 'Was prepared for things being bad but not so bad and every prospect of them getting worse.' She was 'Tired and sick of rationing. The shopkeepers' worries are twice as many as during the war.' She was also anxious about 'being poor'. American hegemony did not impress her favourably, nor the atom bomb. 'To sum up, am tired of life in general as lived in England in 1946. Nothing to look forward to, present irritations enormous. And also fed up with private relationships and see no prospect of alteration there.'

There was little to cheer about in 1946. The grip of austerity was largely unrelieved; the rationing of bread, which had been avoided during the war, was introduced in July 1946, causing grocers no small grief and much public unease. Anti-American sentiments were often heard, certainly from members of the local working class. 'Victory' was seeming stale, if not in London, at least in Dewsbury. A sense of weariness characterises much of Kathleen's diary. On 16 June 1946 she seemed to be sighing out loud as she wrote, 'One of these days I am going to check just what proportion of each day I spend in thinking, talking and planning about food. I even dream about it sometimes, selling it especially, and count endless coupons if I am out of sorts or over-tired. Bread rationing will be a nightmare.' She felt she was on a sort of treadmill. 'Each day becomes more and more automatic – bed and work' (23 June). On 10 July 1946 she felt 'More depressed than at any time since 1940 when Churchill said it would be a five years war'. Words of discontent recur. On 17 July her brother-in-law, Bert, looked into a business in another town. 'We are all fed up with living here, what with the stairs and what with the low class of people around.'* Without doubt, a grocer's life was a hard one – and made worse by the complexities of bread rationing. The next day she reported that she had been 'Sleepless at night, wondering whatever we shall do if Margaret has to go to hospital. It is a nightmare, fearing one of us may break down.' On 27 July she felt 'utterly exhausted and fed up'.

These weeks of (mostly) gloom induced Kathleen to write one passage of unusual introspection. 'Have even laughed a little about the bread rationing today,' she wrote on 14 July. 'But I have read three novels in a week ("Flight from reality", as [the psychologist Alfred] Adler would say), a sure sign I am

---

* On 29 June 1946 she reflected on these people's feelings concerning the Labour Government. 'Supporters (nearly everyone round here) careful not to complain outright against it but work off their spleen rather against other countries. But really at bottom they are dumbfounded. Many prophecies of revolution this winter, and talk of general strikes.' Kathleen's own class-sensitivity was occasionally recorded. On 22 July she wished 'the Government spokesmen would not keep uttering threats and gibes as if we were all (except the manual labourers) potential criminals'. She regretted that some Labour leaders talked 'as if it were something to be ashamed of to be thrifty enough to save up for one's own house'. As various diary passages attest, she thought that many of her working-class neighbours and customers were deficient in foresight and planning.

"unbraced".* This led her to a deeper questioning of her life. 'I wonder if the time will ever come when I may meditate on things that really matter – indulge in a little contemplation from afar, I mean. At present I niggle through the days, sometimes stopping a minute to be astonished at the petty details that fill them, and escape for an hour in the evening into the garden. Then it is that I should do my thinking, and adjusting myself to my circumstances, plan my life according to "things as they are". But "things as they are" will not bear looking at, and in any case I am too tired to do anything but poke in the soil and kill caterpillars, without anything much in my mind at all.'

Kathleen Hey's life, as recorded for Mass Observation, was about to conclude. Her diary was ending. Its final two sentences, on 31 July 1946, were: 'Have bought a half share in a sweep ticket but, alas, the race is not until October. Oh for a win and release from this purgatory.'

* * *

Kathleen Hey died of cancer on 11 June 1984, aged 78, in St Gemma's Hospice, Harrogate Road, in Leeds. Her death certificate lists her usual and presumably most recent address as 26 Belmont Grange, Liversedge, a recently constructed residence for seniors, and her occupation as 'Receptionist (retired)'. The informant on this certificate was Emily Naylor, 'cousin', a relative who does not (as best we can tell) appear in Kathleen's wartime diary. All of her immediate family members predeceased her. She had no niece or nephew.

---

* This testimony of Kathleen's bookishness was only intermittently disclosed. The following week she went one day to Bradford (22 July 1946). 'Nothing much to see. Fortunate in obtaining two out of the eight books I wanted.'

There is little in Kathleen's writing before 1945 about her (shall we call them?) deeper worries and concerns for the future. One exception is a passage in her Directive Response for January 1943, when she reflected on her feelings about 'security'. 'I should actually like a little home of my own and enough to live on in my old age. The dread of being a burden to anyone haunts many moments of my life. Being a "weakling", the thought of serious illness is ever at the back of my mind – coming out of hospital and having nowhere to go to get strength up and such like – for why should my relations have to bear burdens for me, however willing they are?' It is likely, in fact, that her last years involved few family relations at all. One hopes that after the war she may at least have made a few like-minded friends.

Appendix

Mass Observation and its Diarists

A half-year before the outbreak of war, a Penguin Special was published, *Britain by Mass-Observation* (1939), written by Charles Madge and Tom Harrisson, the two key founders of MO. In it they declared how vital it was to study the 'normal and everyday problems of our own lives, as actually lived in the houses and factories, pubs and chapels and shops of this sort of civilisation' (p. 231). This was a central commitment in its sociological mission. And as they and others in MO were discovering, facts and testimony could be obtained in various ways, one of which, they determined in the late summer of that year, was to encourage its volunteers to keep diaries. The result, by the later 1940s, was one of the largest collections of diaries in existence, now housed in The Keep in Brighton, since late 2013 home to the Mass Observation Archive.

It was almost four decades after the end of the war before much was known about this collection. The first of these diaries to be brought to the attention of a public readership was that of Nella Last, a housewife in Barrow-in-Furness, whose massive diary was first edited and selections published as *Nella*

Last's War: A Mother's Diary 1939–45 (Falling Wall Press, 1981; Sphere Books paperback, 1983), edited by Richard Broad and Suzie Fleming. A little later the MO diary of the well-known writer Naomi Mitchison was edited by Dorothy Sheridan and published as *Among You Taking Notes . . .: The Wartime Diary of Naomi Mitchison, 1939–1945* (London: Victor Gollancz, 1985). During these years – and later – selections from some of the most interesting diaries appeared in various anthologies, such as Dorothy Sheridan's edited volume, *Wartime Women* (London: Heinemann, 1990) and the three anthologies edited by Simon Garfield,* usually with their authors anonymised or their identities altered. MO's Observers during the war had been promised anonymity, a provision that in later years was sometimes dropped with the approval of the diarist him- or herself, or the approval of close family members, or when the diarist had been dead for some time and there were no surviving close family members (this is most likely to occur when a diarist, like Kathleen Hey, was childless).

Television served to raise the profile of MO's collection of diaries, especially the 2006 production of *Housewife, 49*, starring Victoria Wood and based on Nella Last's diary. The success of this film was the stimulus for several subsequent trade books, notably a second edition (2006) of Nella Last's wartime diary from 1981 plus three editions of both her post-war writing and her wartime writing that had not previously been printed. These volumes were all published by Profile Books, the latter three edited by Patricia and Robert Malcolmson: *Nella Last's Peace* (2008), *Nella Last in the 1950s*

---

* Garfield's books were all published by Ebury Press: *Our Hidden Lives: The Everyday Diaries of a Forgotten Britain 1945–1948* (2004); *We Are at War: The Diaries of Five Ordinary People in Extraordinary Times* (2005); and *Private Battles: How the War Almost Defeated Us* (2006).

(2010), and *The Diaries of Nella Last: Writing in War and Peace* (2012). Profile is also the publisher of Sandra Koa Wing's fine anthology, *Our Longest Days: A People's History of the Second World War, by the Writers of Mass Observation* (2008). Selections from the writings of another MO diarist are forthcoming: Simon Garfield, ed., *A Notable Woman: The Romantic Journals of Jean Lucey Pratt* (Canongate, November 2015).

With the arrival of the twenty-first century, there was growing interest in the idea of producing scholarly editions of wartime diaries, with suitable annotations and commentaries. Most of the prospective publishers turned out to be record societies. The first of these publications was edited by Robert Malcolmson and Peter Searby, *Wartime Norfolk: The Diary of Rachel Dhonau 1941–1942* (Norfolk Record Society, 2004), who some years later edited another East Anglian volume, *Wartime in West Suffolk: The Diary of Winifred Challis, 1942–1943* (Suffolk Records Society, 2012). Several other scholarly editions have been edited by Patricia and Robert Malcolmson: *A Woman in Wartime London: The Diary of Kathleen Tipper, 1941–1945* (London Record Society, 2006); *A Soldier in Bedfordshire, 1941–1942: The Diary of Private Denis Argent, Royal Engineers* (Bedfordshire Historical Record Society, 2009); *Dorset in Wartime: The Diary of Phyllis Walther, 1941–1942* (Dorset Record Society, 2009); *Warriors at Home 1940–1942: Three Surrey Diarists* (Surrey Record Society, 2012; one of the three wrote for MO); and *A Free-Spirited Woman: The London Diaries of Gladys Langford 1936–1940* (London Record Society, 2014; she wrote for MO in 1939). Other editions are forthcoming, including the diary of Annie Holness for 1941–1943, to be published by the Record Society of Lancashire and Cheshire, and a short volume on Leeds in 1939–1940 to be published by the Thoresby Society. One other MO diarist has been published,

Love and War in London: A Woman's Diary, 1939–1942, by Olivia Cockett, edited by Robert Malcolmson (Waterloo, Ontario: Wilfred Laurier University Press, 2005; second edition, Stroud, Gloucestershire: The History Press, 2008, under the title of *Love and War in London: The Mass Observation Wartime Diary of Olivia Crockett.*). A stimulating account of some of MO's diarists has been written by James Hinton, *Nine Wartime Lives: Mass-Observation and the Making of the Modern Self* (Oxford University Press, 2010).

Acknowledgements

A number of people have given us vital support as we worked on this book. The staff of Special Collections at the University of Sussex, which is now housed in a magnificent new archive, The Keep, has, as always, been highly attentive and efficient. We are especially grateful to Jessica Scantlebury, who has assisted our research in all sorts of ways, both when we were in Brighton and when we were working at home. Others at Sussex, notably Rose Lock, Adam Harwood, Lisa Towner, Owen Emmerson, Jo Baines, and Fiona Courage, have worked on our behalf, and we wish to express our appreciation to them all. Another person whose help has been invaluable is Christine Stearn at the Dewsbury Library. She has on many occasions answered our queries and aided us in tracking down sources, as well as facilitating our research trips to West Yorkshire. Indeed, we would say that her assistance since 2012 has been crucial, given how distant we normally are from Dewsbury. Assistance with specific questions was provided by Graeme Garvey, Sheila Young, John Widdowson, Will Ryan, Malcolm Mathieson of the West Yorkshire Archives

Service, Katie Ankers of the BBC Written Archives Centre, Tony Sharkey of the Blackpool Central Library, and Nicola Herbert of the Hull History Centre, and we thank them all. We have also benefited from our visits to the British Library, especially its newspaper collection in Colindale before its closure in November 2013, and the Leeds Public Library; from information given to us by Anne Wickes at the Second World War Experience Centre in Wetherby, West Yorkshire; and from the advice and initiatives of Gordon Wise at Curtis Brown.

We are pleased to recognise several other people as important to the production of this edition. We are much indebted to Ann Stephenson for her careful research into Kathleen Hey's family history, which yielded much useful information. She generously did this work voluntarily. Ann also put us in touch with Diane Oldfield, a resident of Batley, who very kindly drove one of us around Dewsbury and several nearby towns one afternoon in October 2013, helping us to identify places mentioned in the diary and understand better the topography of the region. Heather Goldick at the Nelson Public Library handled very efficiently our many interlibrary loan requests (which are managed through an excellent provincial programme); Trevor Henderson in Nelson advised us on a number of computer matters that threatened to grind us down; and in late 2013 two anonymous readers of a draft of this book, both associated with the Yorkshire Archaeological Society, offered us many helpful comments and criticisms.

Finally, we are indebted to our editor, Sally Partington, for her fine work in helping us prepare this text for publication. She spotted numerous stigmata in our typescript and identified passages that would benefit from elaboration or clarification. Her extensive knowledge of wartime society prodded us to make several changes for the better that otherwise we would not have made; and she took the leading role in locating suitable illustrations. We very much appreciate her constructive contributions to this book.

Nelson, British Columbia
September 2015